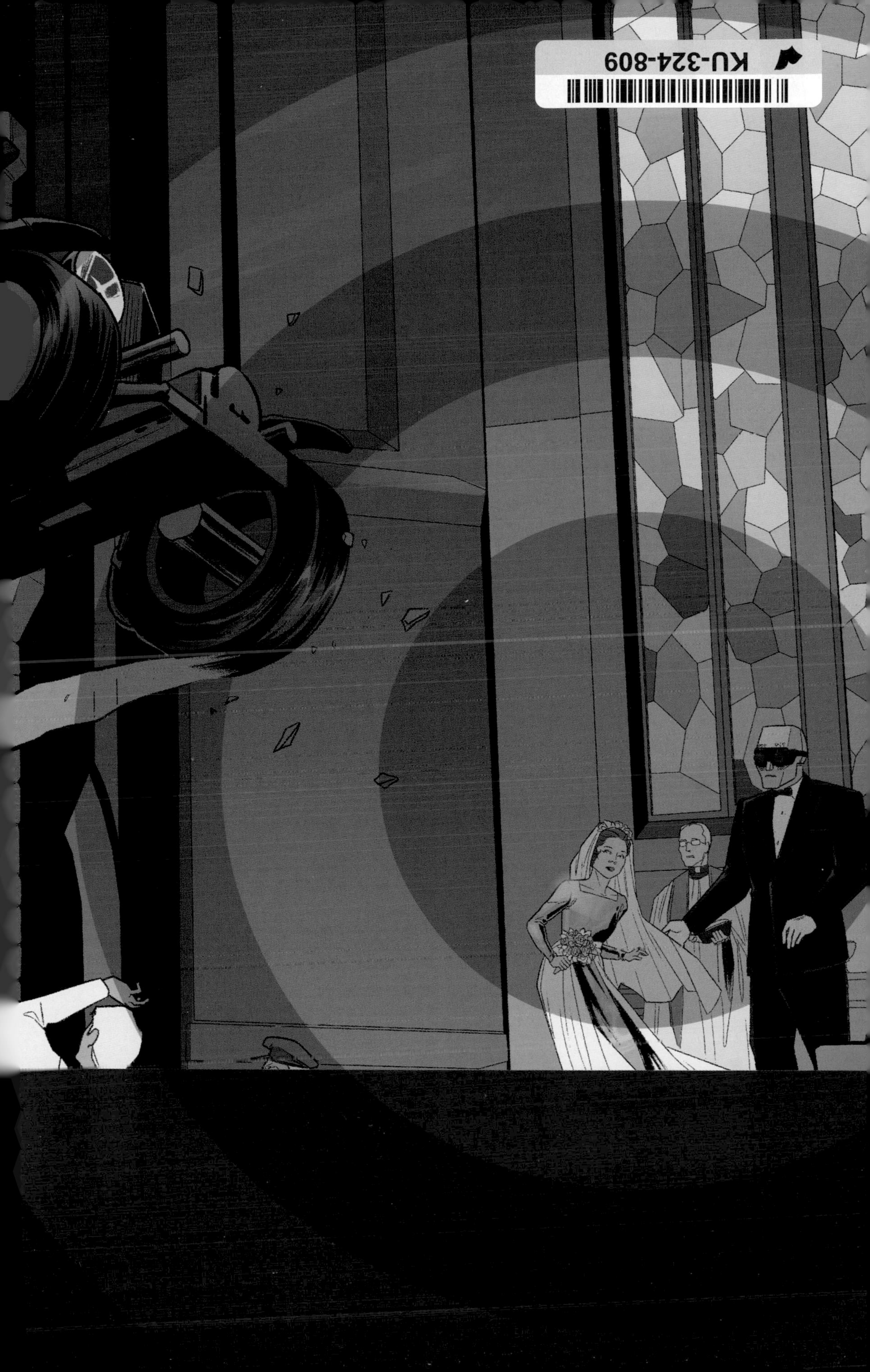

WRITTEN BY
CALEB MONROE

ART BY
YASMIN LIANG

COLORS BY
RON RILEY

LETTERS BY
ED DUKESHIRE

COVER BY
JOSEPH MICHAEL LINSNER

ASSISTANT EDITOR
CHRIS ROSA

EDITOR
MATT GAGNON

TRADE DESIGN
KELSEY DIETERICH

STEED and Mrs PEEL

THE RETURN OF THE MONSTER

SOUTHWARK LIBRARIES

SK 2534548 6

BOOM! STUDIOS

ROSS RICHIE CEO & Founder • JACK CUMMINS President & COO • MARK SMYLIE Chief Creative Officer • MATT GAGNON Editor-in-Chief • FILIP SABLIK VP of Publishing & Marketing • STEPHEN CHRISTY VP of Development
LANCE KREITER VP of Licensing & Merchandising • PHIL BARBARO VP of Finance • BRYCE CARLSON Managing Editor • MEL CAYLO Marketing Manager • SCOTT NEWMAN Production Design Manager • IRENE BRADISH Operations Manager • DAFNA PLEBAN Editor
SHANNON WATTERS Editor • ERIC HARBURN Editor • REBECCA TAYLOR Editor • CHRIS ROSA Assistant Editor • ALEX GALER Assistant Editor • WHITNEY LEOPARD Assistant Editor • JASMINE AMIRI Assistant Editor • CAMERON CHITTOCK Assistant Editor
HANNAH NANCE PARTLOW Production Designer • DEVIN FUNCHES E-Commerce & Inventory Coordinator • BRIANNA HART Executive Assistant • AARON FERRARA Operations Assistant • JOSÉ MEZA Sales Assistant • ELIZABETH LOUGHRIDGE Accounting Assistant

STEED AND MRS. PEEL: The Return Of The Monster, April 2014. Published by BOOM! Studios, a division of Boom Entertainment, Inc. The Avengers and Steed and Mrs. Peel are trademarks of StudioCanal S.A. All Rights Reserved. Copyright © 2014 StudioCanal S.A. Previously published in single magazine form as STEED AND MRS. PEEL ONGOING No. 8-11. ™ & © 2013 StudioCanal S.A. All rights reserved. BOOM! Studios™ and the BOOM! Studios logo are trademarks of Boom Entertainment, Inc., registered in various countries and categories. All characters, events, and institutions depicted herein are fictional. Any similarity between any of the names, characters, persons, events, and/or institutions in this publication to actual names, characters, and persons, whether living or dead, events, and/or institutions is unintended and purely coincidental. BOOM! Studios does not read or accept unsolicited submissions of ideas, stories, or artwork.

A catalog record of this book is available from OCLC and the BOOM! Studios website, www.boom-studios.com, on the Librarians Page.

BOOM! Studios, 5670 Wilshire Boulevard, Suite 450, Los Angeles, CA 90036-5679. Printed in China. First Printing.
ISBN: 978-1-60886-363-1, eISBN: 978-1-61398-217-4

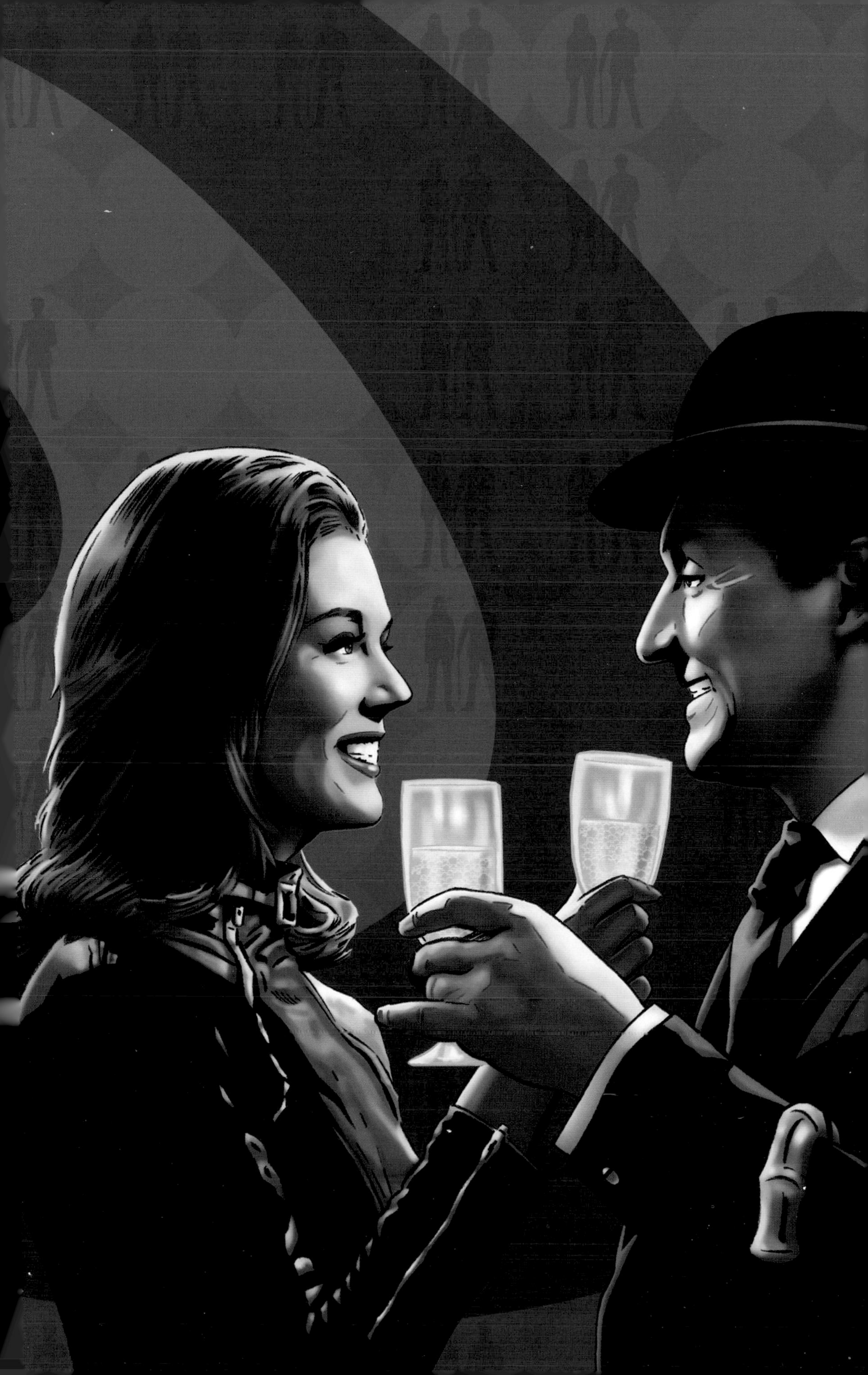

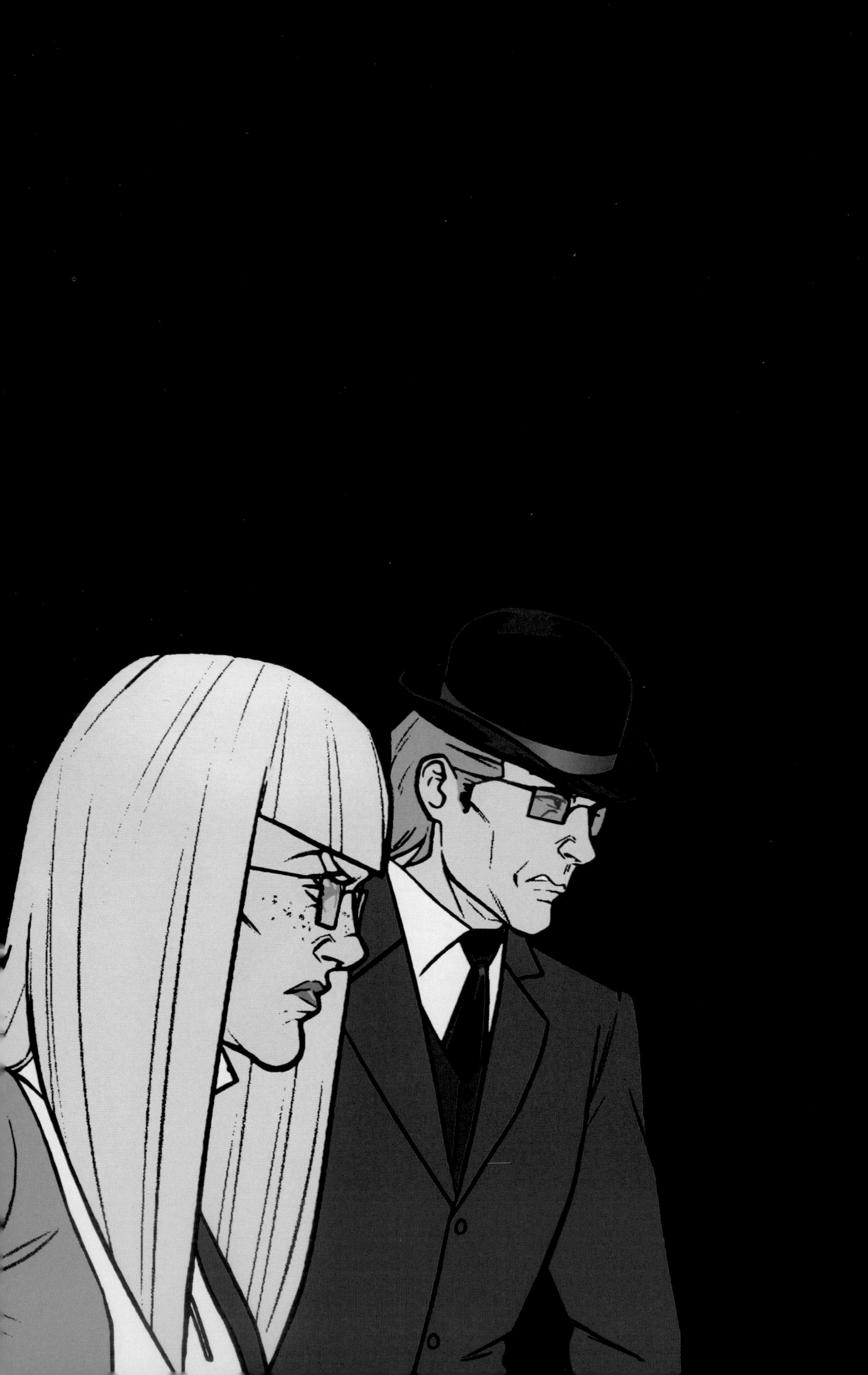

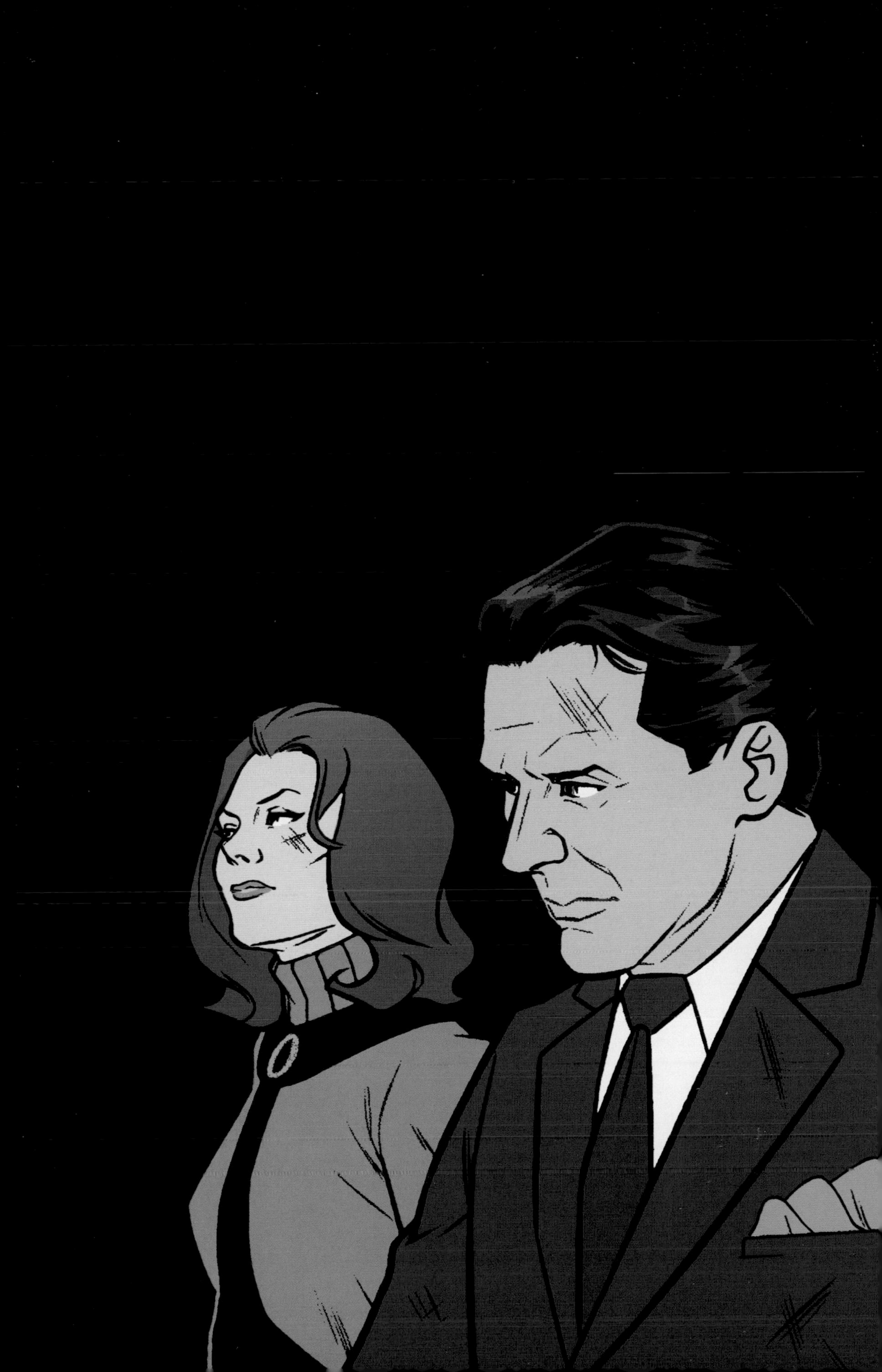

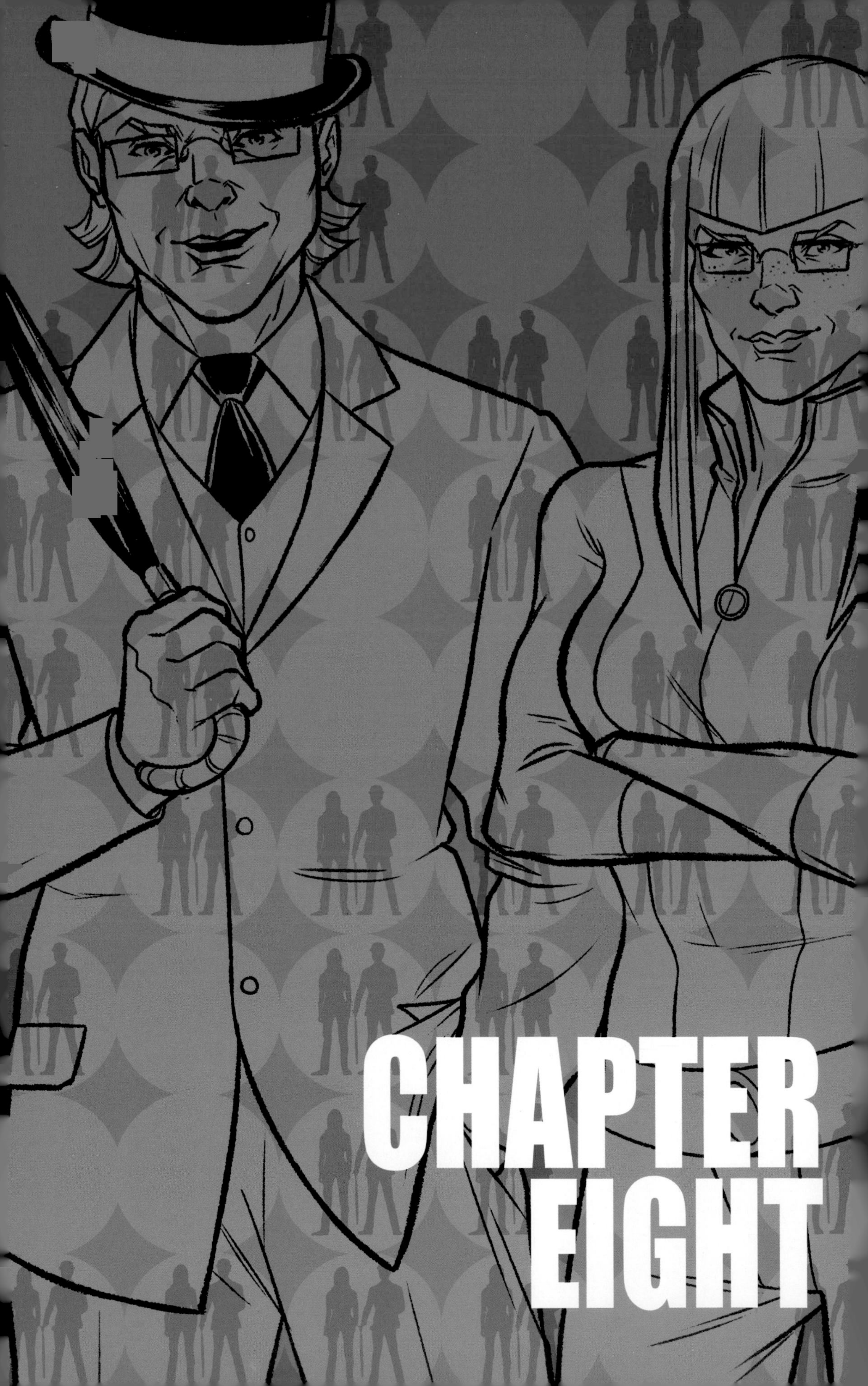

CHAPTER EIGHT

THE ART OF RESURRECTION

STEED SEES DOUBLE
EMMA IS ALL WET

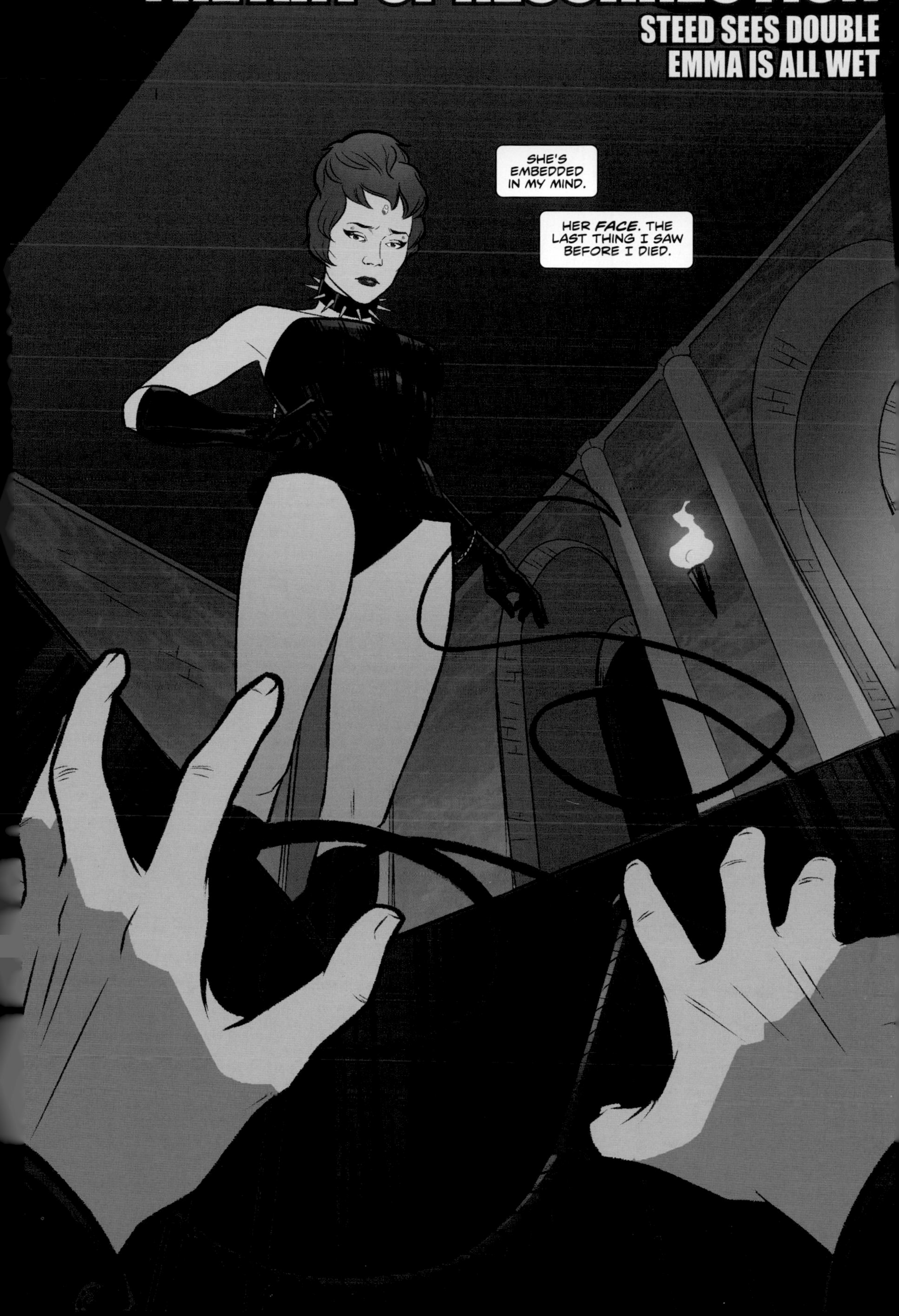
SHE'S EMBEDDED IN MY MIND.
HER FACE. THE LAST THING I SAW BEFORE I DIED.

YES, "DIED."

I MUST HAVE DIED.

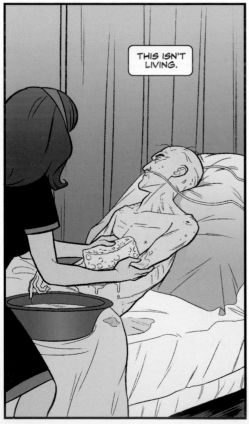

THIS ISN'T LIVING.

THIS IS HELL.

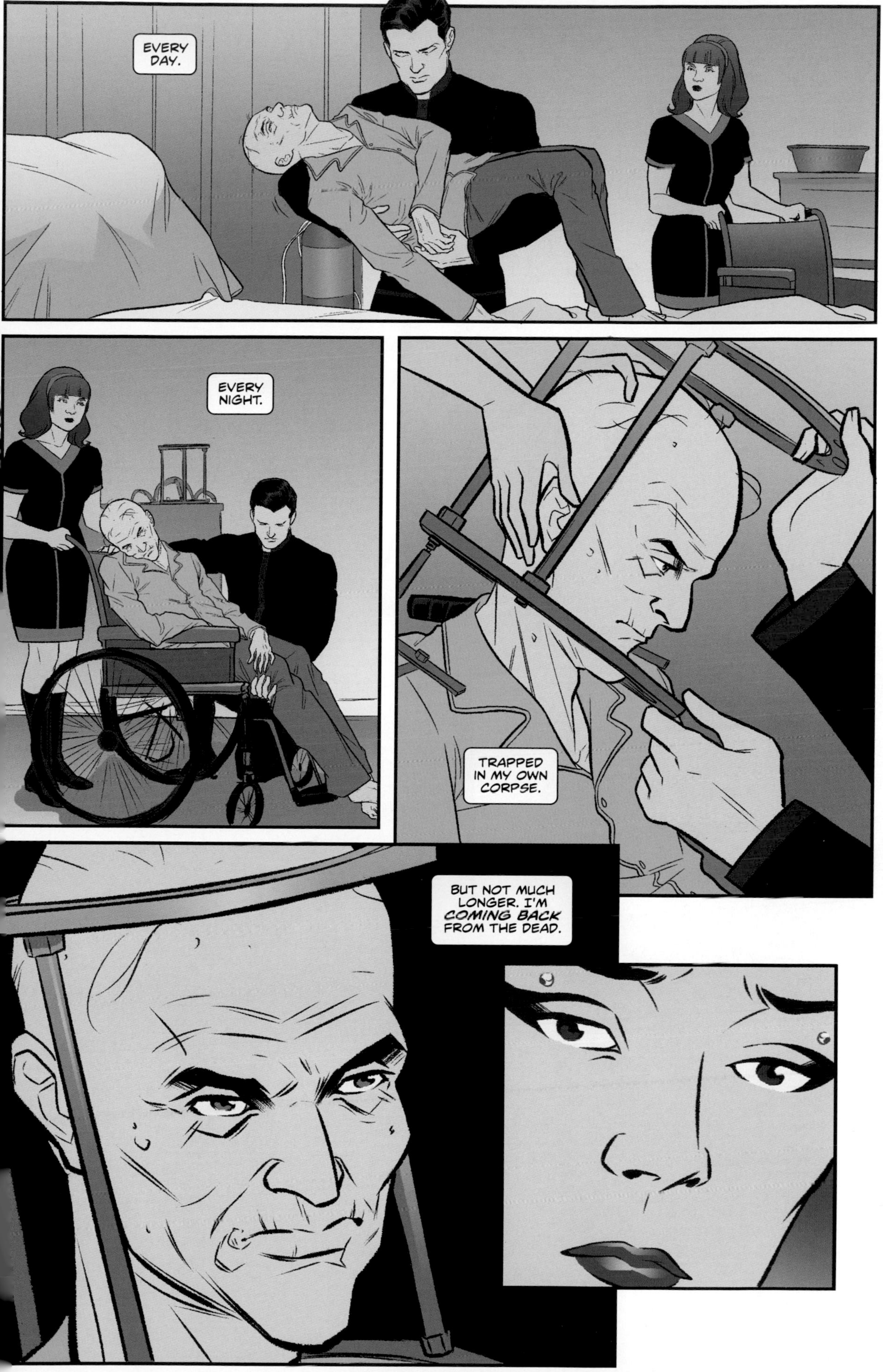
EVERY DAY.
EVERY NIGHT.
TRAPPED IN MY OWN CORPSE.
BUT NOT MUCH LONGER. I'M *COMING BACK* FROM THE DEAD.

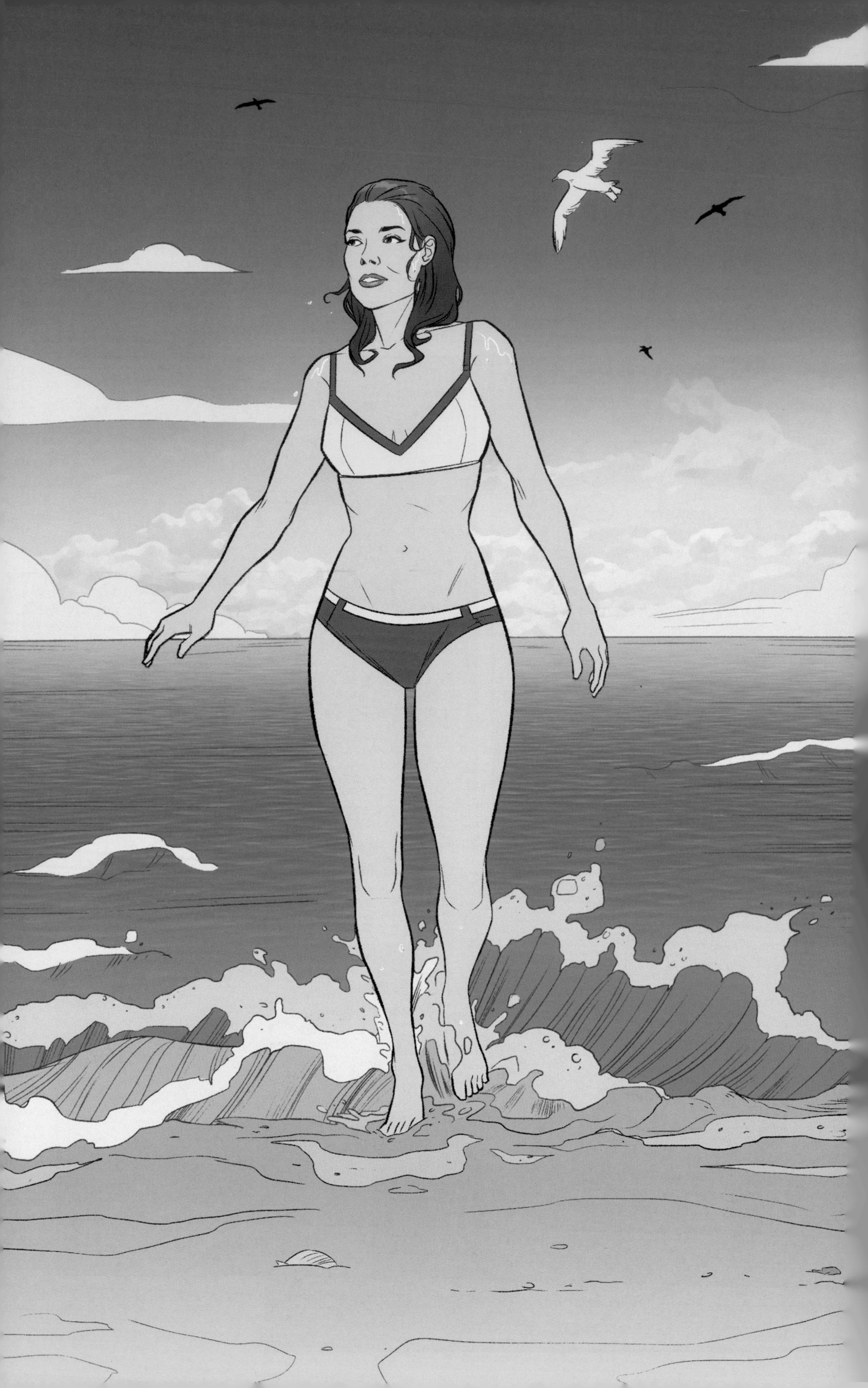

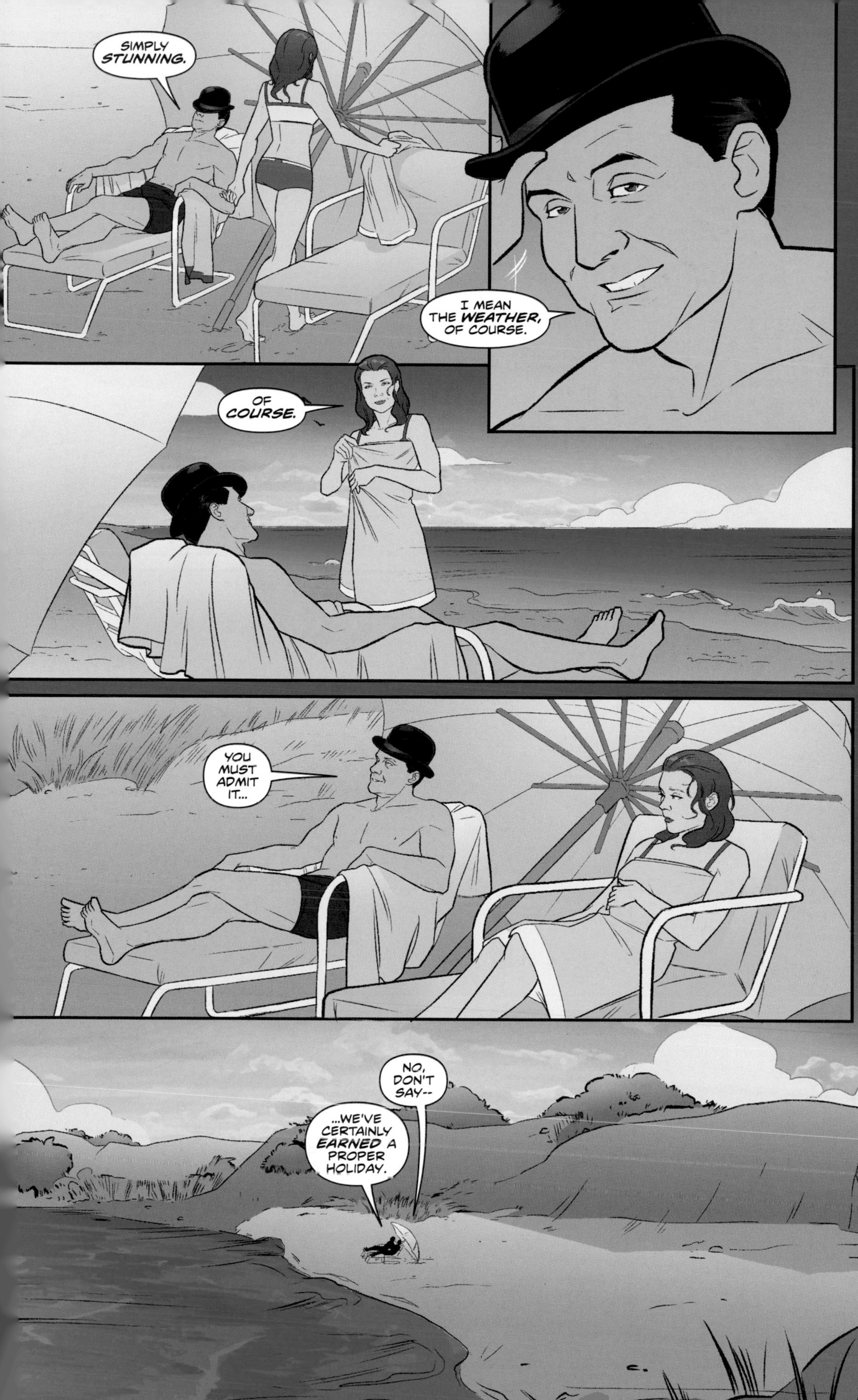
SIMPLY STUNNING.
I MEAN THE WEATHER, OF COURSE.
OF COURSE.
YOU MUST ADMIT IT...
NO, DON'T SAY--
...WE'VE CERTAINLY EARNED A PROPER HOLIDAY.

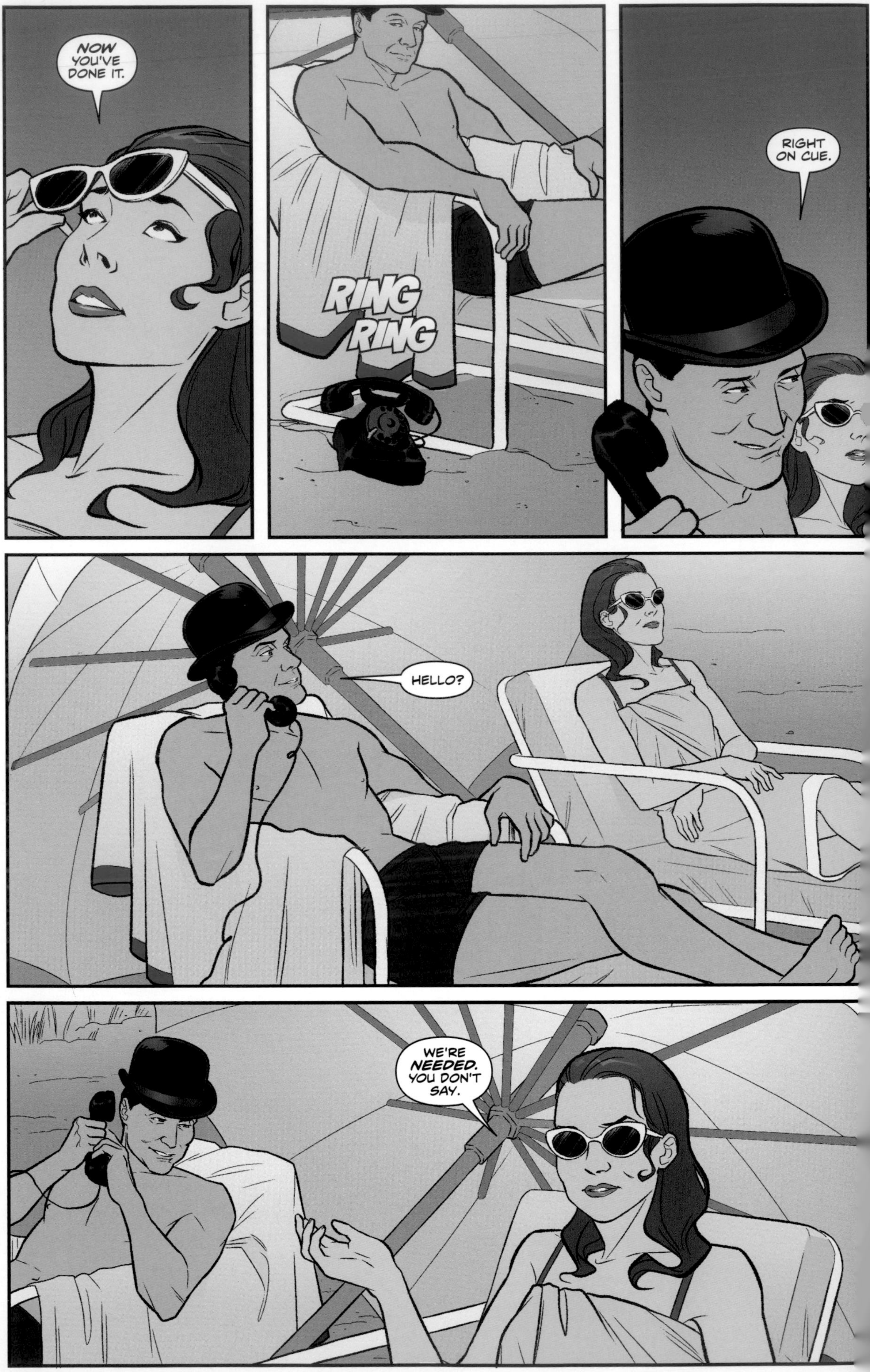
NOW YOU'VE DONE IT.
RING RING
RIGHT ON CUE.
HELLO?
WE'RE NEEDED. YOU DON'T SAY.

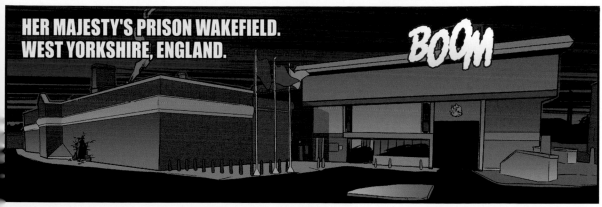

HER MAJESTY'S PRISON WAKEFIELD.
WEST YORKSHIRE, ENGLAND.

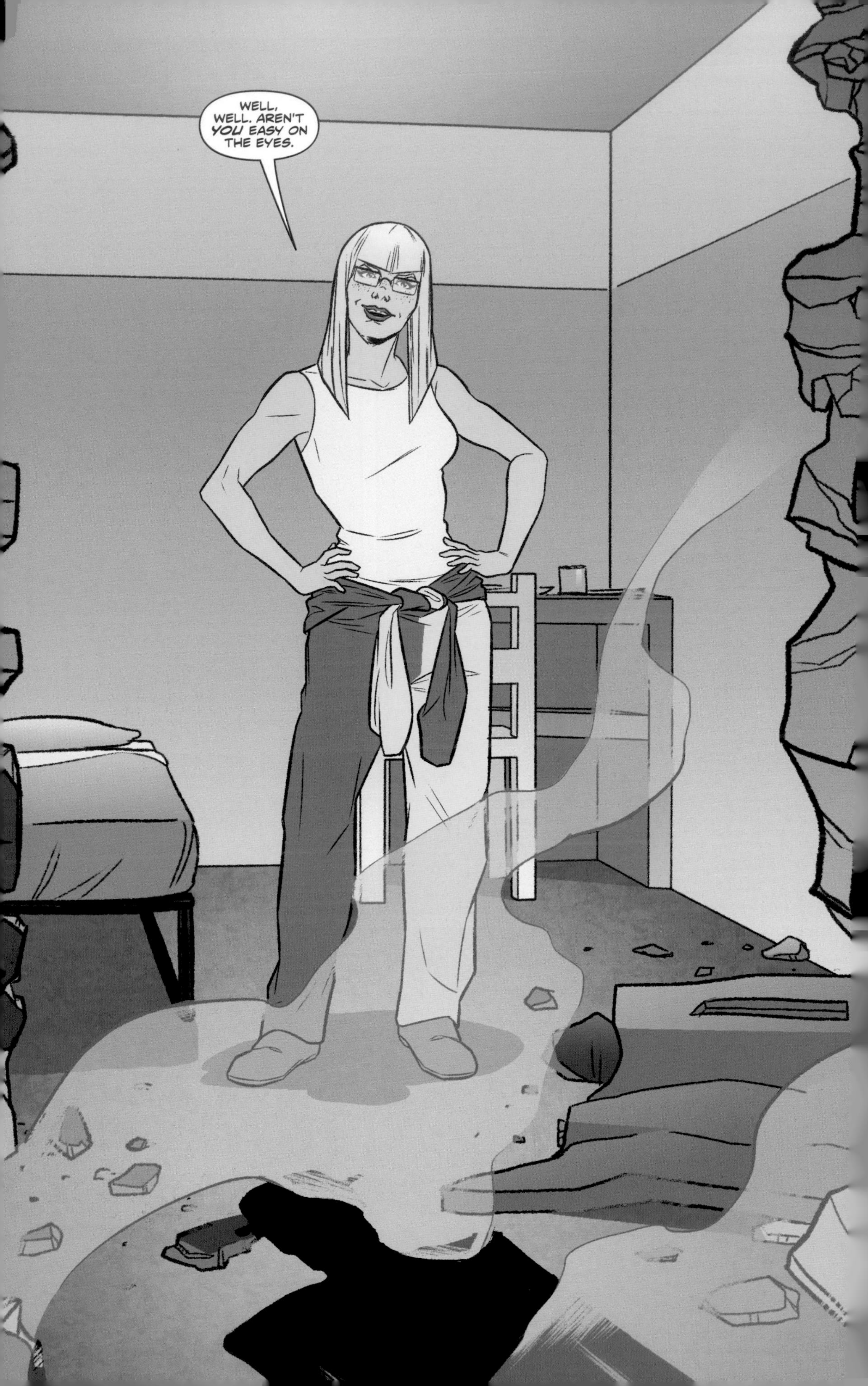
WELL, WELL. AREN'T YOU EASY ON THE EYES.

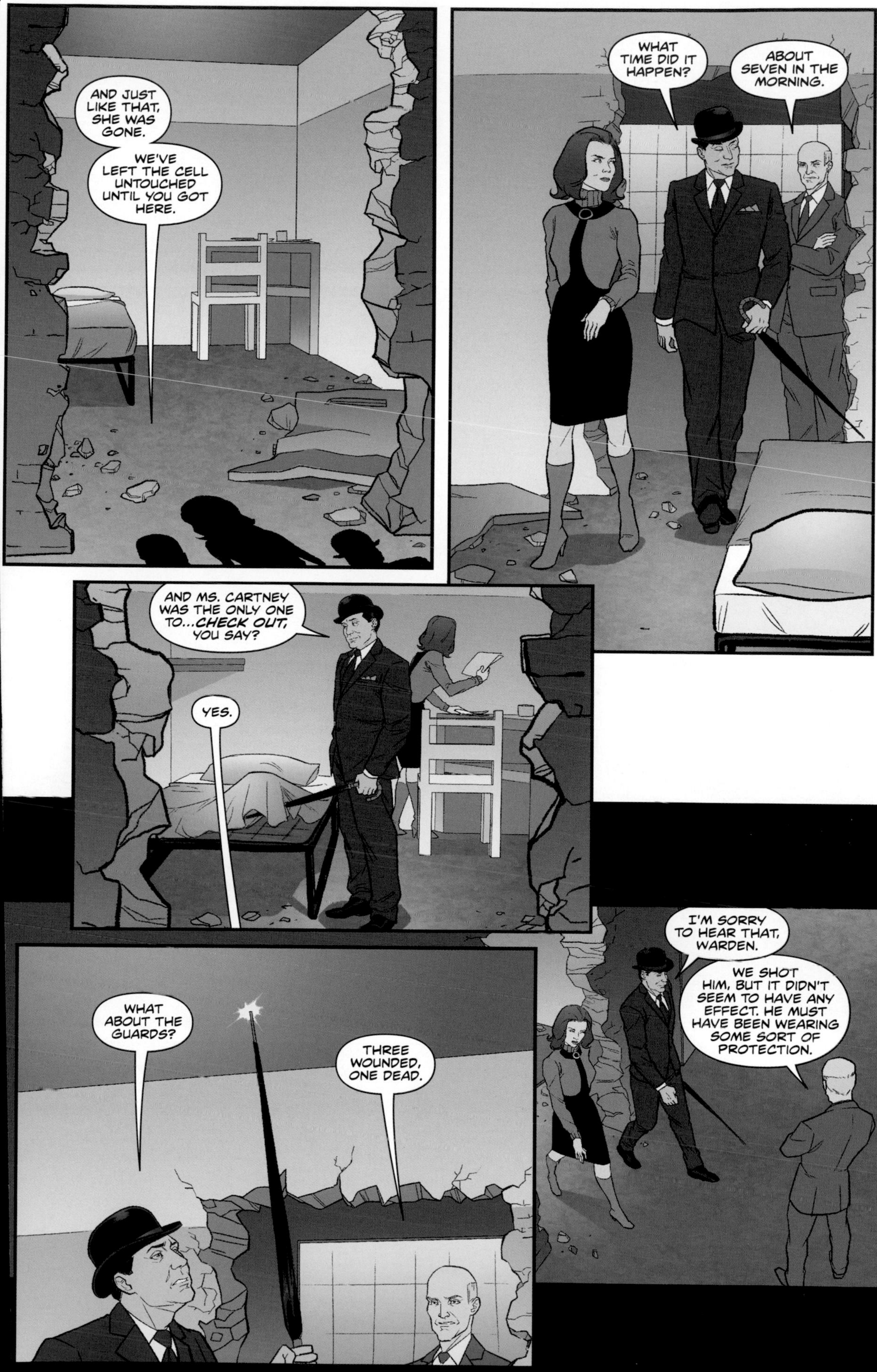
AND JUST LIKE THAT, SHE WAS GONE.
WE'VE LEFT THE CELL UNTOUCHED UNTIL YOU GOT HERE.
WHAT TIME DID IT HAPPEN?
ABOUT SEVEN IN THE MORNING.
AND MS. CARTNEY WAS THE ONLY ONE TO...CHECK OUT, YOU SAY?
YES.
WHAT ABOUT THE GUARDS?
THREE WOUNDED, ONE DEAD.
I'M SORRY TO HEAR THAT, WARDEN.
WE SHOT HIM, BUT IT DIDN'T SEEM TO HAVE ANY EFFECT. HE MUST HAVE BEEN WEARING SOME SORT OF PROTECTION.

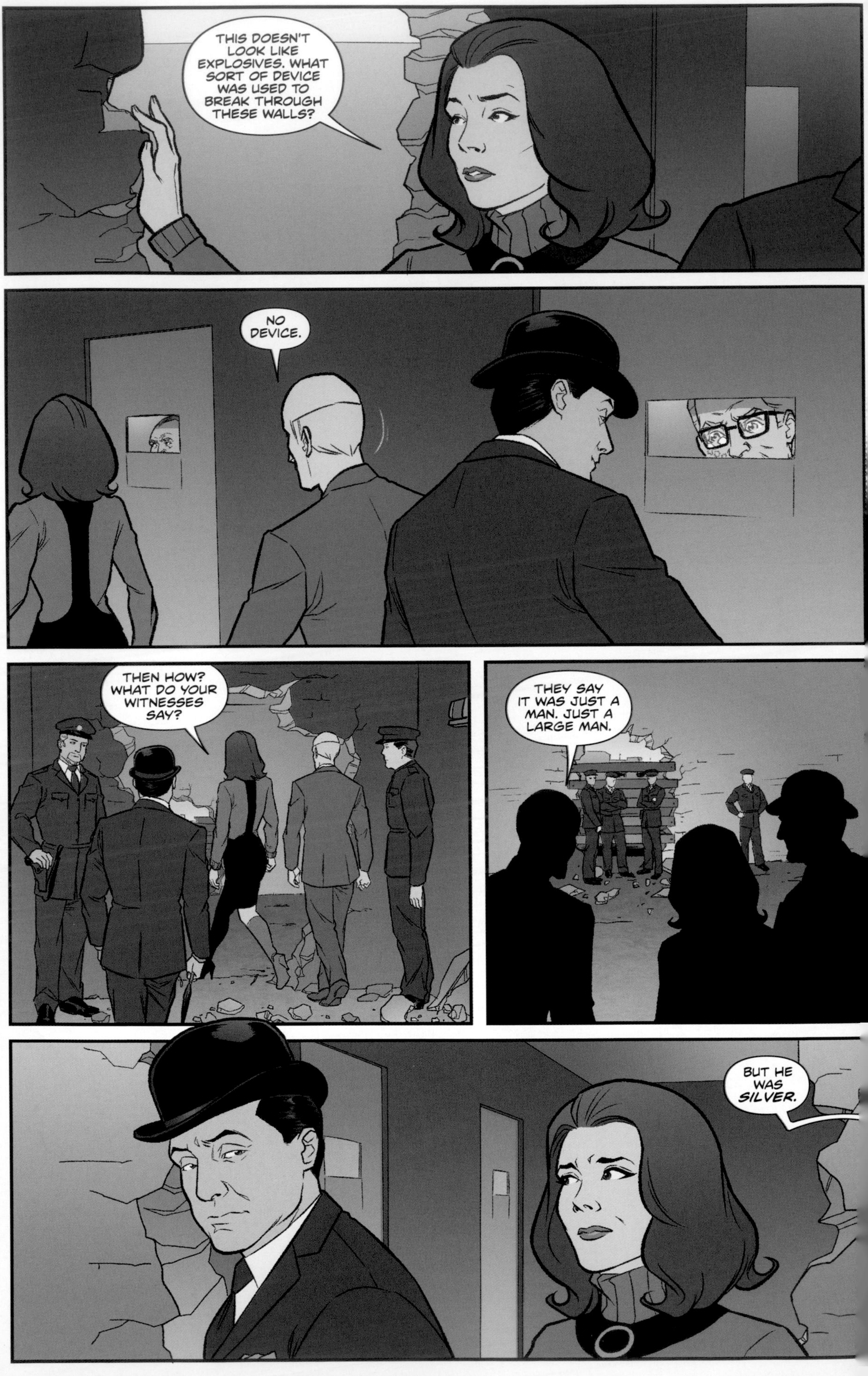
THIS DOESN'T LOOK LIKE EXPLOSIVES. WHAT SORT OF DEVICE WAS USED TO BREAK THROUGH THESE WALLS?
NO DEVICE.
THEN HOW? WHAT DO YOUR WITNESSES SAY?
THEY SAY IT WAS JUST A MAN. JUST A LARGE MAN.
BUT HE WAS SILVER.

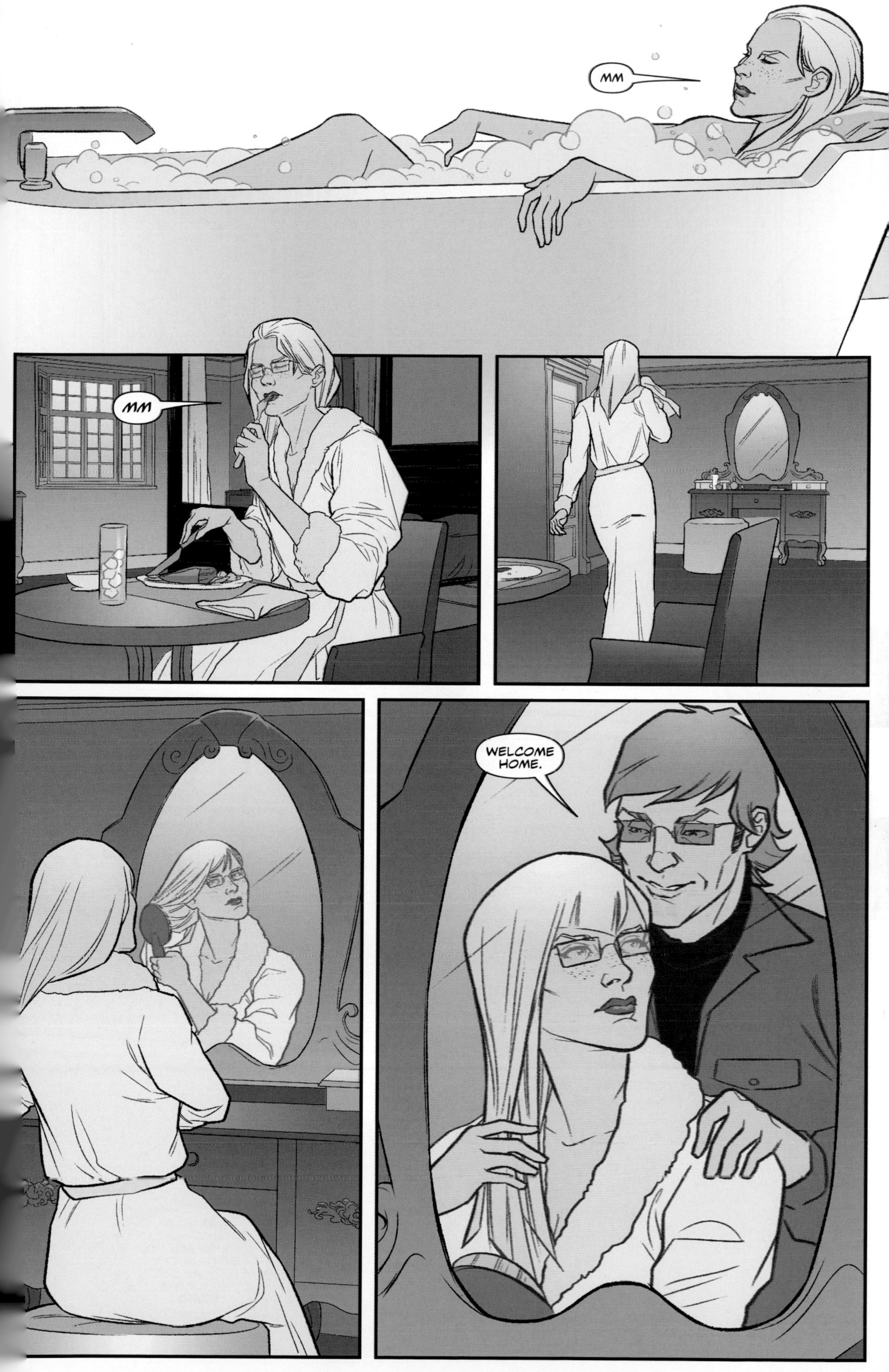
MM
MM
WELCOME HOME.

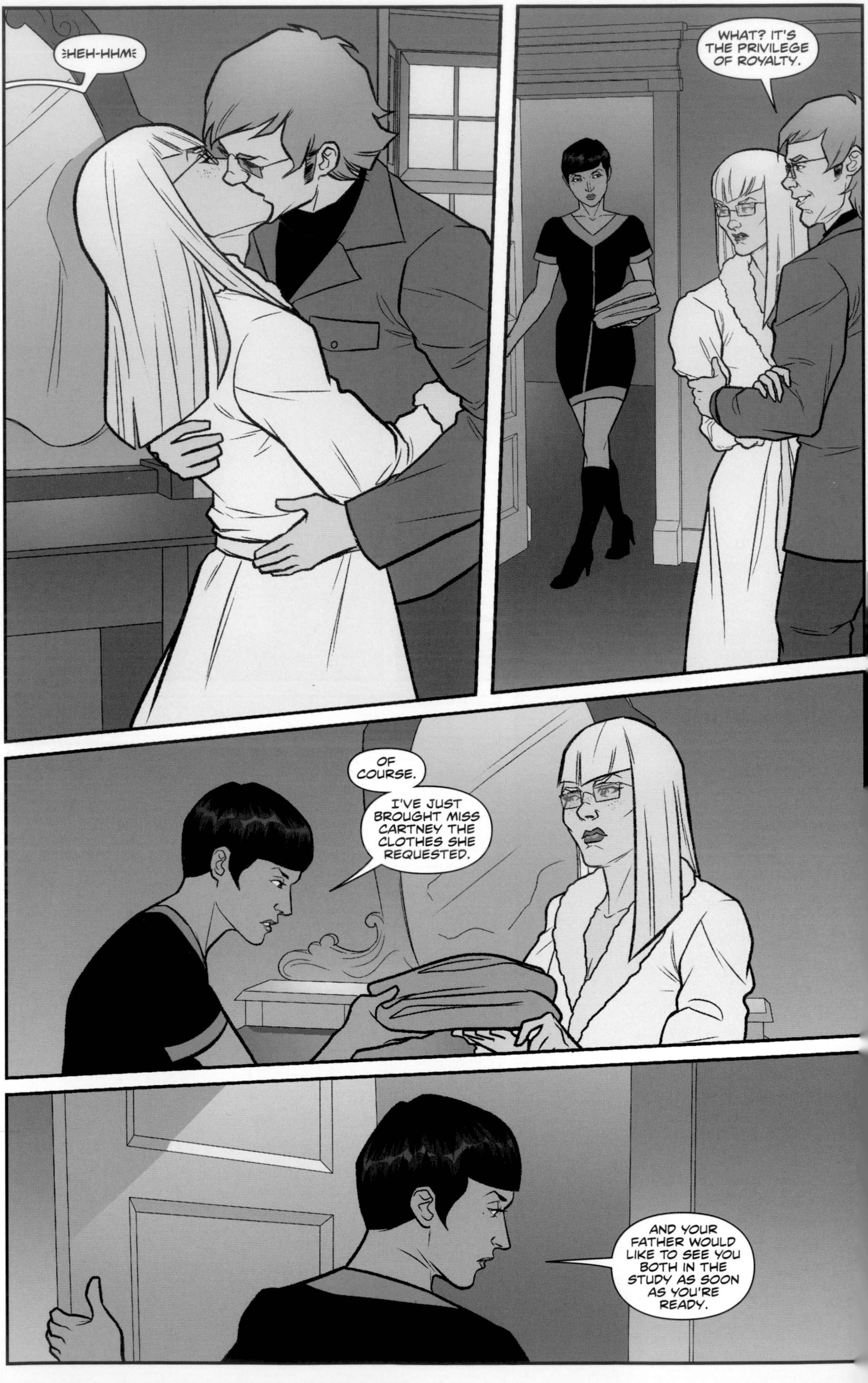

HEH-HHM
WHAT? IT'S THE PRIVILEGE OF ROYALTY.
OF COURSE.
I'VE JUST BROUGHT MISS CARTNEY THE CLOTHES SHE REQUESTED.
AND YOUR FATHER WOULD LIKE TO SEE YOU BOTH IN THE STUDY AS SOON AS YOU'RE READY.

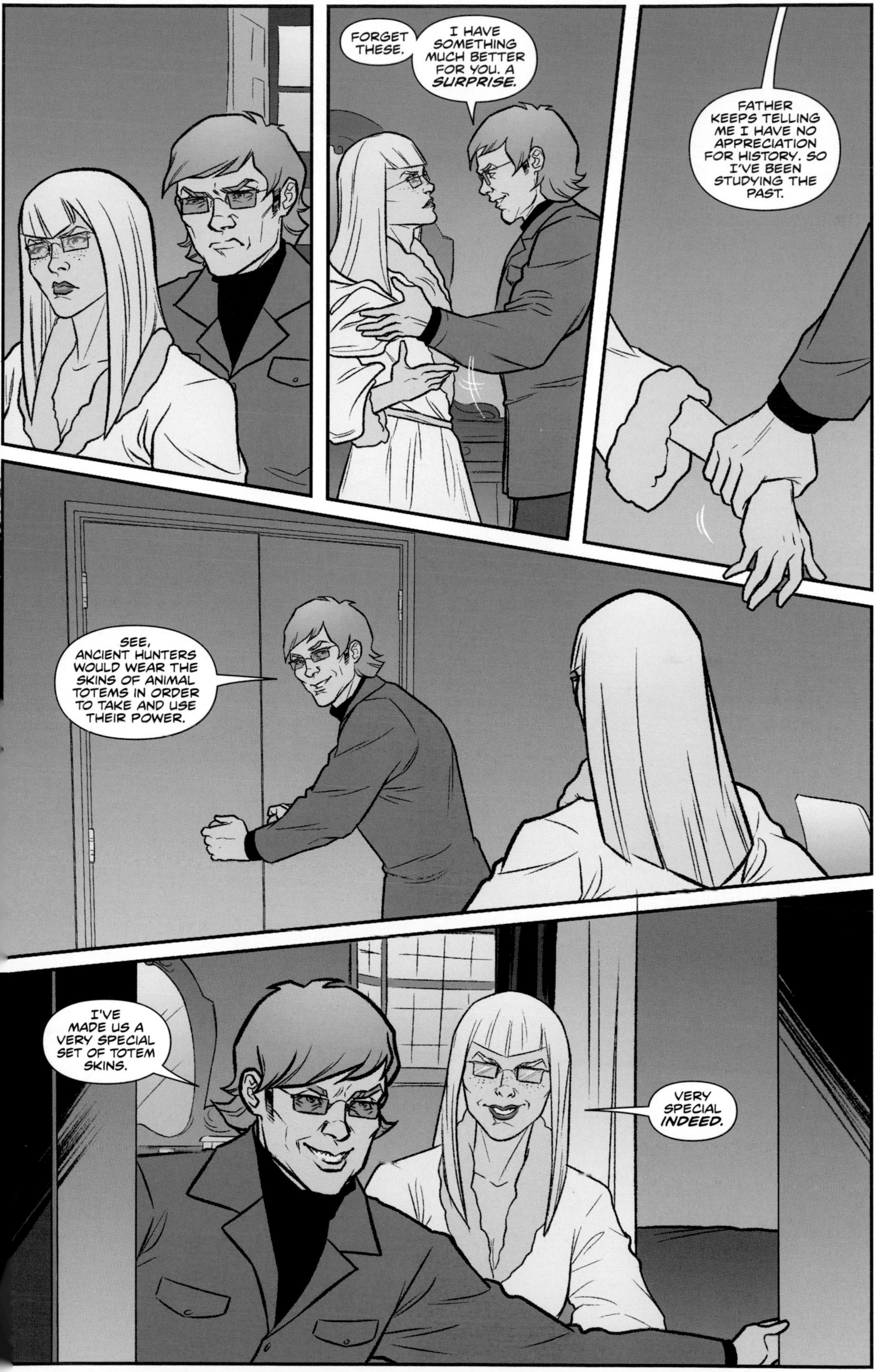
FORGET THESE.
I HAVE SOMETHING MUCH BETTER FOR YOU. A *SURPRISE.*
FATHER KEEPS TELLING ME I HAVE NO APPRECIATION FOR HISTORY. SO I'VE BEEN STUDYING THE PAST.
SEE, ANCIENT HUNTERS WOULD WEAR THE SKINS OF ANIMAL TOTEMS IN ORDER TO TAKE AND USE THEIR POWER.
I'VE MADE US A VERY SPECIAL SET OF TOTEM SKINS.
VERY SPECIAL *INDEED.*

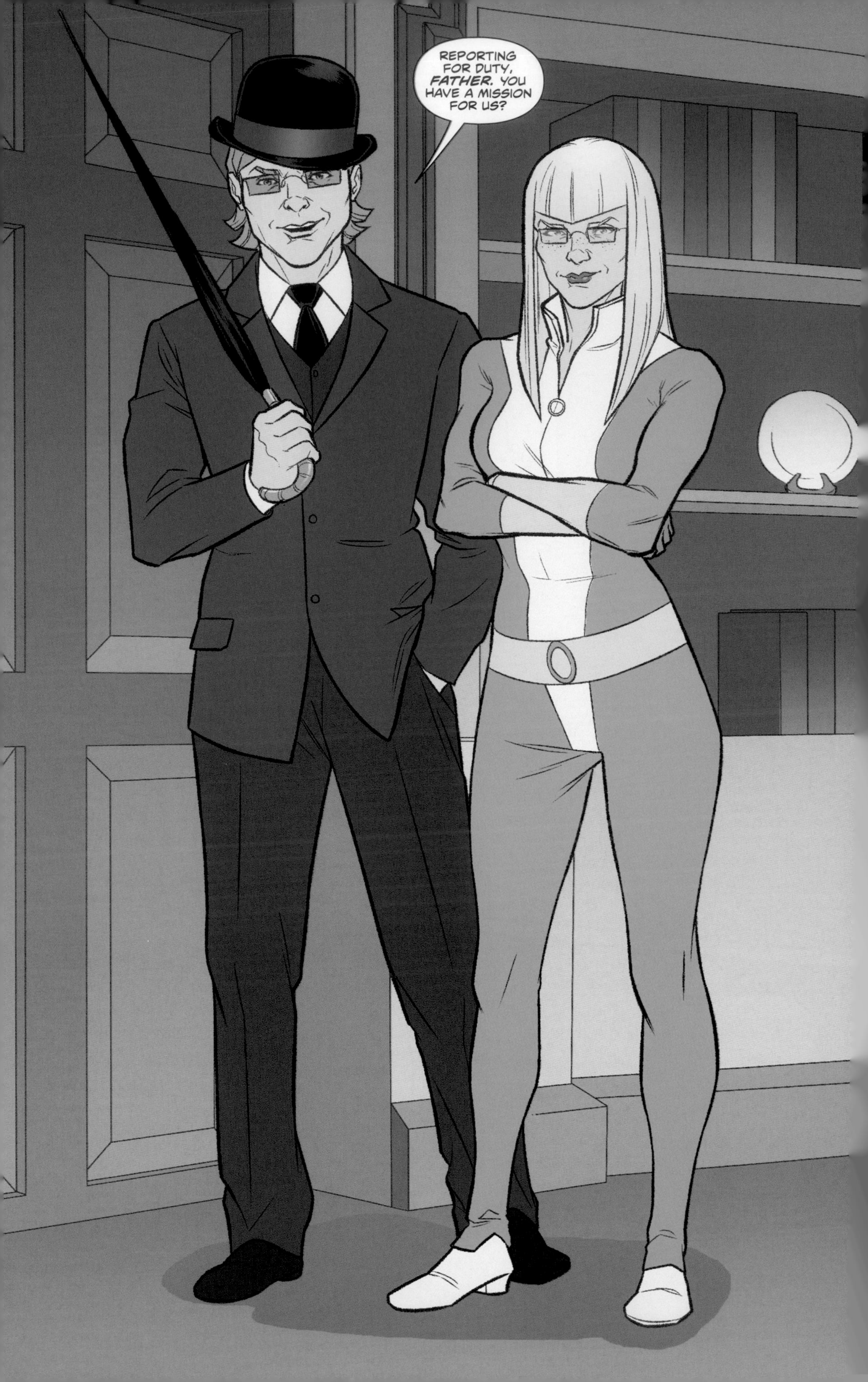
REPORTING FOR DUTY, FATHER. YOU HAVE A MISSION FOR US?

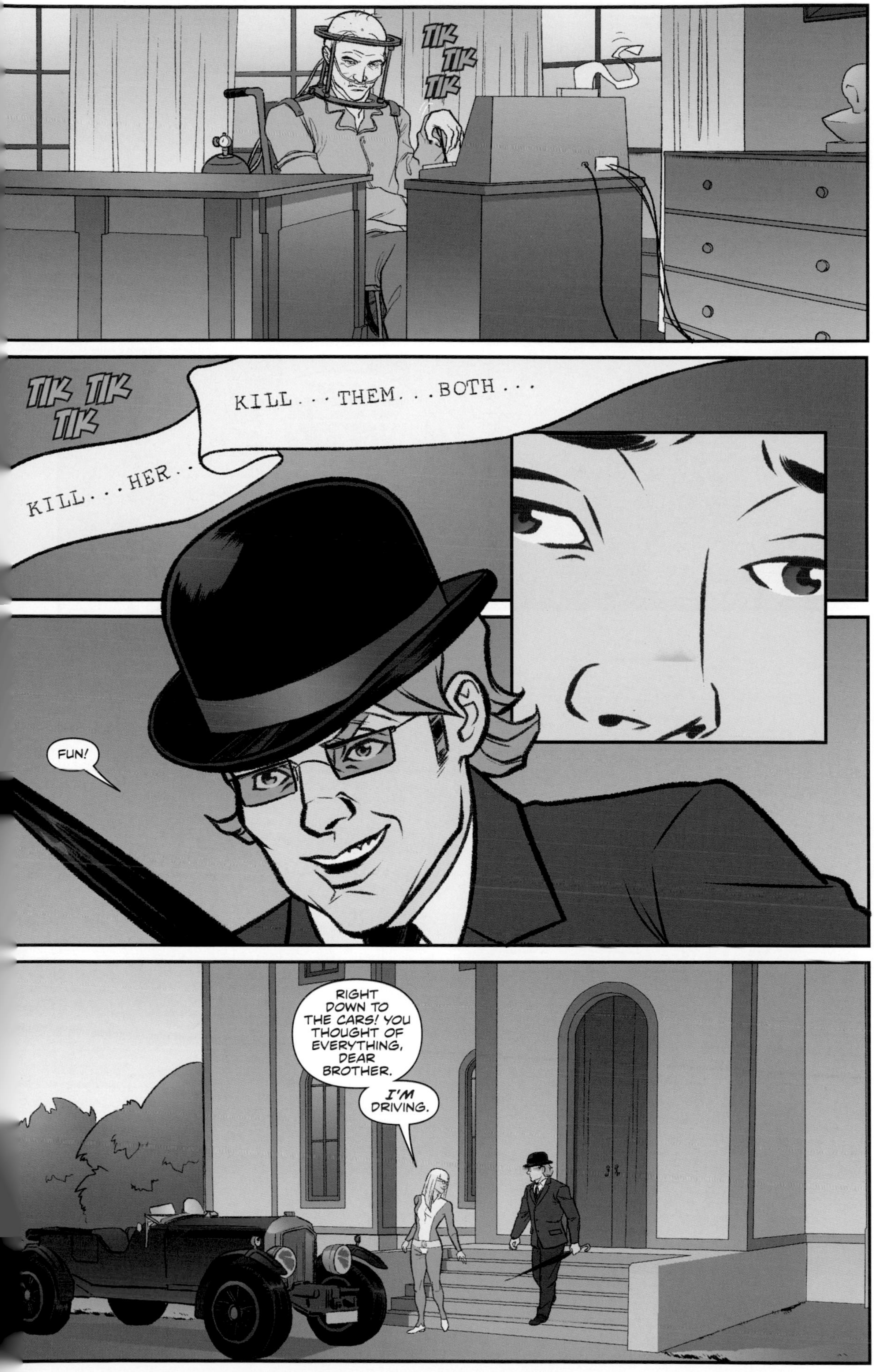
TIK
TIK
TIK
TIK TIK
TIK
KILL...HER...
KILL...THEM...BOTH...
FUN!
RIGHT DOWN TO THE CARS! YOU THOUGHT OF EVERYTHING, DEAR BROTHER.
I'M DRIVING.

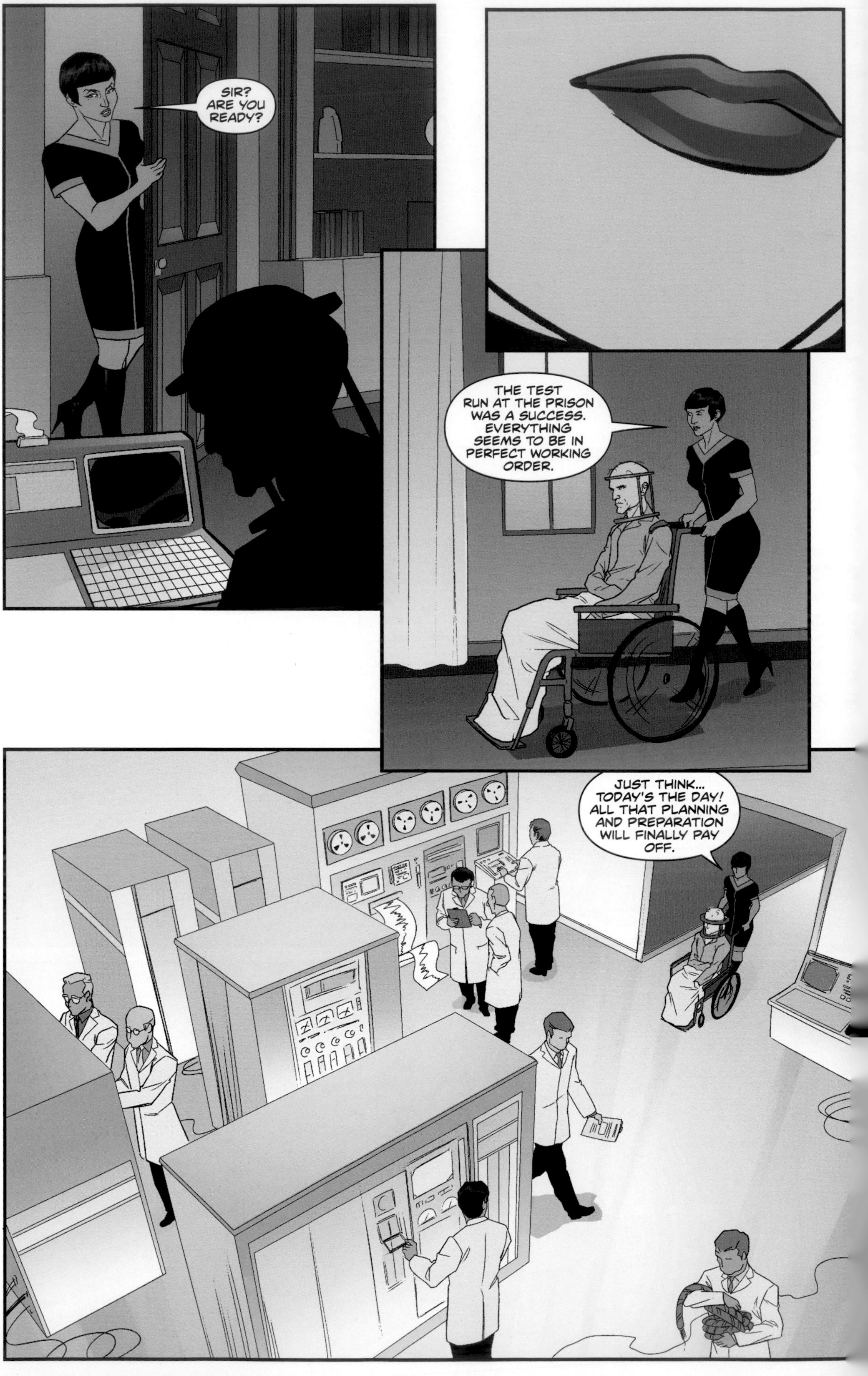
SIR? ARE YOU READY?
THE TEST RUN AT THE PRISON WAS A SUCCESS. EVERYTHING SEEMS TO BE IN PERFECT WORKING ORDER.
JUST THINK... TODAY'S THE DAY! ALL THAT PLANNING AND PREPARATION WILL FINALLY PAY OFF.

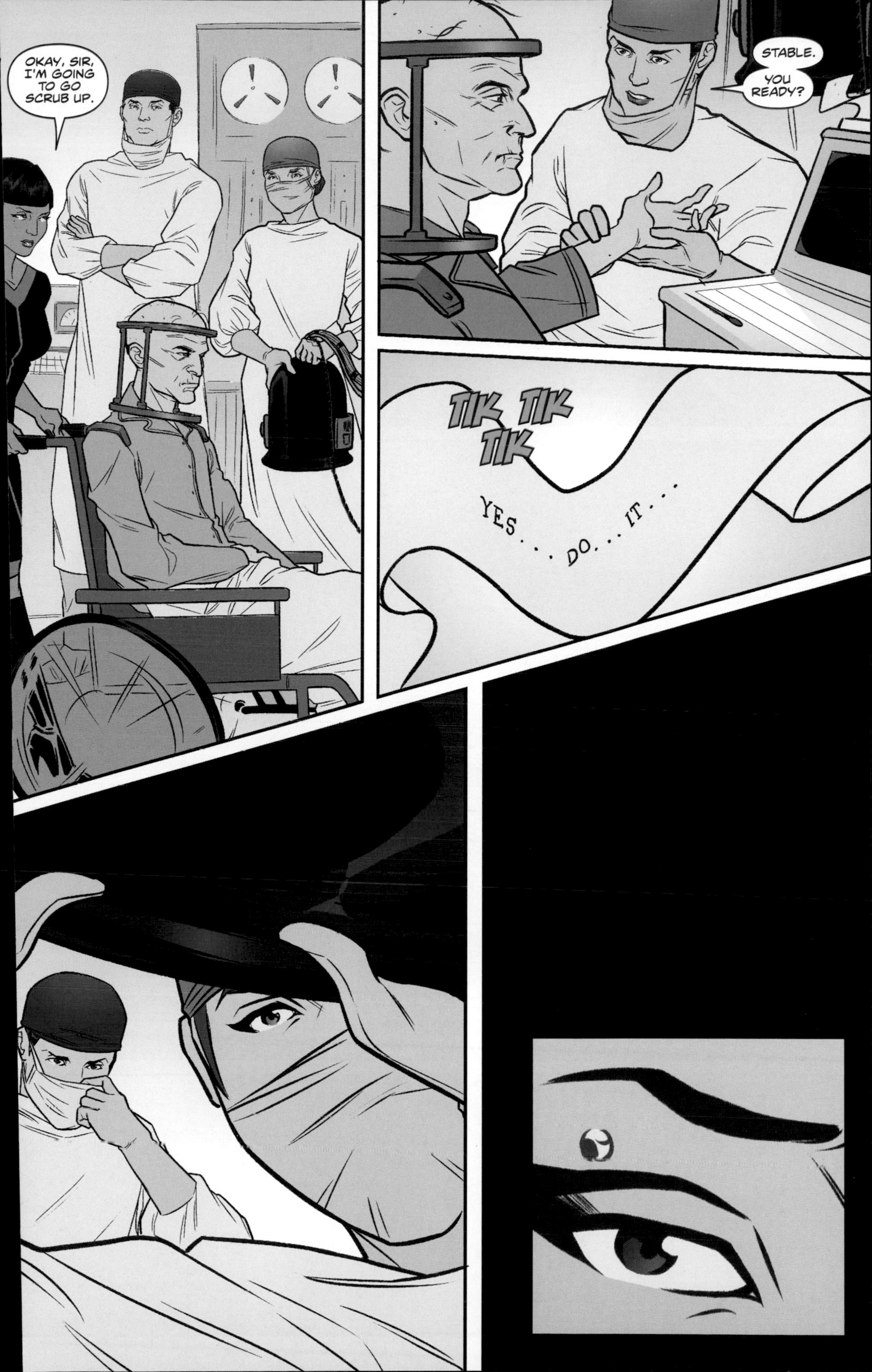

OKAY, SIR, I'M GOING TO GO SCRUB UP.
STABLE.
YOU READY?
TIK TIK TIK
YES... DO... IT...

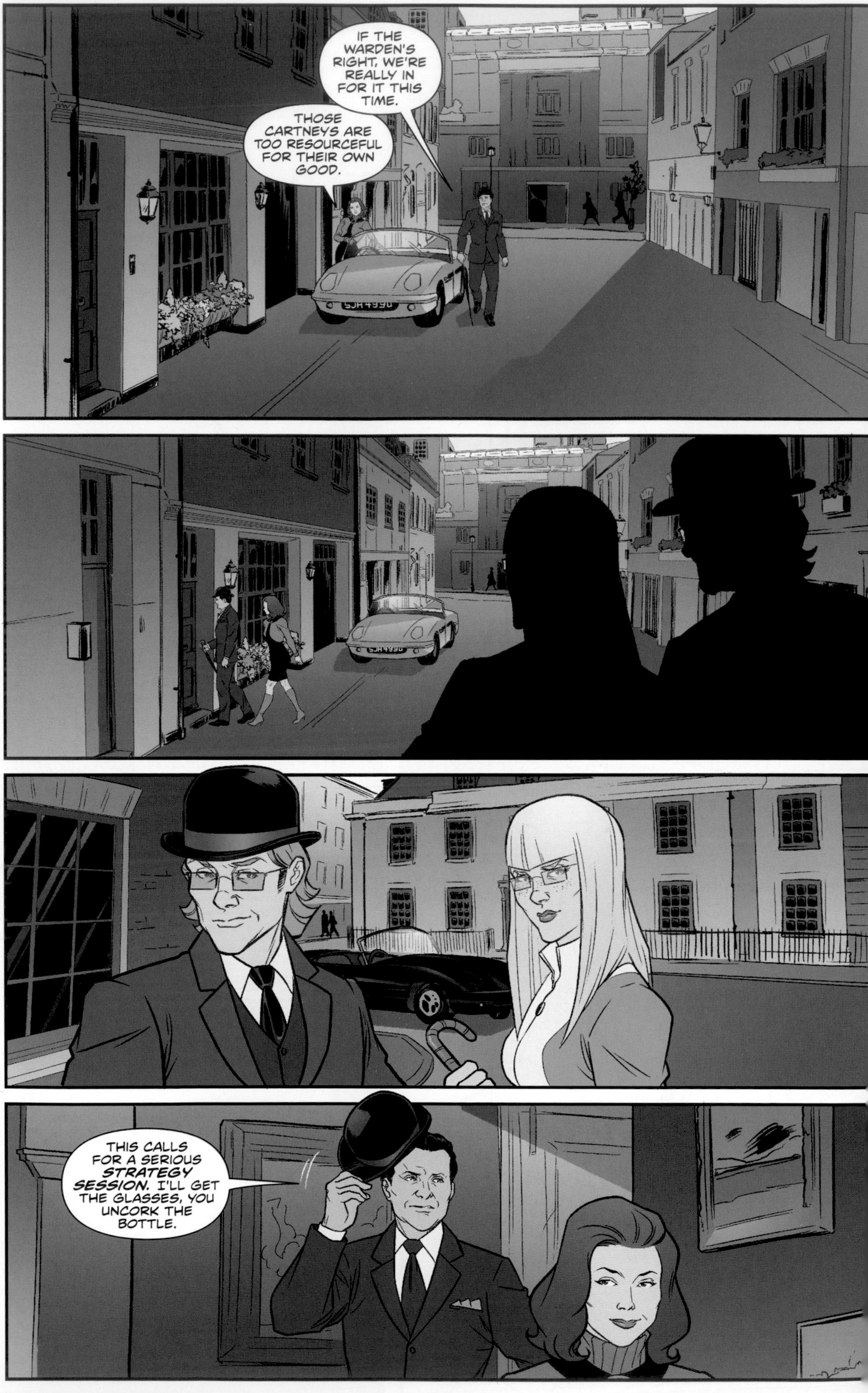
IF THE WARDEN'S RIGHT, WE'RE REALLY IN FOR IT THIS TIME.
THOSE CARTNEYS ARE TOO RESOURCEFUL FOR THEIR OWN GOOD.
THIS CALLS FOR A SERIOUS STRATEGY SESSION. I'LL GET THE GLASSES, YOU UNCORK THE BOTTLE.

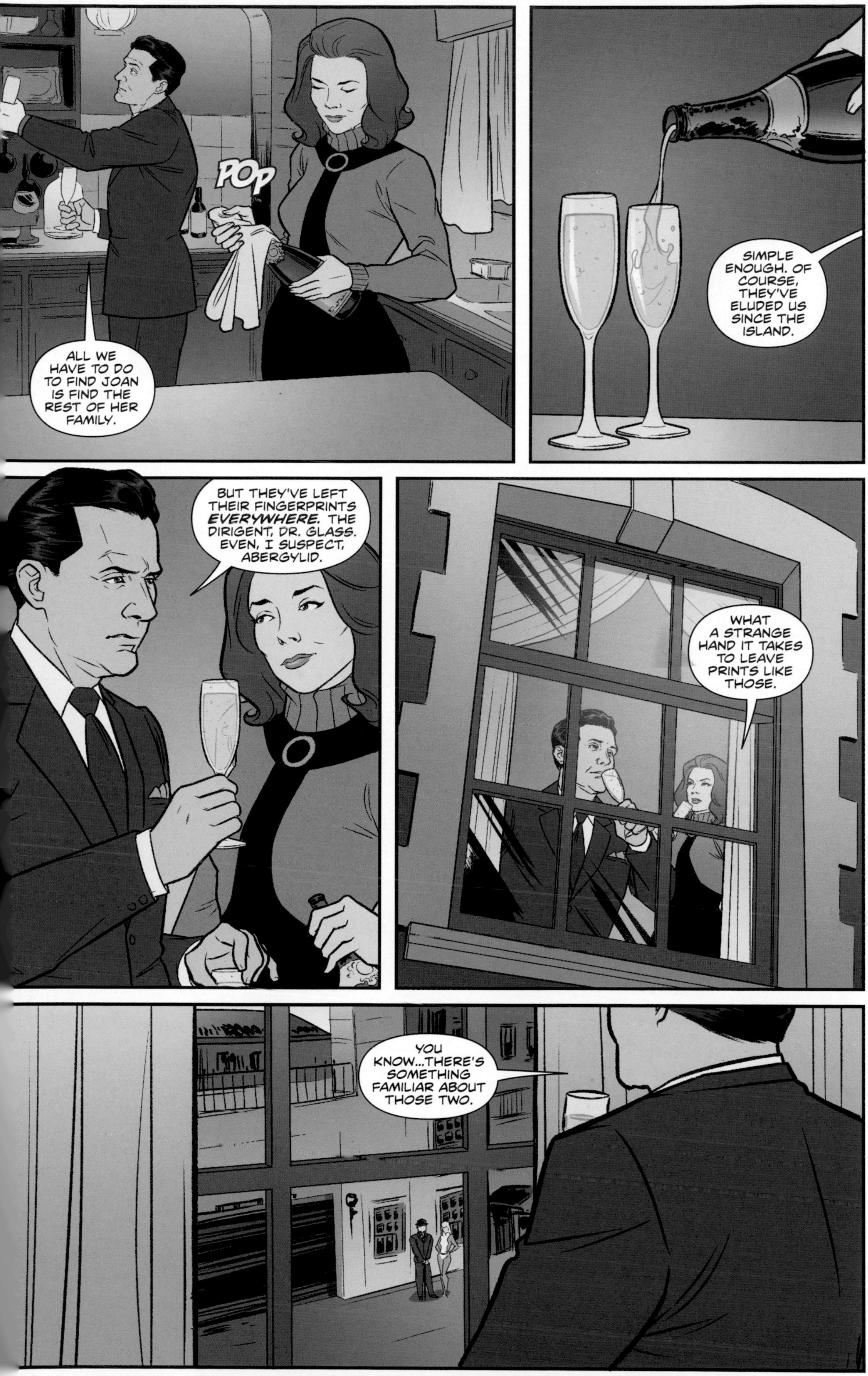
POP
ALL WE HAVE TO DO TO FIND JOAN IS FIND THE REST OF HER FAMILY.
SIMPLE ENOUGH. OF COURSE, THEY'VE ELUDED US SINCE THE ISLAND.
BUT THEY'VE LEFT THEIR FINGERPRINTS **EVERYWHERE.** THE DIRIGENT, DR. GLASS. EVEN, I SUSPECT, ABERGYLID.
WHAT A STRANGE HAND IT TAKES TO LEAVE PRINTS LIKE THOSE.
YOU KNOW...THERE'S SOMETHING FAMILIAR ABOUT THOSE TWO.

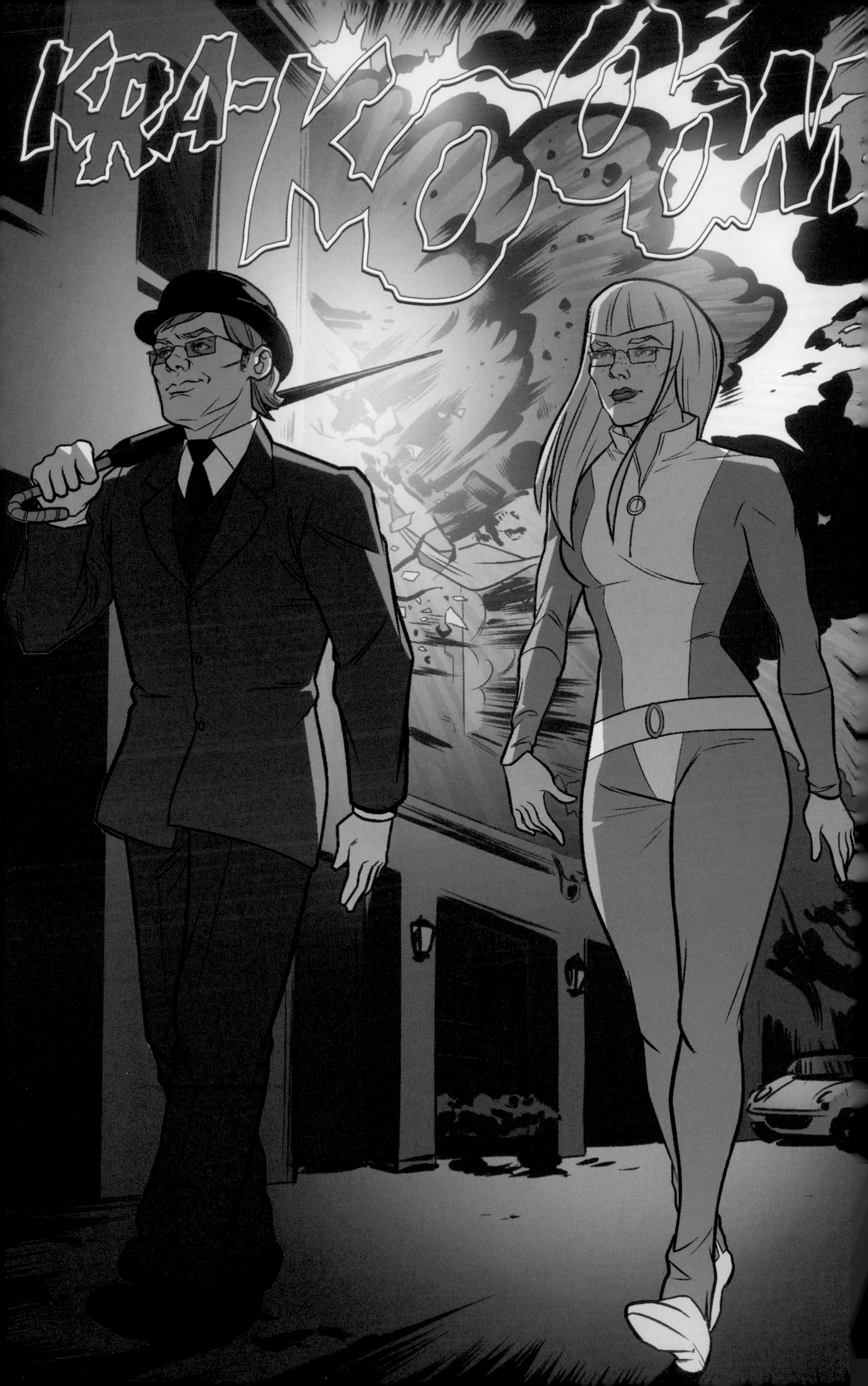
KRA-KOOOOM

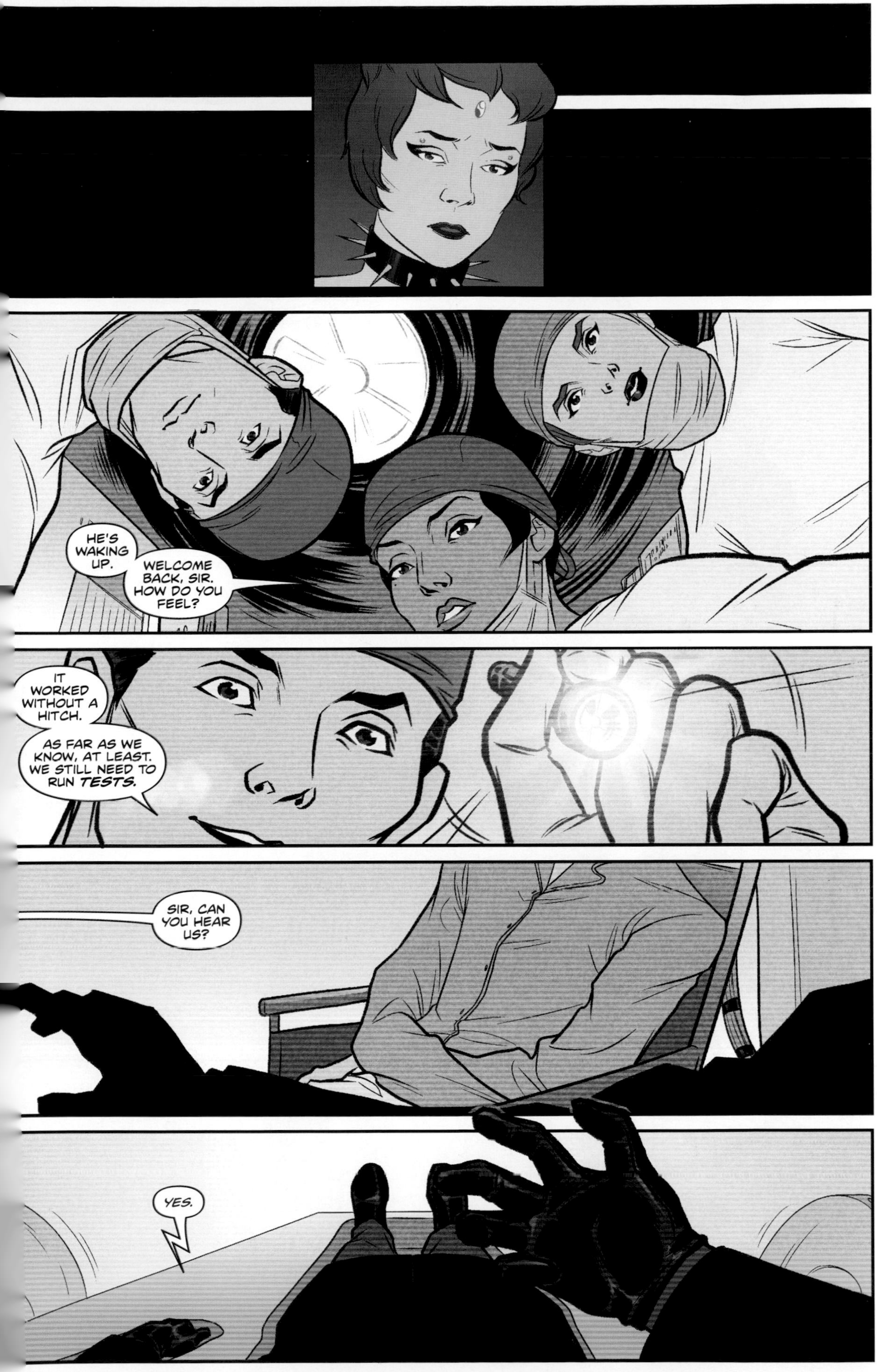

HE'S WAKING UP.
WELCOME BACK, SIR. HOW DO YOU FEEL?
IT WORKED WITHOUT A HITCH.
AS FAR AS WE KNOW, AT LEAST. WE STILL NEED TO RUN *TESTS.*
SIR, CAN YOU HEAR US?
YES.

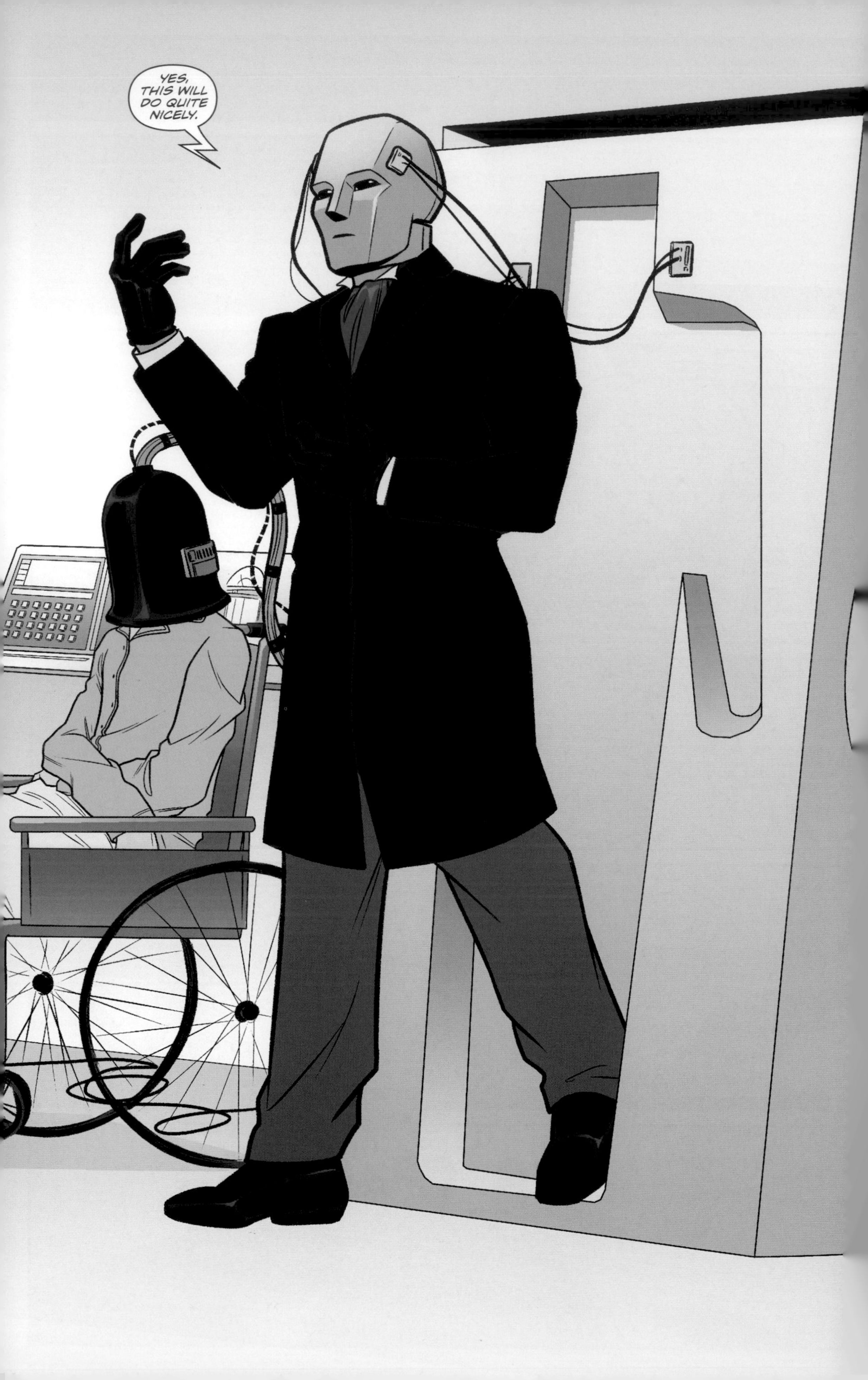
YES, THIS WILL DO QUITE NICELY.

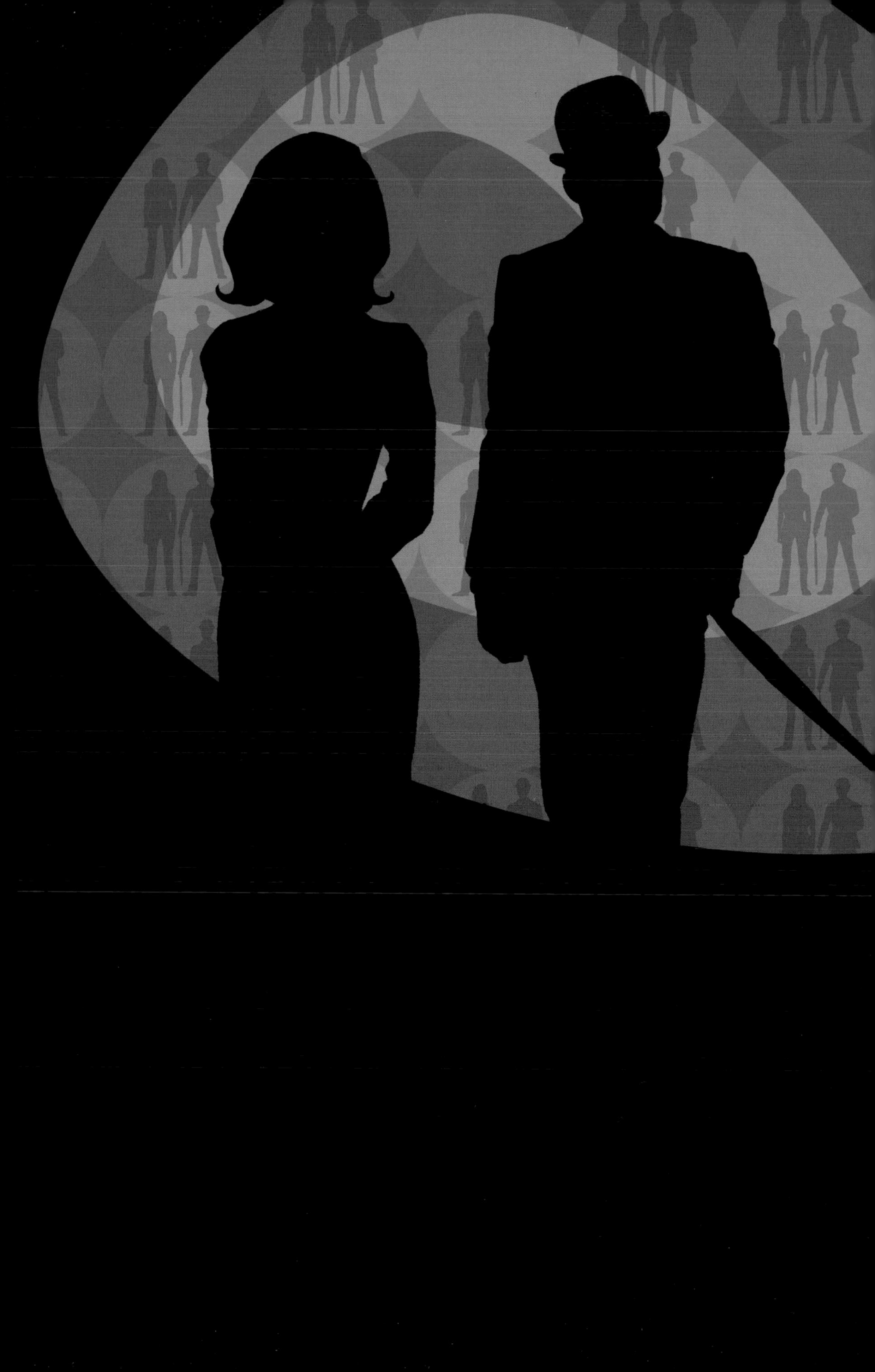

CHAPTER NINE

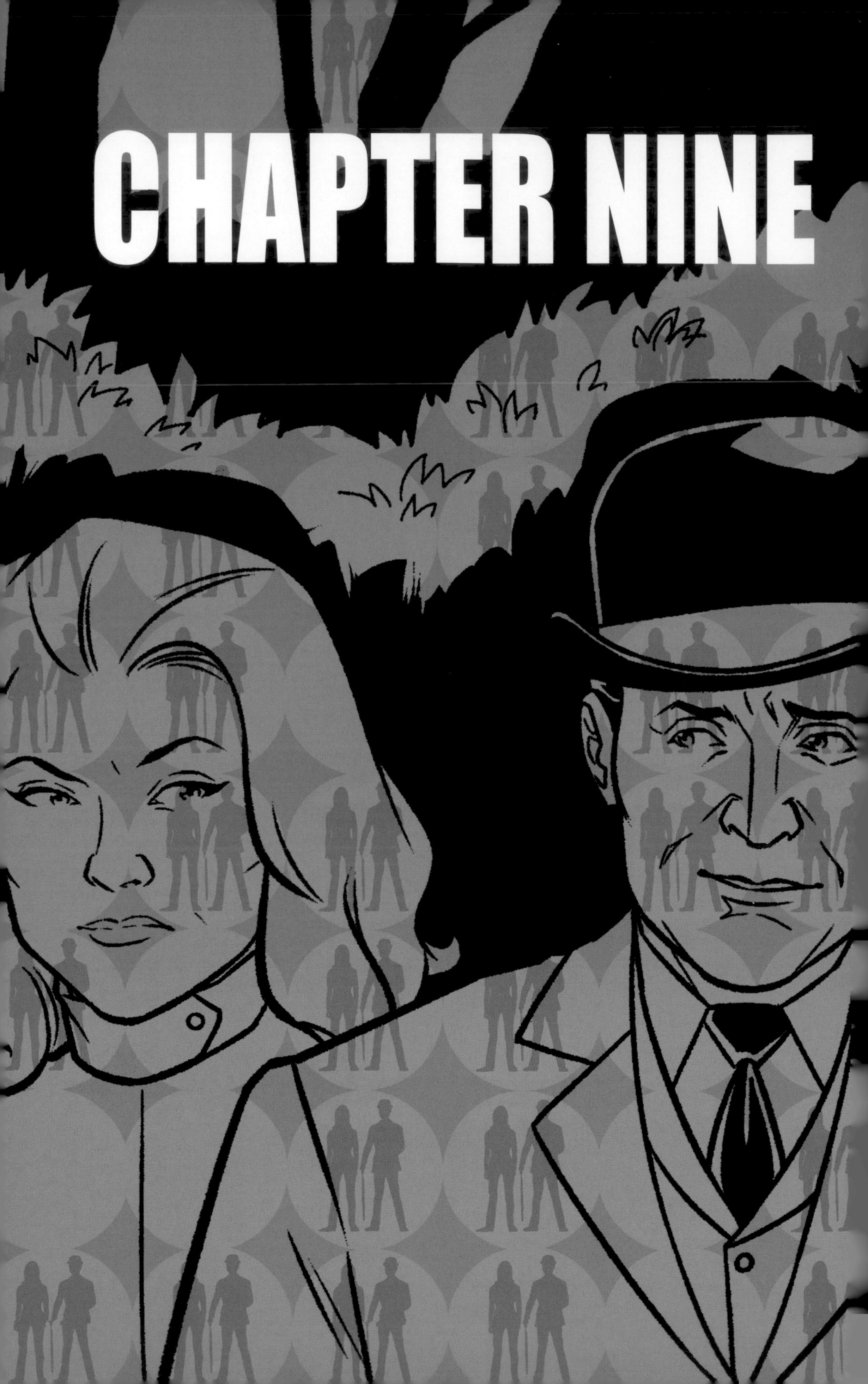

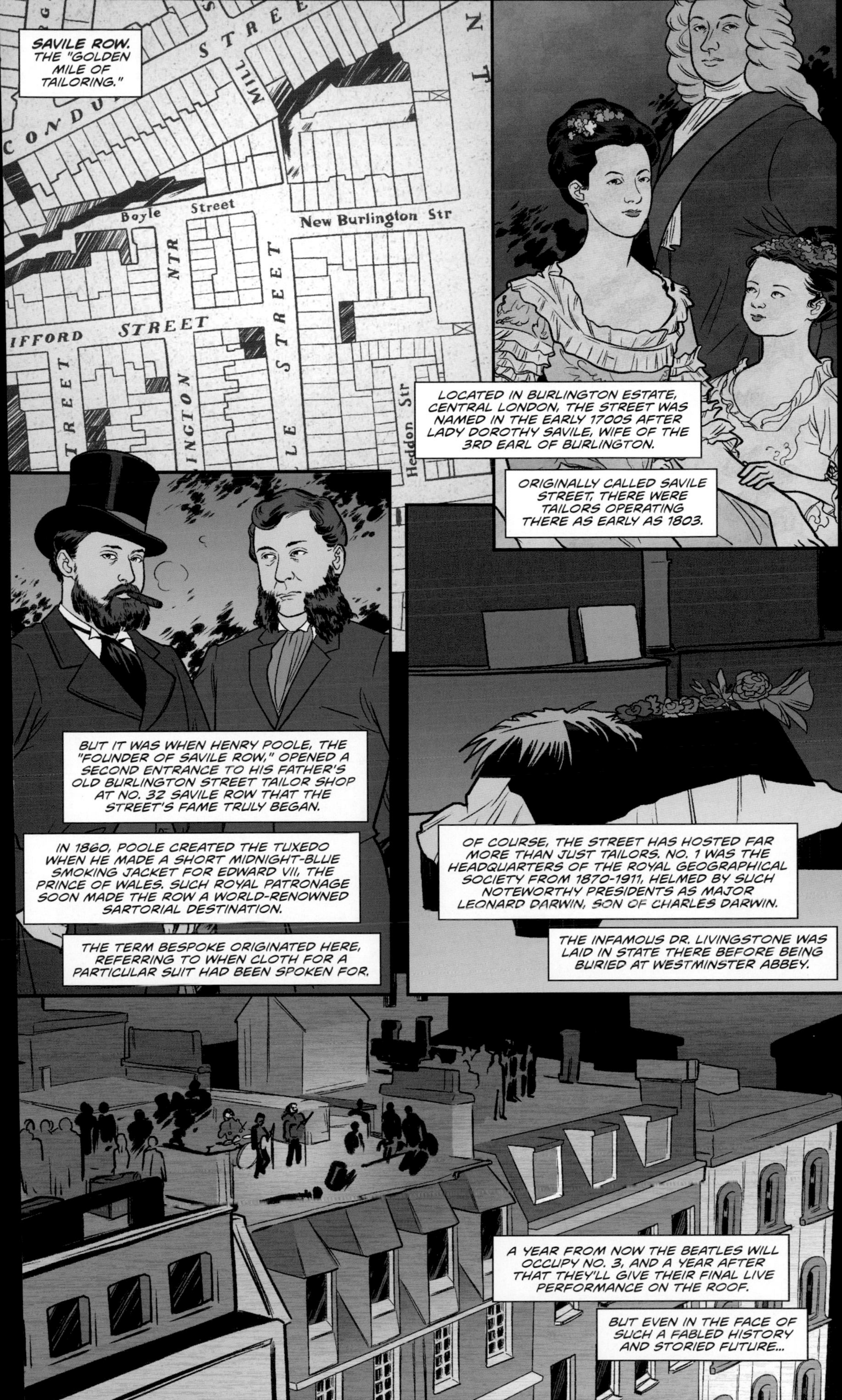
SAVILE ROW. THE "GOLDEN MILE OF TAILORING."
STREET
CONDUIT
MILL
Boyle Street
New Burlington Str
NTR
STREET
CLIFFORD STREET
STREET
BURLINGTON
SAVILE STREET
Heddon Str
LOCATED IN BURLINGTON ESTATE, CENTRAL LONDON, THE STREET WAS NAMED IN THE EARLY 1700S AFTER LADY DOROTHY SAVILE, WIFE OF THE 3RD EARL OF BURLINGTON.
ORIGINALLY CALLED SAVILE STREET, THERE WERE TAILORS OPERATING THERE AS EARLY AS 1803.
BUT IT WAS WHEN HENRY POOLE, THE "FOUNDER OF SAVILE ROW," OPENED A SECOND ENTRANCE TO HIS FATHER'S OLD BURLINGTON STREET TAILOR SHOP AT NO. 32 SAVILE ROW THAT THE STREET'S FAME TRULY BEGAN.
IN 1860, POOLE CREATED THE TUXEDO WHEN HE MADE A SHORT MIDNIGHT-BLUE SMOKING JACKET FOR EDWARD VII, THE PRINCE OF WALES. SUCH ROYAL PATRONAGE SOON MADE THE ROW A WORLD-RENOWNED SARTORIAL DESTINATION.
THE TERM BESPOKE ORIGINATED HERE, REFERRING TO WHEN CLOTH FOR A PARTICULAR SUIT HAD BEEN SPOKEN FOR.
OF COURSE, THE STREET HAS HOSTED FAR MORE THAN JUST TAILORS. NO. 1 WAS THE HEADQUARTERS OF THE ROYAL GEOGRAPHICAL SOCIETY FROM 1870-1911, HELMED BY SUCH NOTEWORTHY PRESIDENTS AS MAJOR LEONARD DARWIN, SON OF CHARLES DARWIN.
THE INFAMOUS DR. LIVINGSTONE WAS LAID IN STATE THERE BEFORE BEING BURIED AT WESTMINSTER ABBEY.
A YEAR FROM NOW THE BEATLES WILL OCCUPY NO. 3, AND A YEAR AFTER THAT THEY'LL GIVE THEIR FINAL LIVE PERFORMANCE ON THE ROOF.
BUT EVEN IN THE FACE OF SUCH A FABLED HISTORY AND STORIED FUTURE...

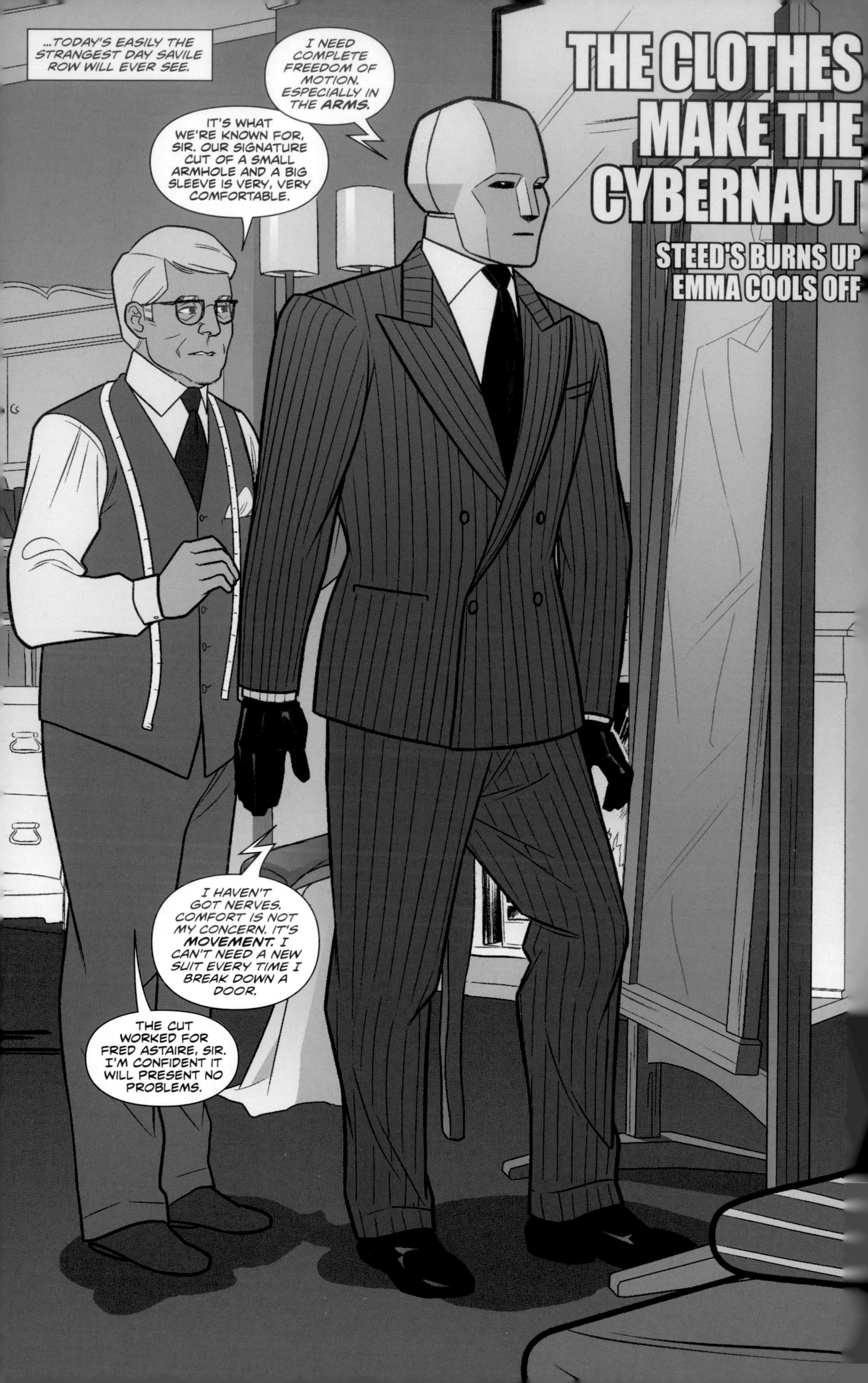
THE CLOTHES MAKE THE CYBERNAUT
STEED'S BURNS UP EMMA COOLS OFF
...TODAY'S EASILY THE STRANGEST DAY SAVILE ROW WILL EVER SEE.
I NEED COMPLETE FREEDOM OF MOTION. ESPECIALLY IN THE ARMS.
IT'S WHAT WE'RE KNOWN FOR, SIR. OUR SIGNATURE CUT OF A SMALL ARMHOLE AND A BIG SLEEVE IS VERY, VERY COMFORTABLE.
I HAVEN'T GOT NERVES. COMFORT IS NOT MY CONCERN. IT'S MOVEMENT. I CAN'T NEED A NEW SUIT EVERY TIME I BREAK DOWN A DOOR.
THE CUT WORKED FOR FRED ASTAIRE, SIR. I'M CONFIDENT IT WILL PRESENT NO PROBLEMS.

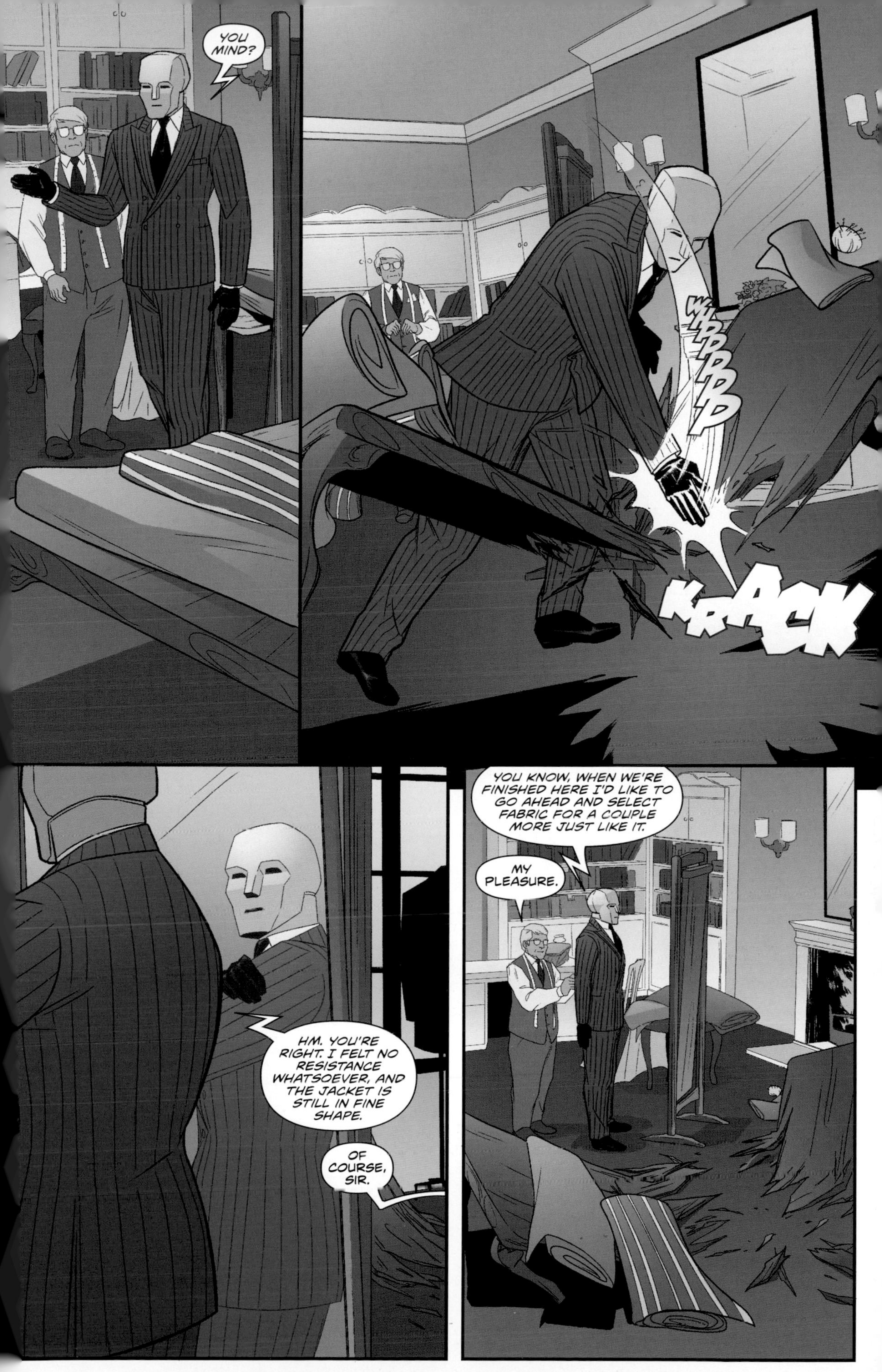
YOU MIND?
WHRRRRP
KRACK
HM. YOU'RE RIGHT. I FELT NO RESISTANCE WHATSOEVER, AND THE JACKET IS STILL IN FINE SHAPE.
OF COURSE, SIR.
YOU KNOW, WHEN WE'RE FINISHED HERE I'D LIKE TO GO AHEAD AND SELECT FABRIC FOR A COUPLE MORE JUST LIKE IT.
MY PLEASURE.

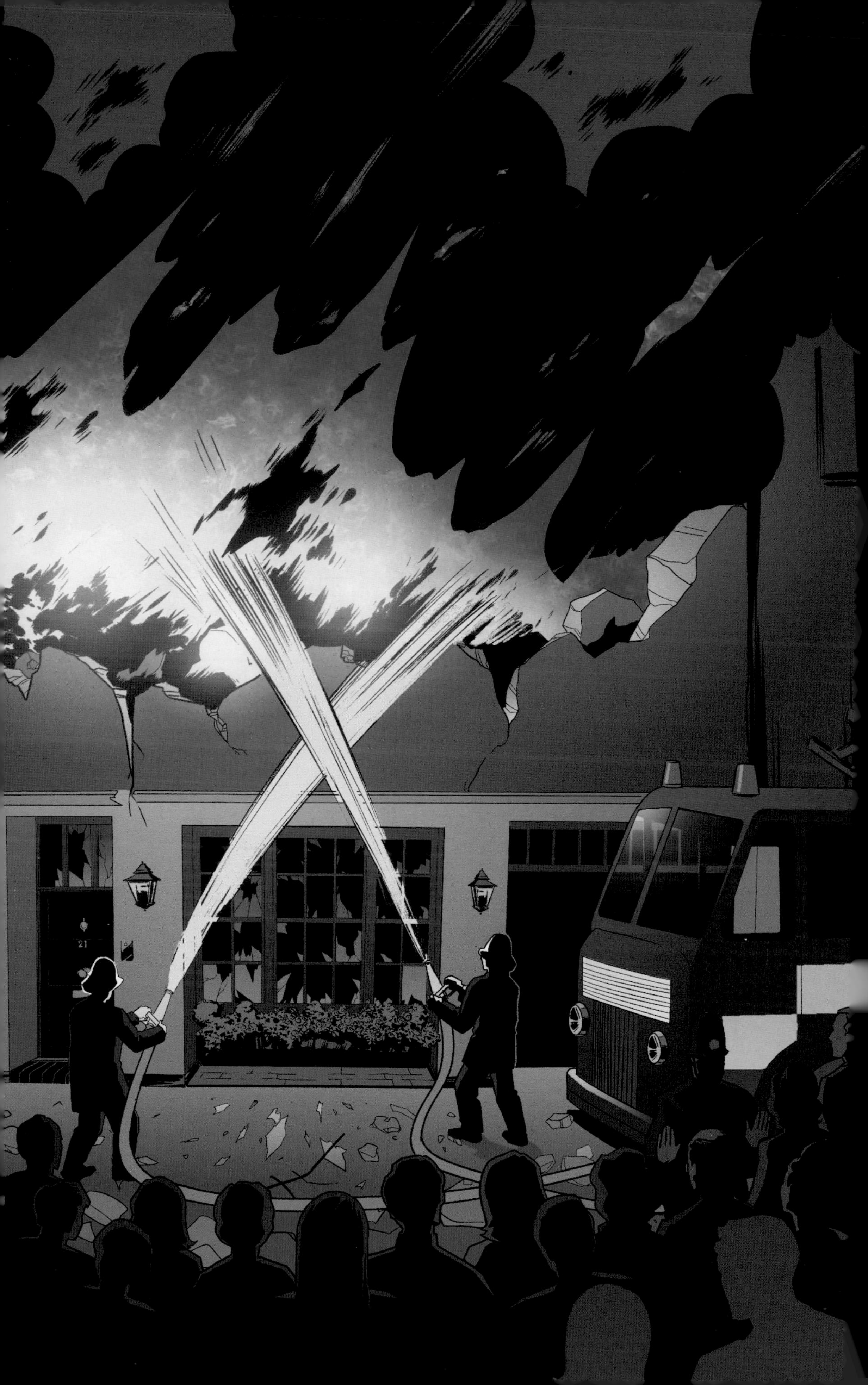
21

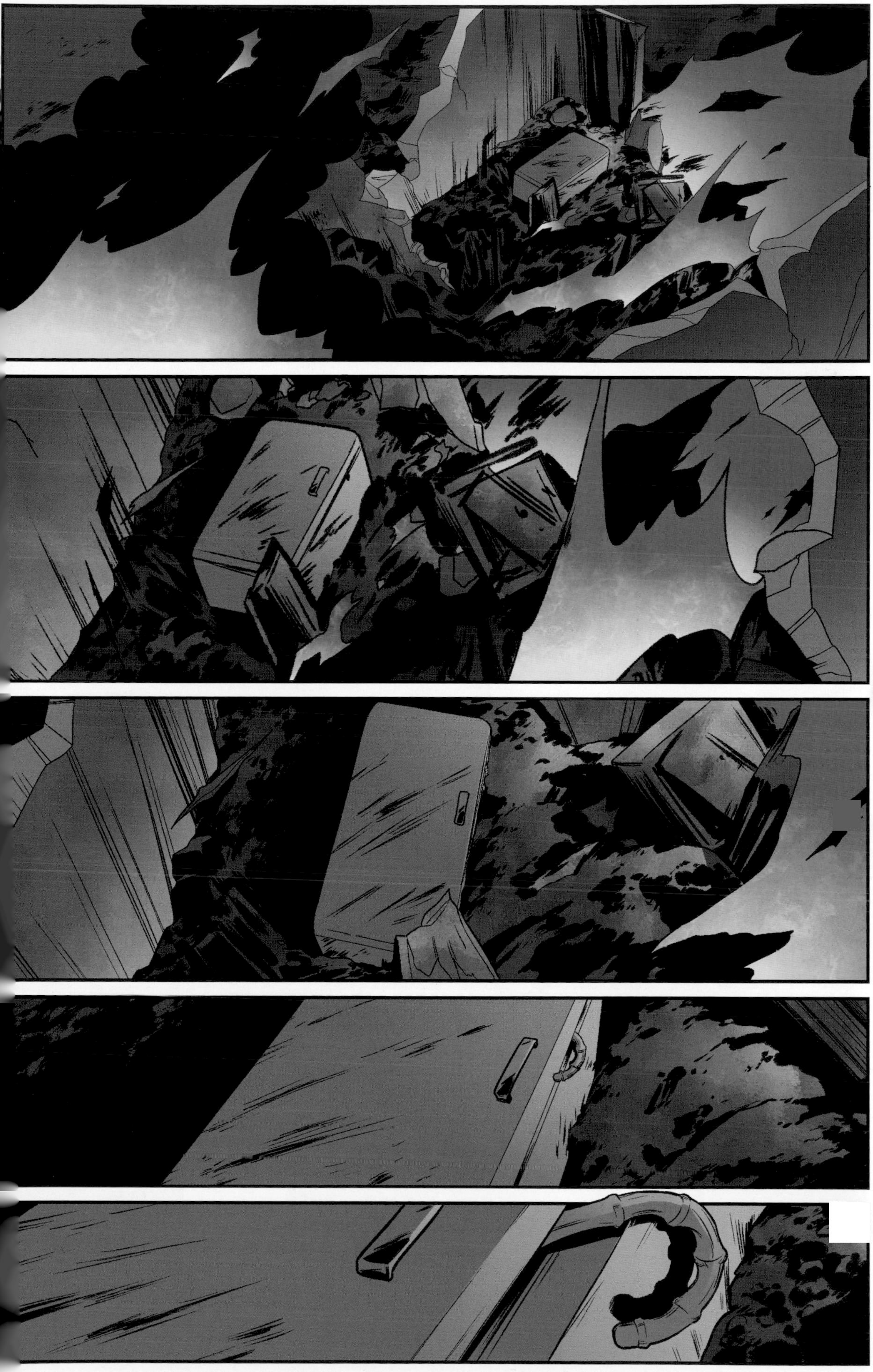

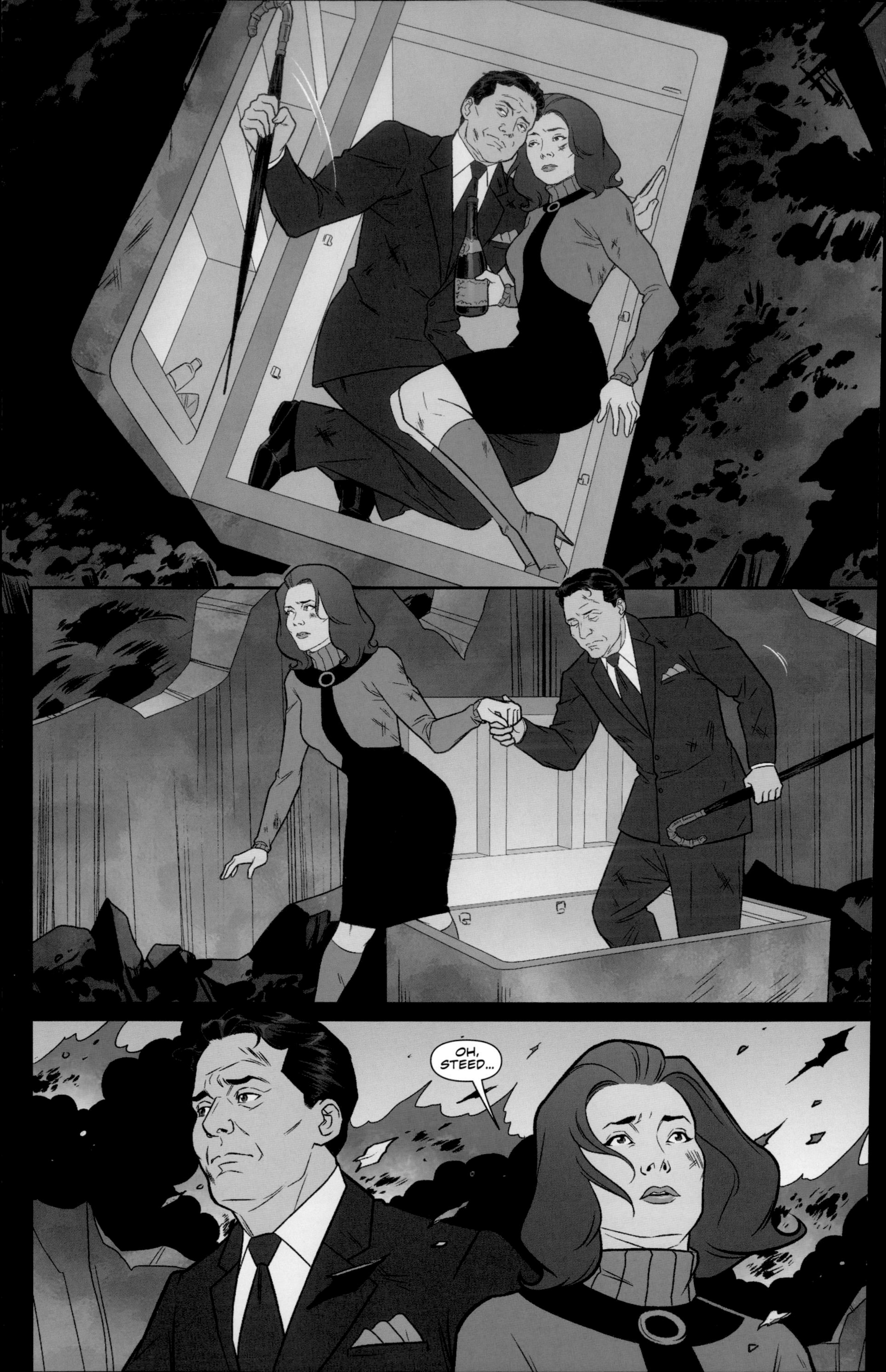
OH, STEED...

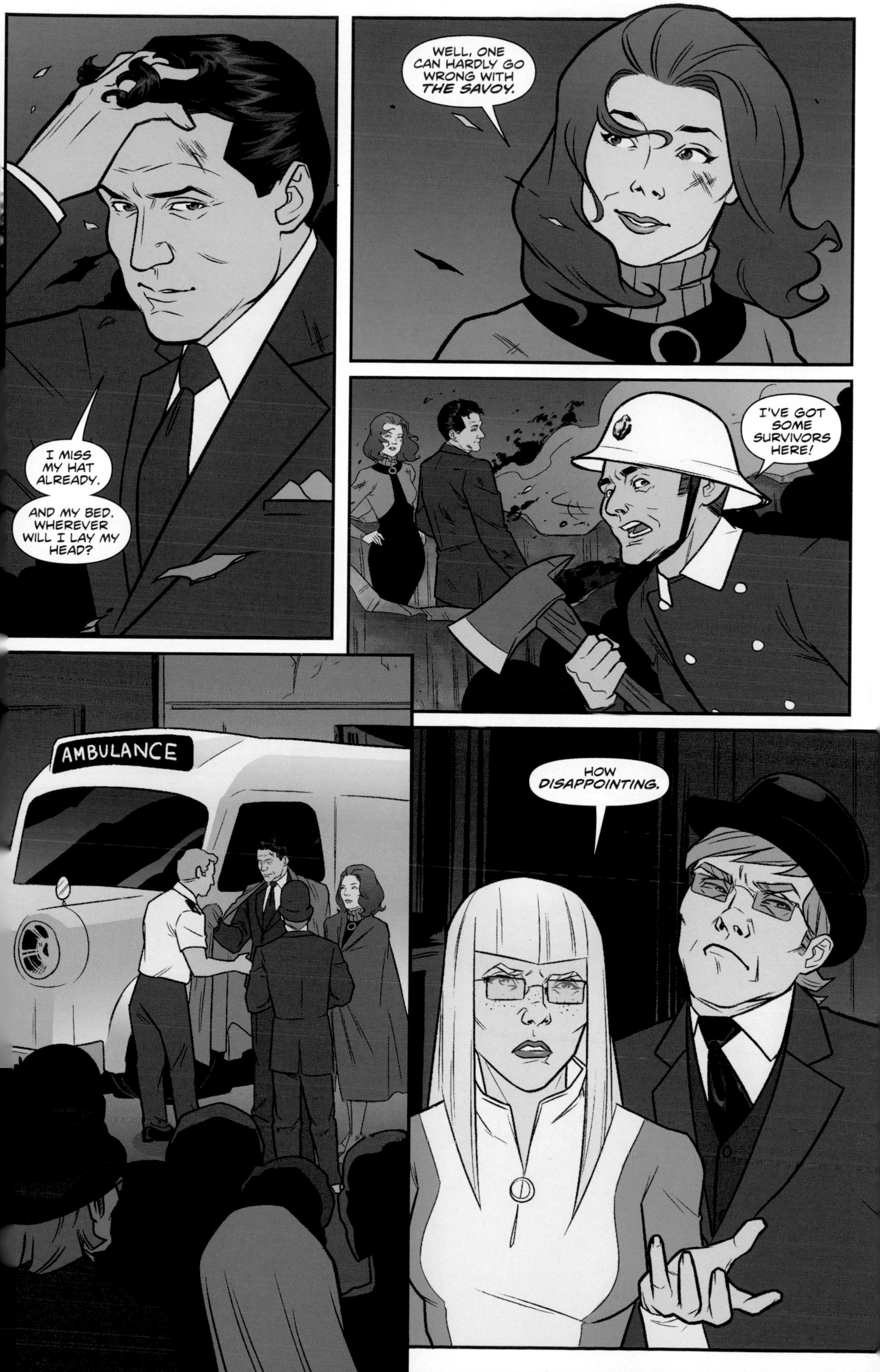

I MISS MY HAT ALREADY.
AND MY BED. WHEREVER WILL I LAY MY HEAD?
WELL, ONE CAN HARDLY GO WRONG WITH *THE SAVOY.*
I'VE GOT SOME SURVIVORS HERE!
AMBULANCE
HOW *DISAPPOINTING.*

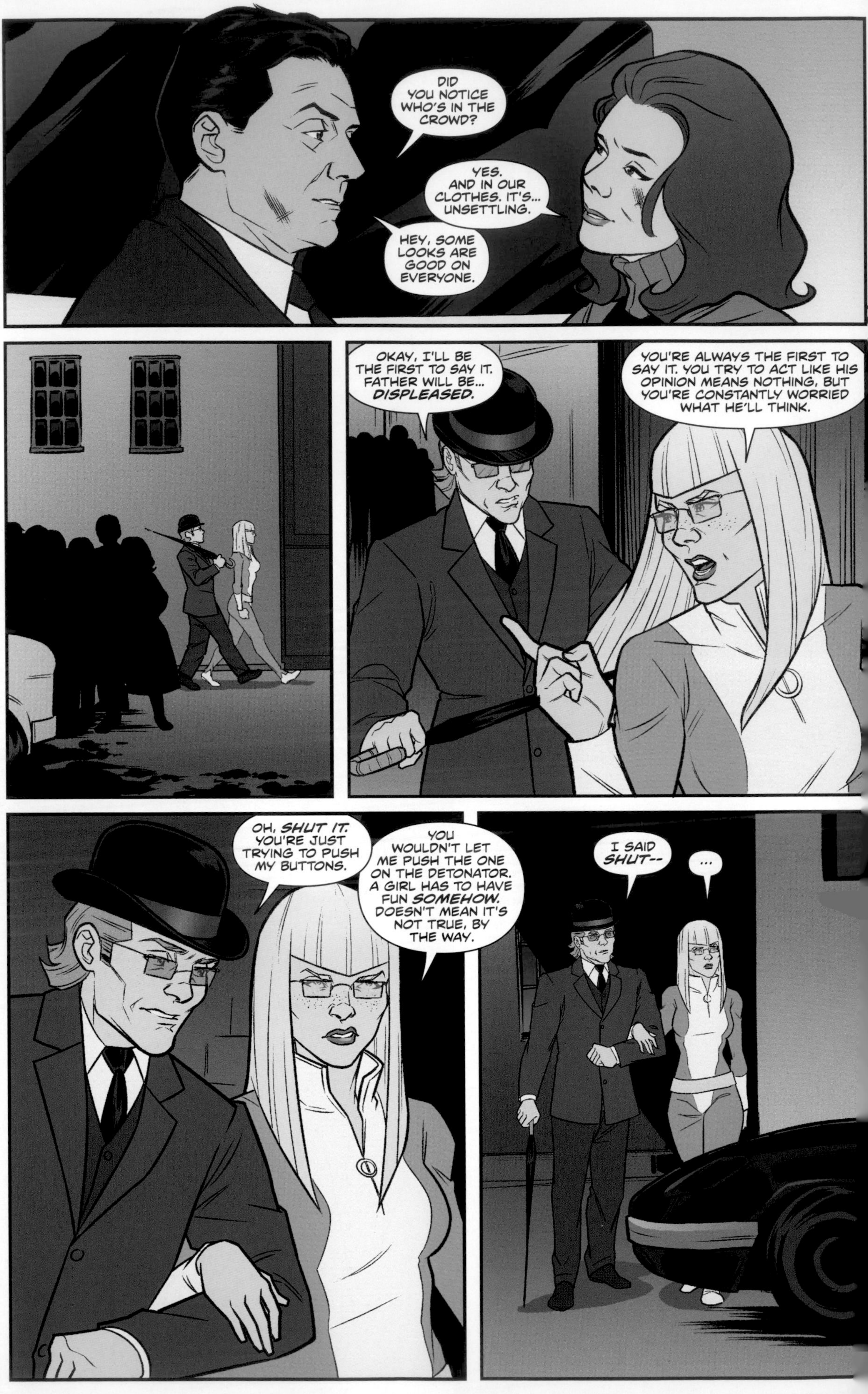
DID YOU NOTICE WHO'S IN THE CROWD?
YES. AND IN OUR CLOTHES. IT'S... UNSETTLING.
HEY, SOME LOOKS ARE GOOD ON EVERYONE.
OKAY, I'LL BE THE FIRST TO SAY IT. FATHER WILL BE... DISPLEASED.
YOU'RE ALWAYS THE FIRST TO SAY IT. YOU TRY TO ACT LIKE HIS OPINION MEANS NOTHING, BUT YOU'RE CONSTANTLY WORRIED WHAT HE'LL THINK.
OH, SHUT IT. YOU'RE JUST TRYING TO PUSH MY BUTTONS.
YOU WOULDN'T LET ME PUSH THE ONE ON THE DETONATOR. A GIRL HAS TO HAVE FUN SOMEHOW. DOESN'T MEAN IT'S NOT TRUE, BY THE WAY.
I SAID SHUT--
...

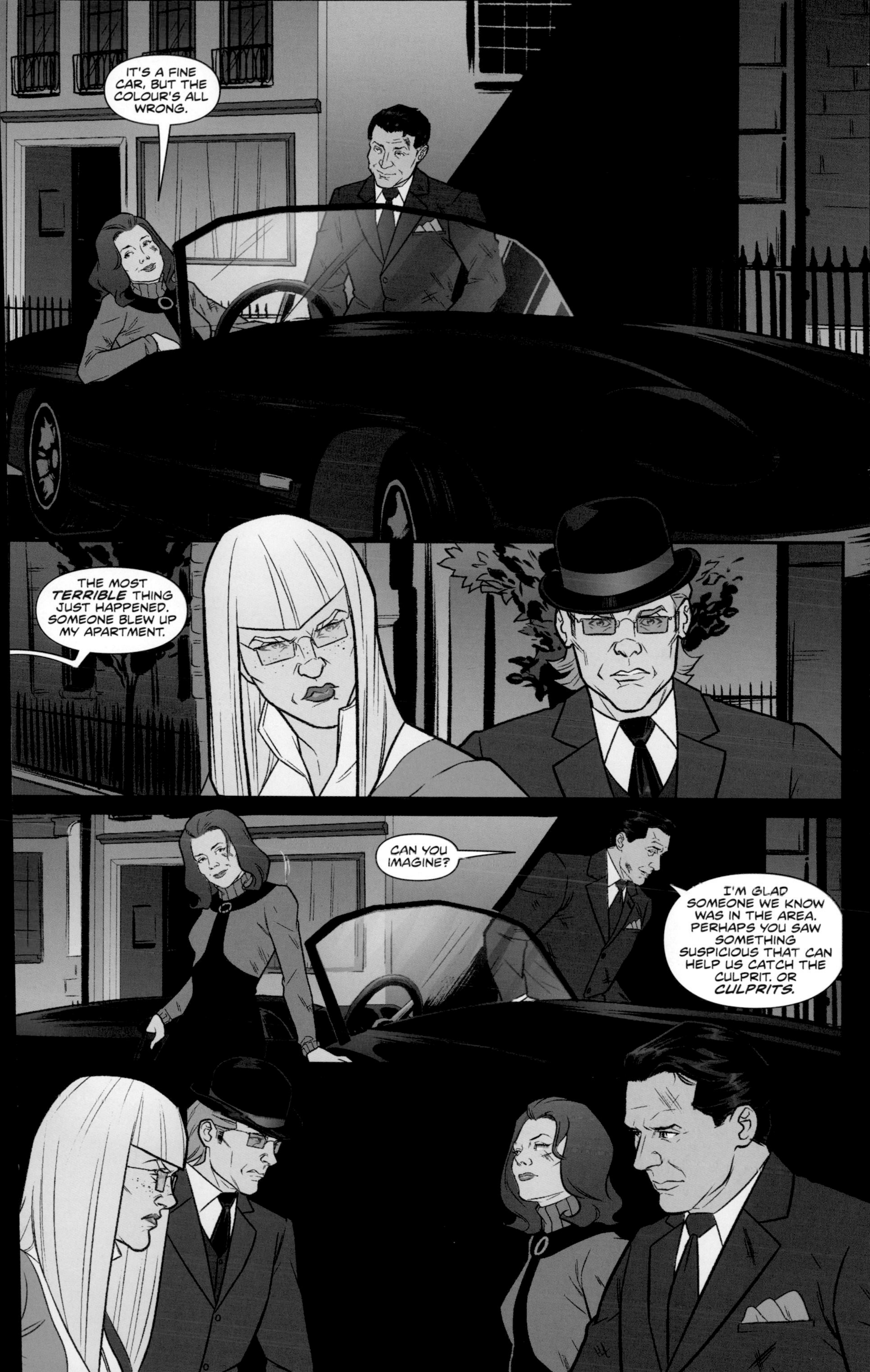
IT'S A FINE CAR, BUT THE COLOUR'S ALL WRONG.
THE MOST TERRIBLE THING JUST HAPPENED. SOMEONE BLEW UP MY APARTMENT.
CAN YOU IMAGINE?
I'M GLAD SOMEONE WE KNOW WAS IN THE AREA. PERHAPS YOU SAW SOMETHING SUSPICIOUS THAT CAN HELP US CATCH THE CULPRIT. OR CULPRITS.

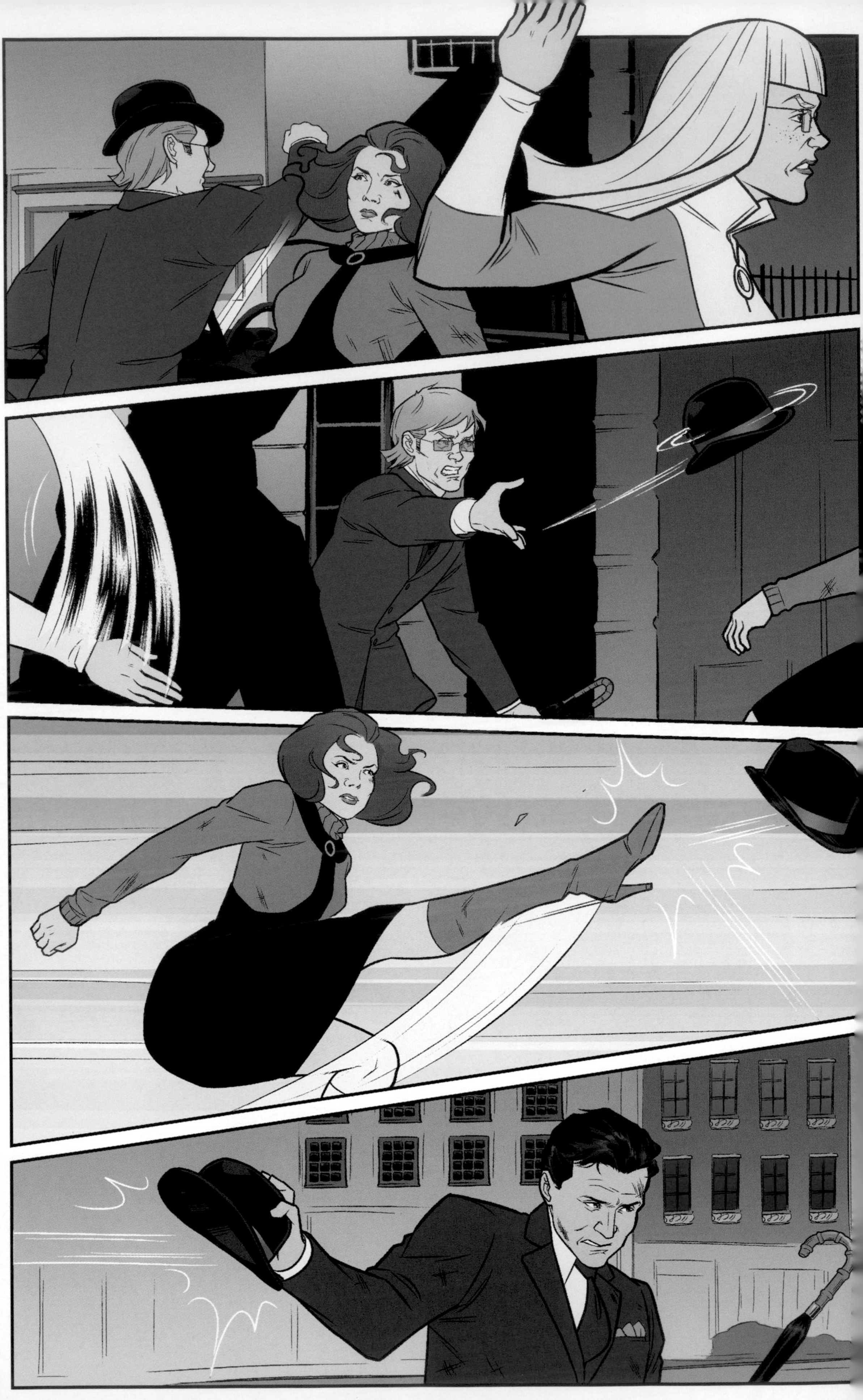

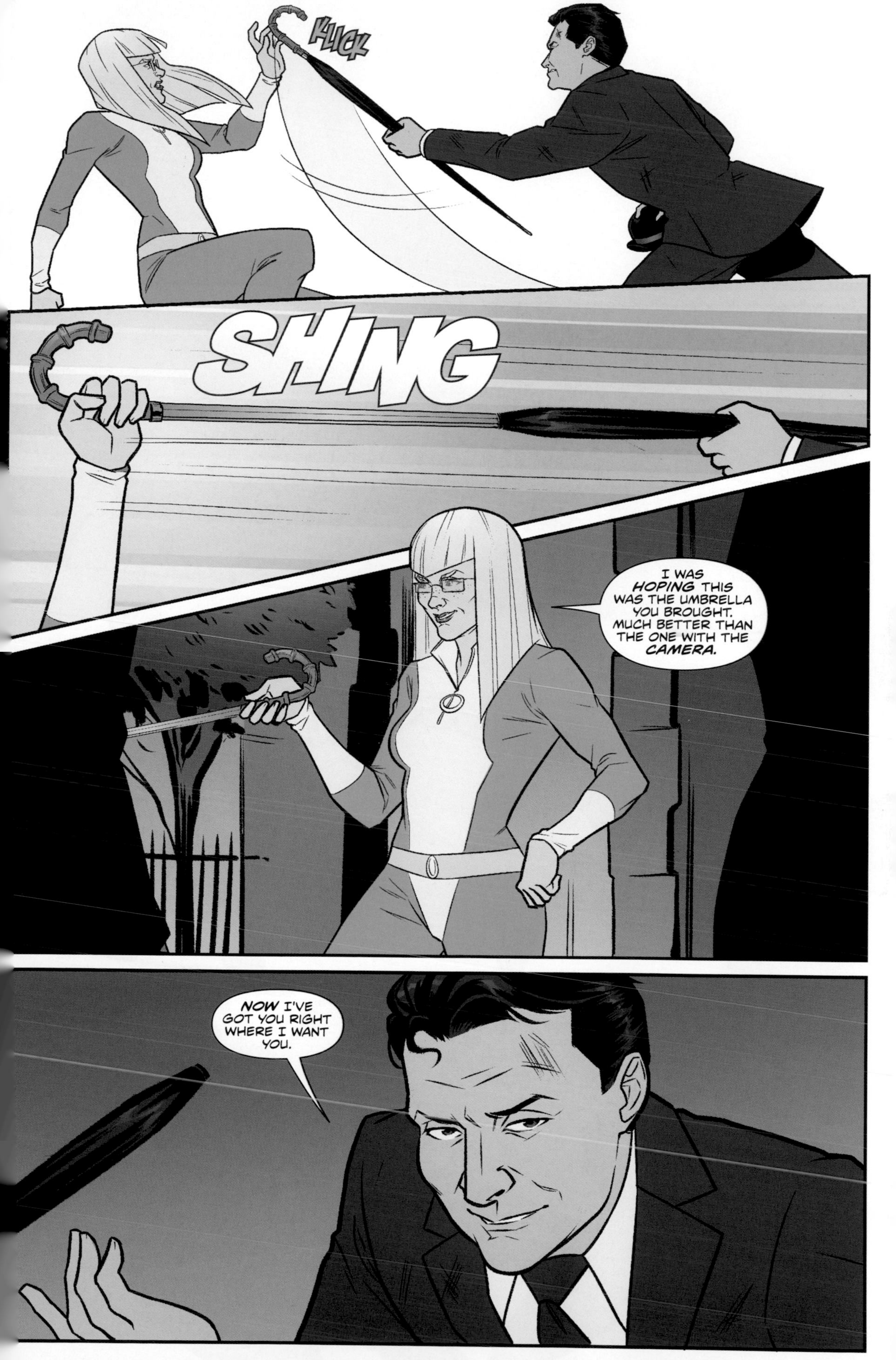
KLICK
SHING
I WAS HOPING THIS WAS THE UMBRELLA YOU BROUGHT. MUCH BETTER THAN THE ONE WITH THE CAMERA.
NOW I'VE GOT YOU RIGHT WHERE I WANT YOU.

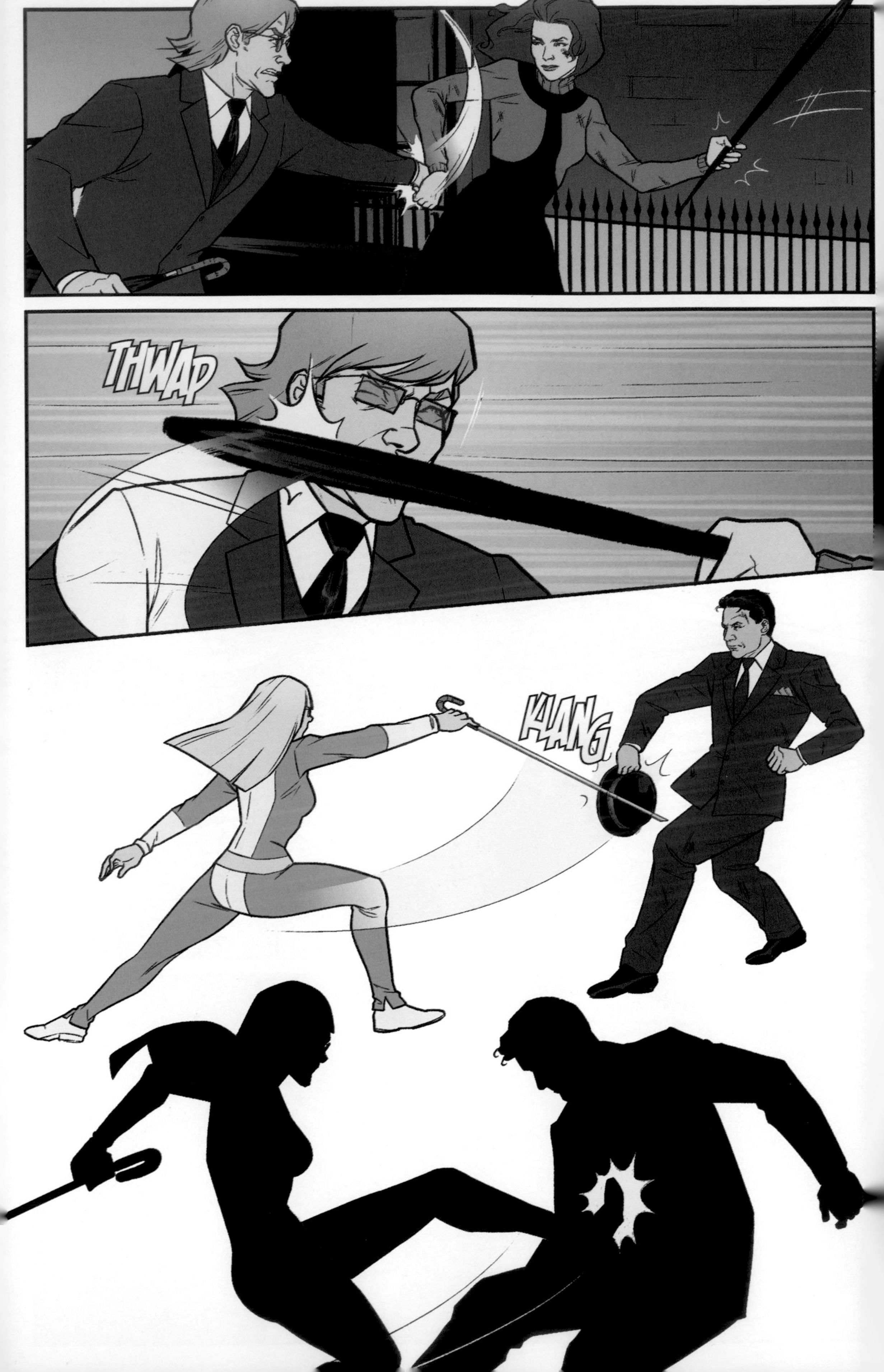
THWAP
KLANG

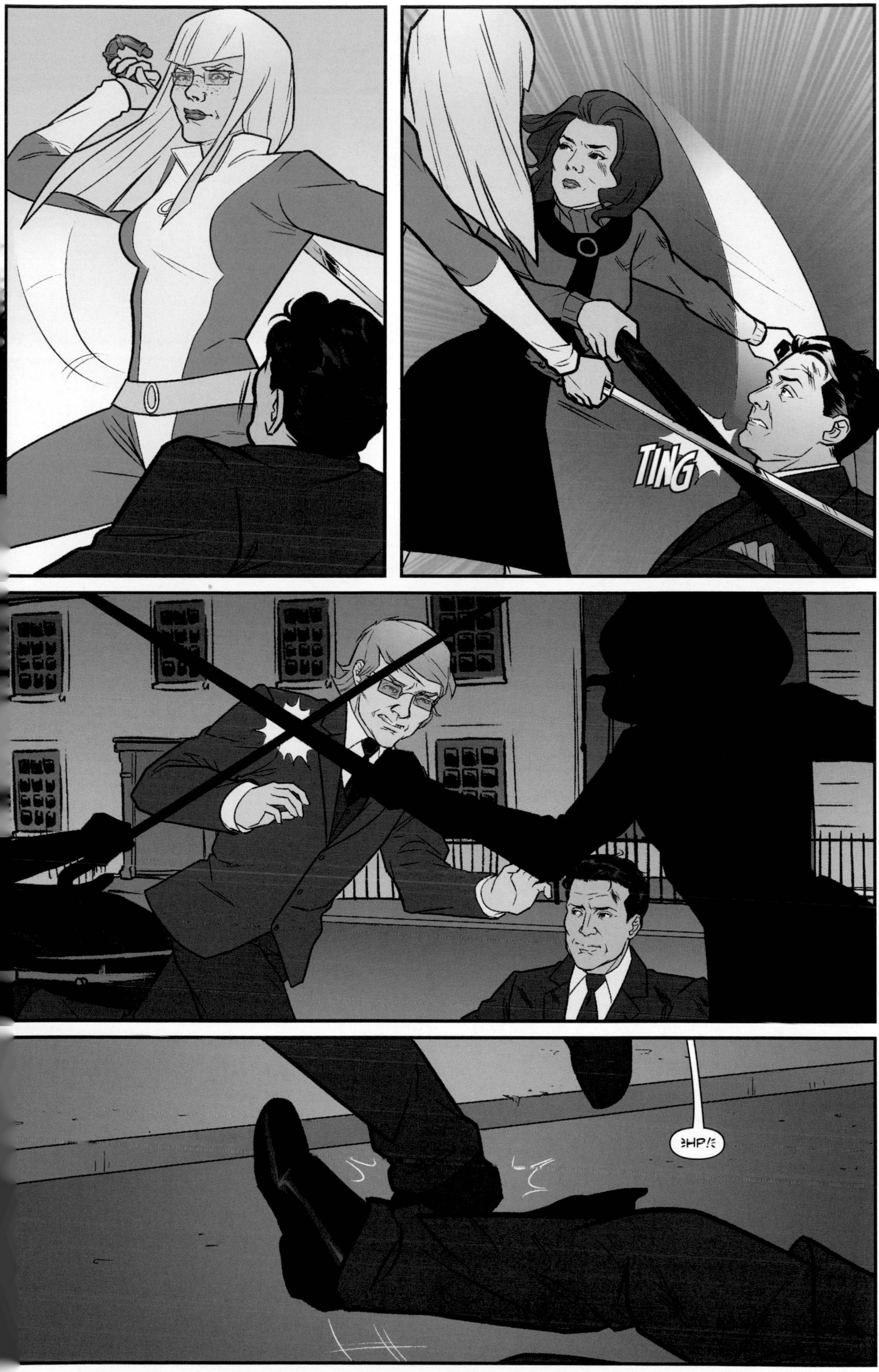
TING
HP!

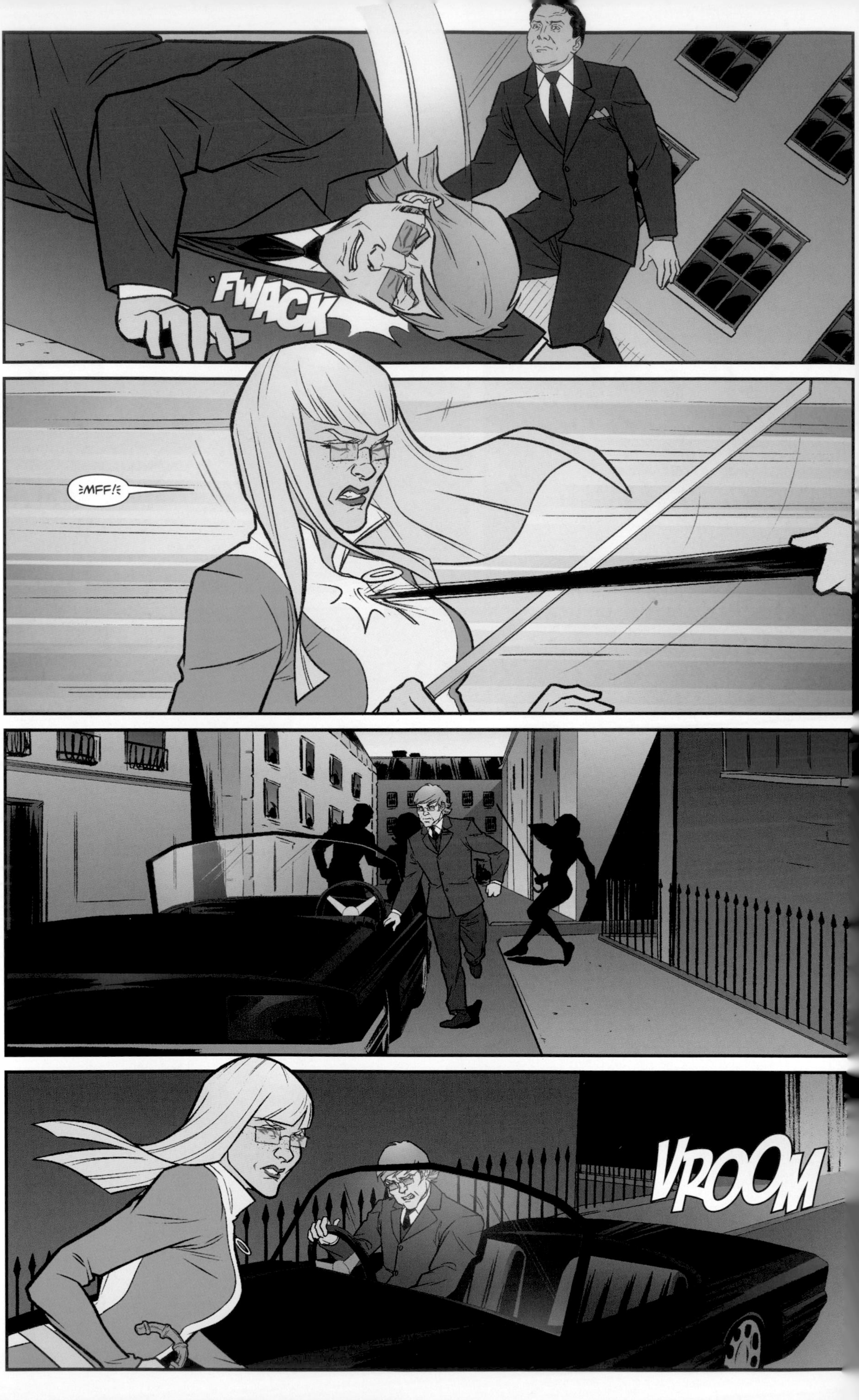
FWACK
MFF!
VROOM

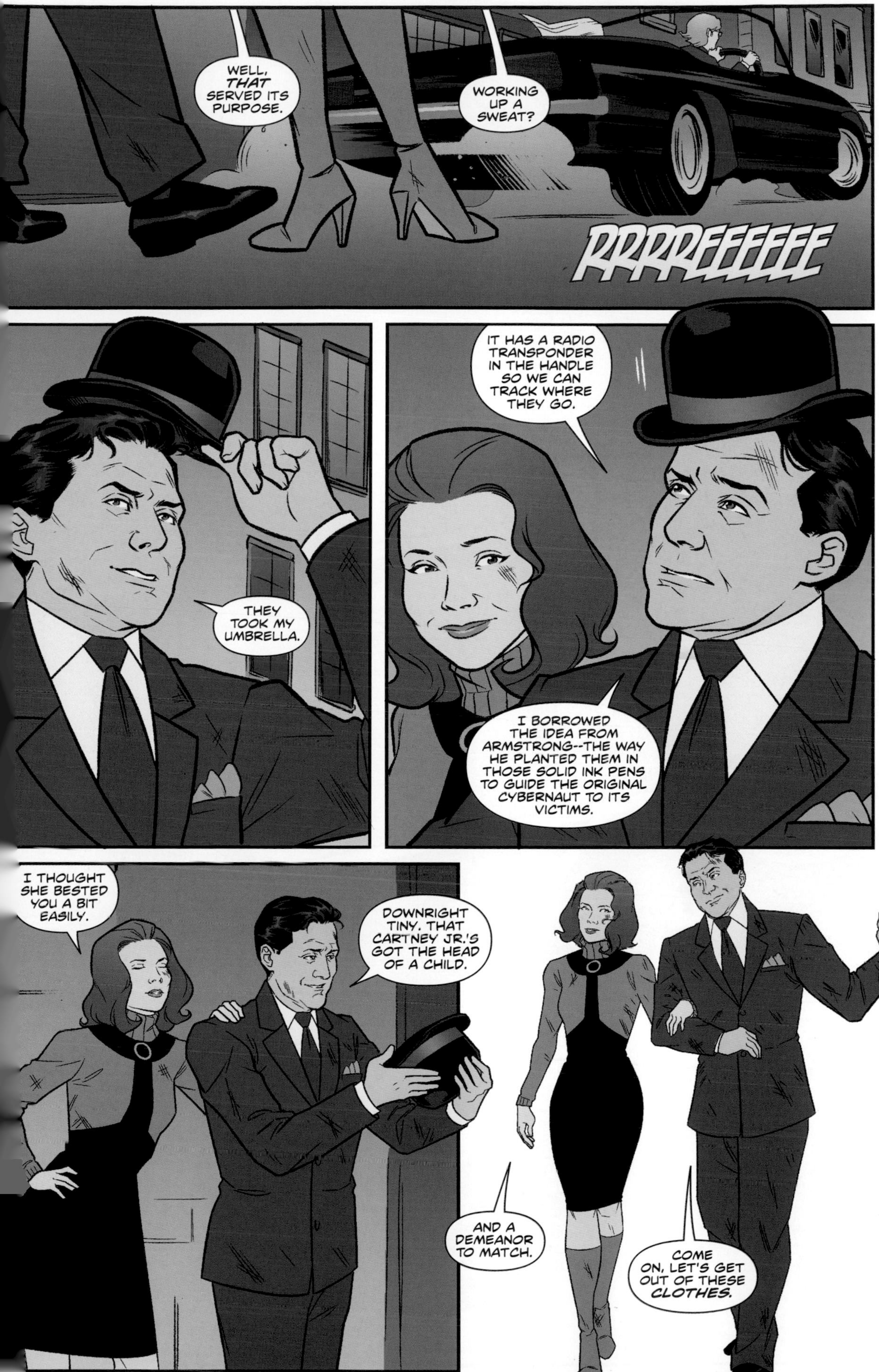

WELL, THAT SERVED ITS PURPOSE.
WORKING UP A SWEAT?
RRRREEEEEE
THEY TOOK MY UMBRELLA.
IT HAS A RADIO TRANSPONDER IN THE HANDLE SO WE CAN TRACK WHERE THEY GO.
I BORROWED THE IDEA FROM ARMSTRONG--THE WAY HE PLANTED THEM IN THOSE SOLID INK PENS TO GUIDE THE ORIGINAL CYBERNAUT TO ITS VICTIMS.
I THOUGHT SHE BESTED YOU A BIT EASILY.
DOWNRIGHT TINY. THAT CARTNEY JR.'S GOT THE HEAD OF A CHILD.
AND A DEMEANOR TO MATCH.
COME ON, LET'S GET OUT OF THESE CLOTHES.

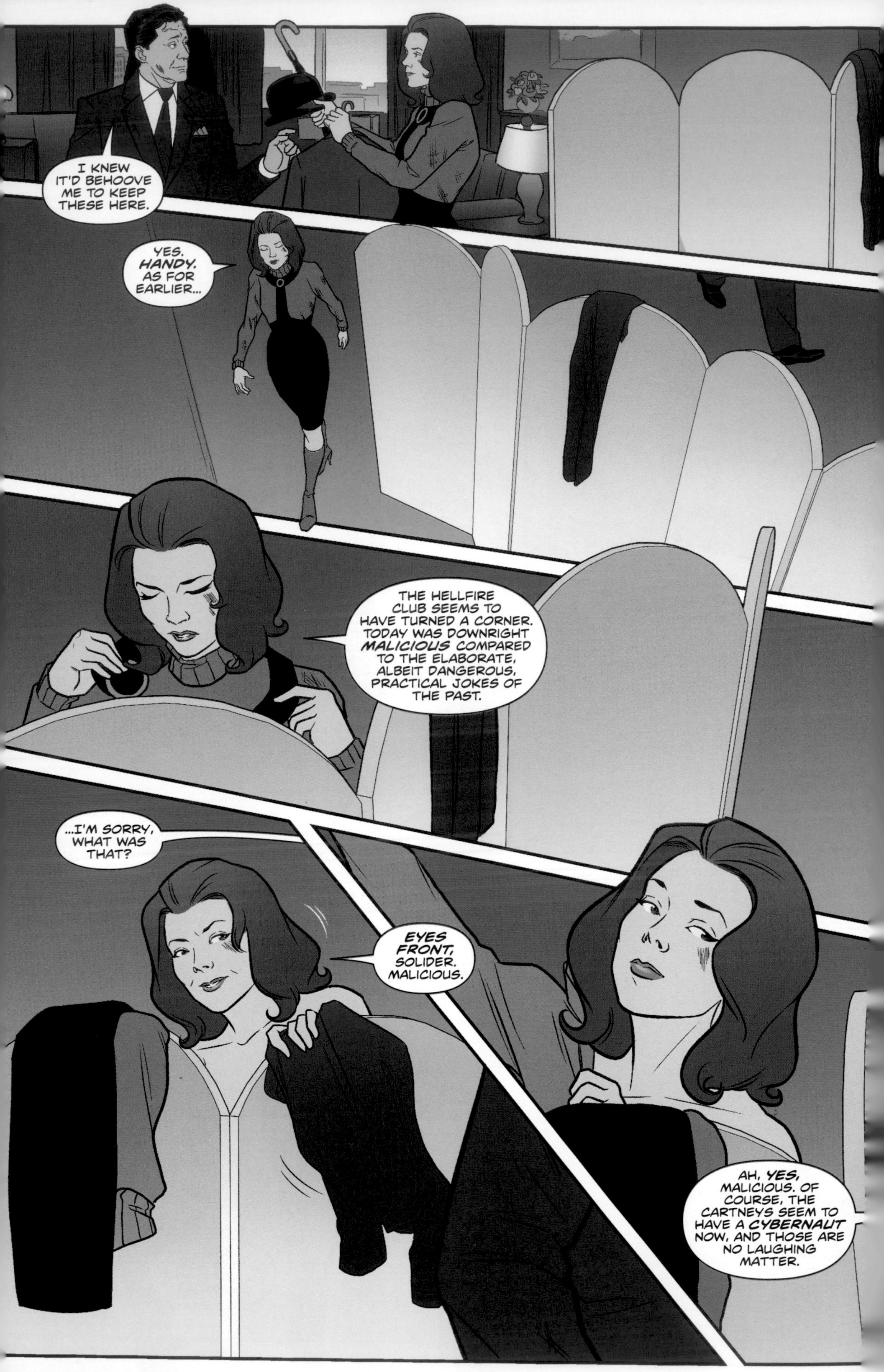
I KNEW IT'D BEHOOVE ME TO KEEP THESE HERE.
YES. *HANDY.* AS FOR EARLIER...
THE HELLFIRE CLUB SEEMS TO HAVE TURNED A CORNER. TODAY WAS DOWNRIGHT *MALICIOUS* COMPARED TO THE ELABORATE, ALBEIT DANGEROUS, PRACTICAL JOKES OF THE PAST.
...I'M SORRY, WHAT WAS THAT?
EYES FRONT, SOLIDER. MALICIOUS.
AH, *YES,* MALICIOUS. OF COURSE, THE CARTNEYS SEEM TO HAVE A *CYBERNAUT* NOW, AND THOSE ARE NO LAUGHING MATTER.

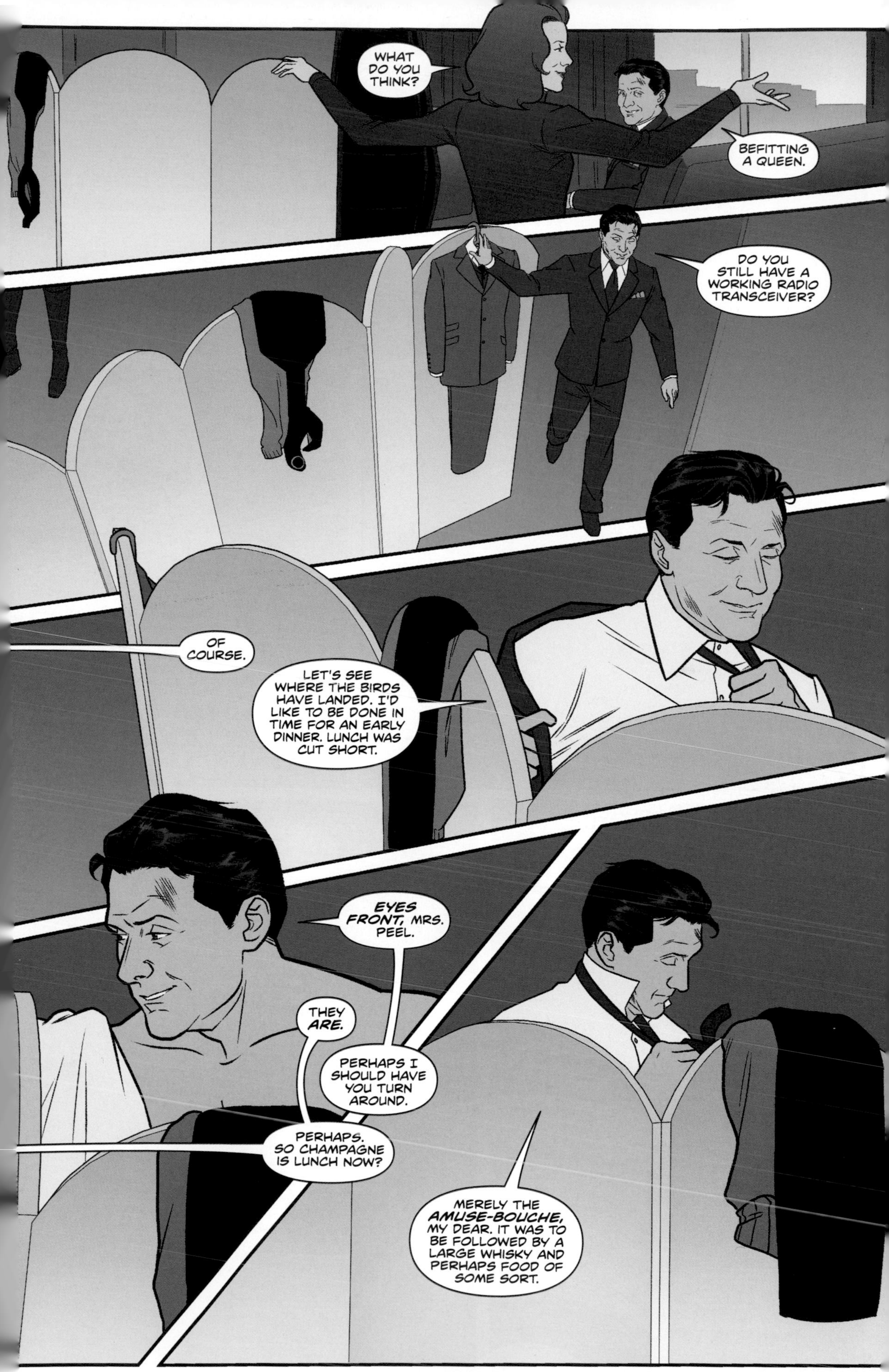
WHAT DO YOU THINK?
BEFITTING A QUEEN.
DO YOU STILL HAVE A WORKING RADIO TRANSCEIVER?
OF COURSE.
LET'S SEE WHERE THE BIRDS HAVE LANDED. I'D LIKE TO BE DONE IN TIME FOR AN EARLY DINNER. LUNCH WAS CUT SHORT.
EYES FRONT, MRS. PEEL.
THEY *ARE.*
PERHAPS I SHOULD HAVE YOU TURN AROUND.
PERHAPS. SO CHAMPAGNE IS LUNCH NOW?
MERELY THE *AMUSE-BOUCHE,* MY DEAR. IT WAS TO BE FOLLOWED BY A LARGE WHISKY AND PERHAPS FOOD OF SOME SORT.

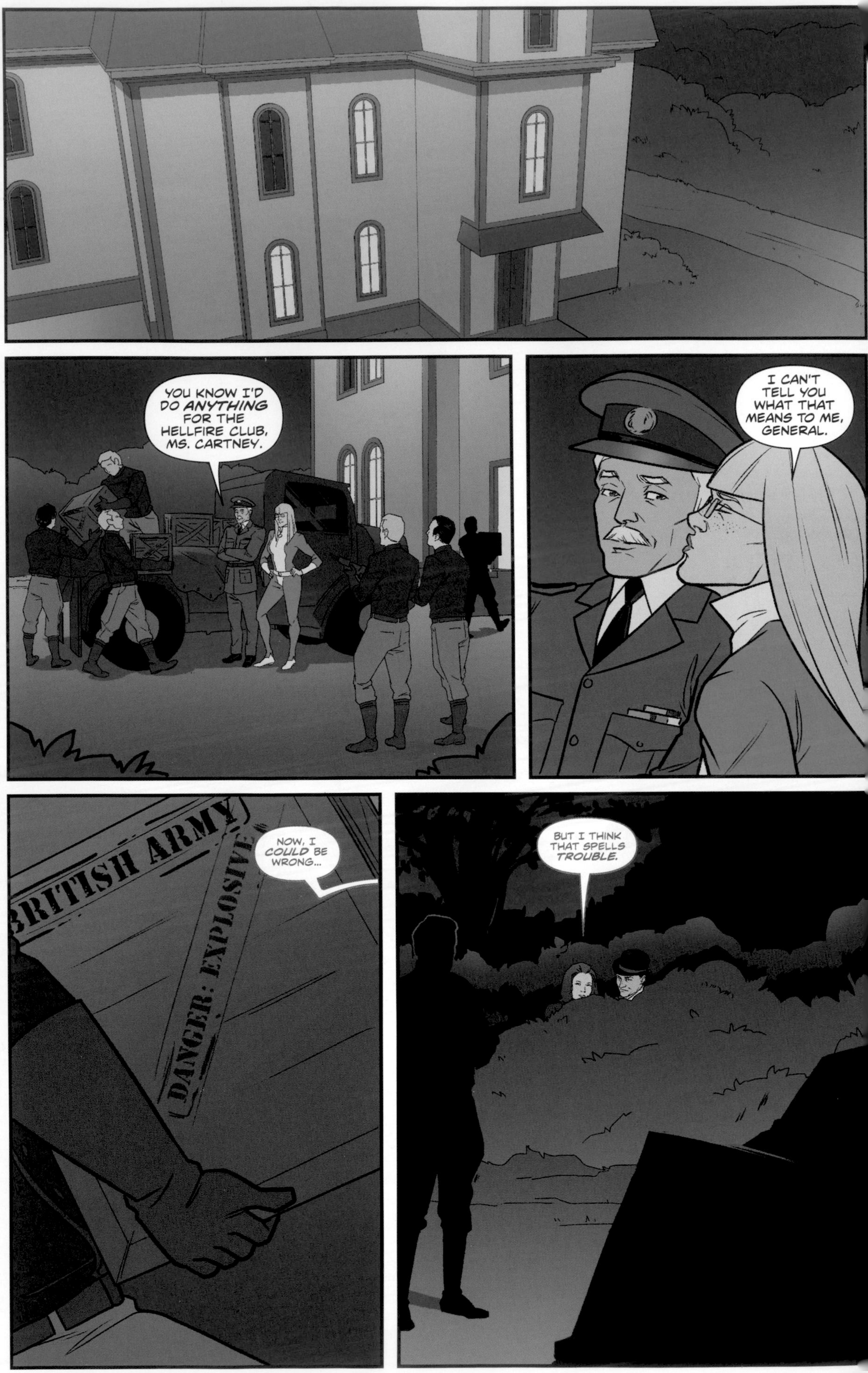
YOU KNOW I'D DO ANYTHING FOR THE HELLFIRE CLUB, MS. CARTNEY.
I CAN'T TELL YOU WHAT THAT MEANS TO ME, GENERAL.
BRITISH ARMY
DANGER: EXPLOSIVE
NOW, I COULD BE WRONG...
BUT I THINK THAT SPELLS TROUBLE.

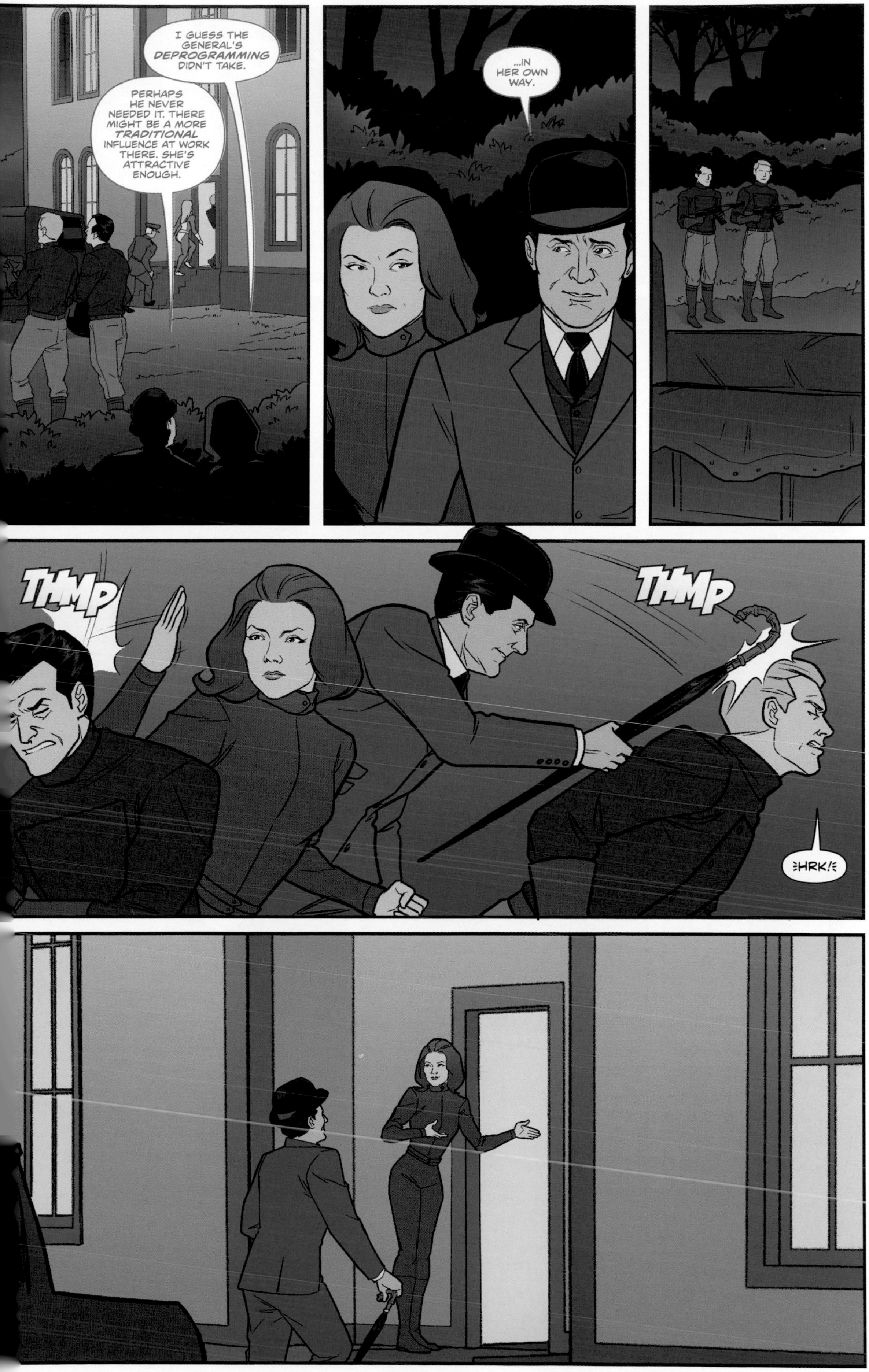
I GUESS THE GENERAL'S *DEPROGRAMMING* DIDN'T TAKE.
PERHAPS HE NEVER NEEDED IT. THERE MIGHT BE A MORE *TRADITIONAL* INFLUENCE AT WORK THERE. SHE'S ATTRACTIVE ENOUGH.
...IN HER OWN WAY.
THMP
THMP
HRK!

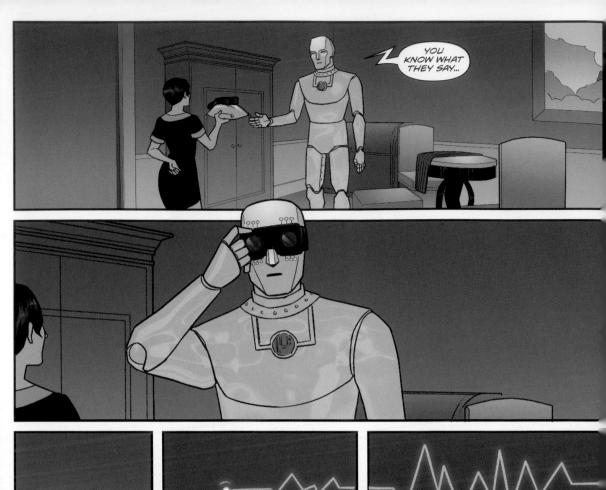

YOU KNOW WHAT THEY SAY...

IT'S THE CLOTHES THAT MAKE THE MAN.

...

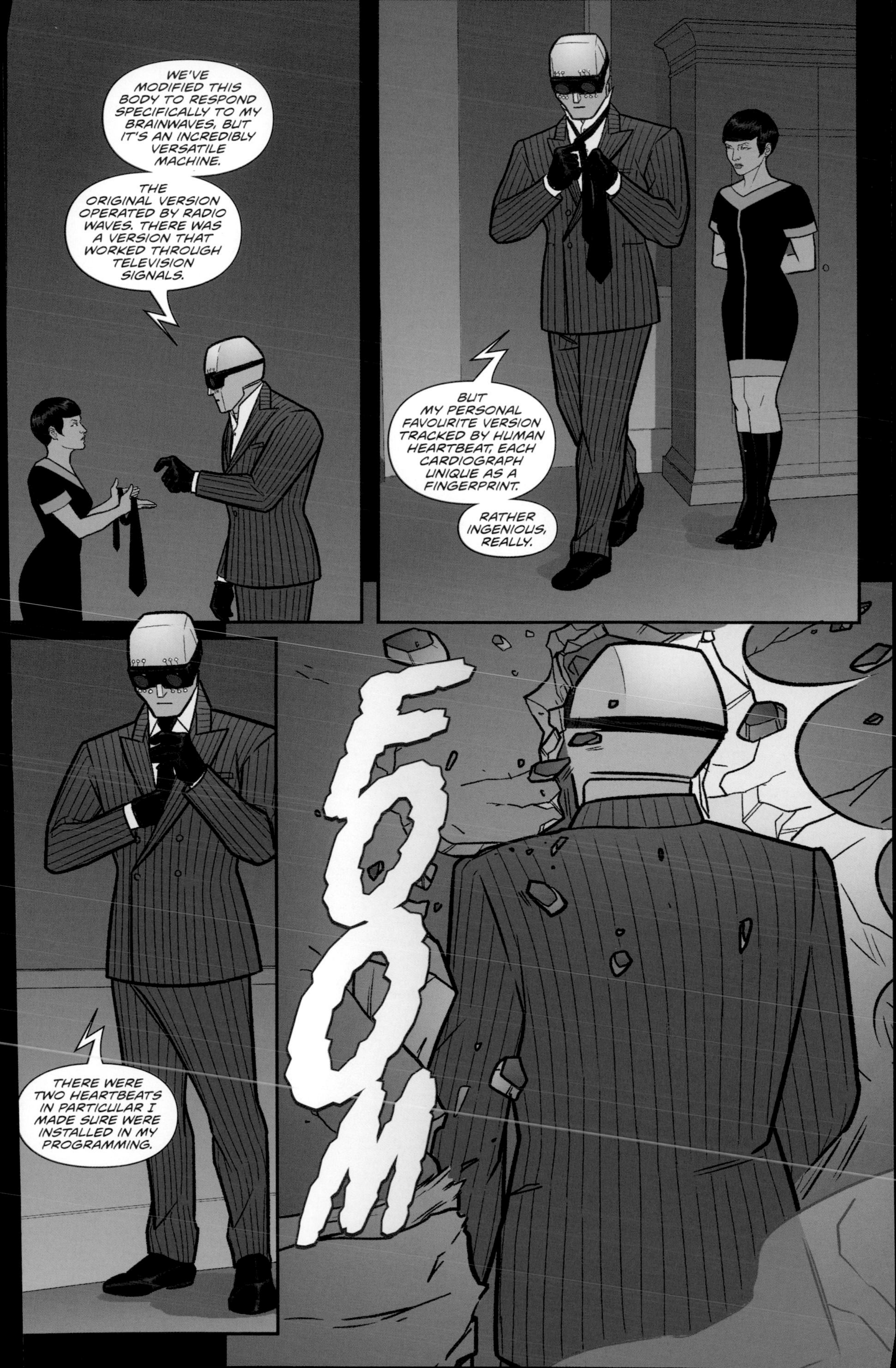
WE'VE MODIFIED THIS BODY TO RESPOND SPECIFICALLY TO MY BRAINWAVES, BUT IT'S AN INCREDIBLY VERSATILE MACHINE.
THE ORIGINAL VERSION OPERATED BY RADIO WAVES. THERE WAS A VERSION THAT WORKED THROUGH TELEVISION SIGNALS.
BUT MY PERSONAL FAVOURITE VERSION TRACKED BY HUMAN HEARTBEAT, EACH CARDIOGRAPH UNIQUE AS A FINGERPRINT.
RATHER INGENIOUS, REALLY.
THERE WERE TWO HEARTBEATS IN PARTICULAR I MADE SURE WERE INSTALLED IN MY PROGRAMMING.
FOOM

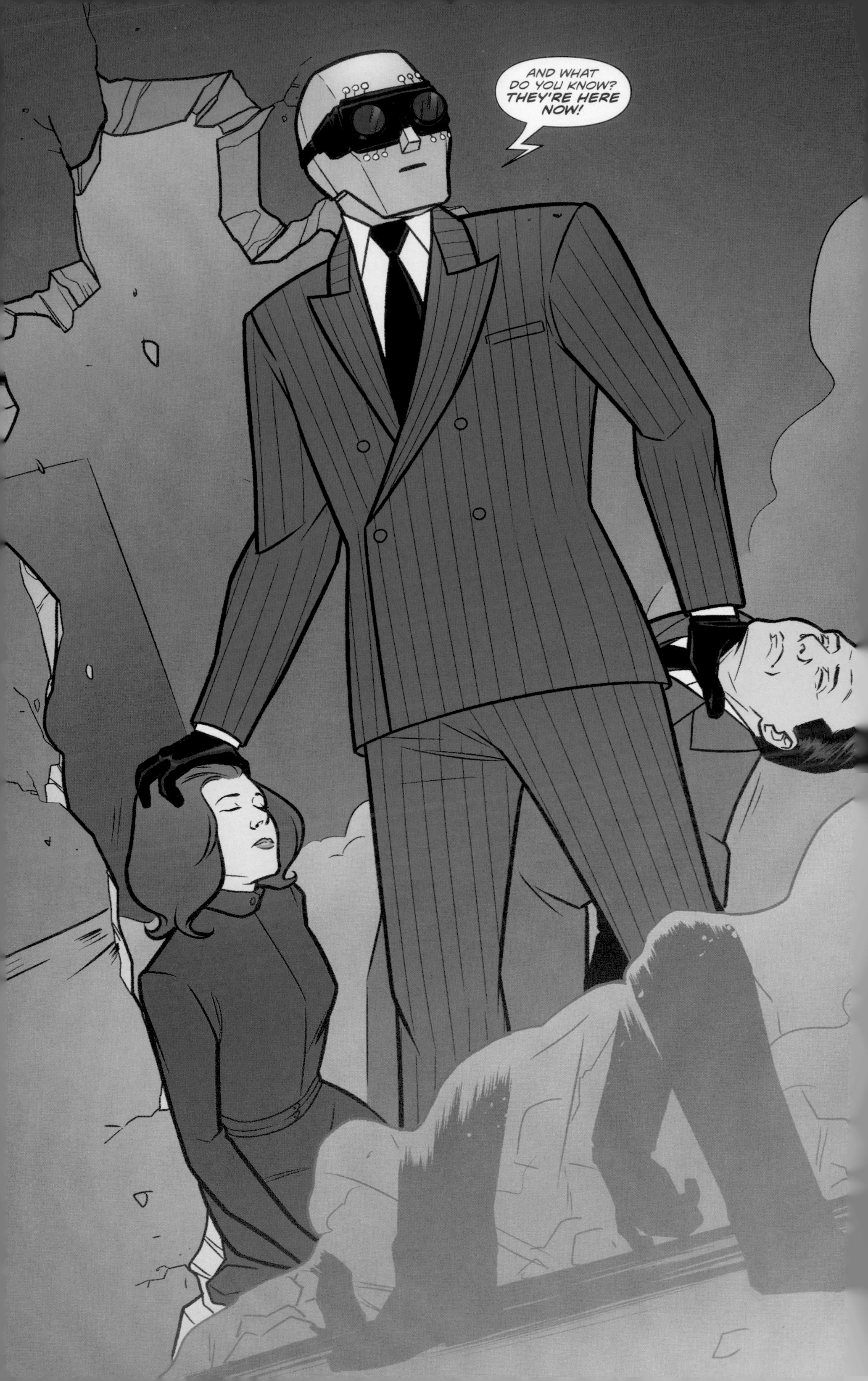
AND WHAT DO YOU KNOW? THEY'RE HERE NOW!

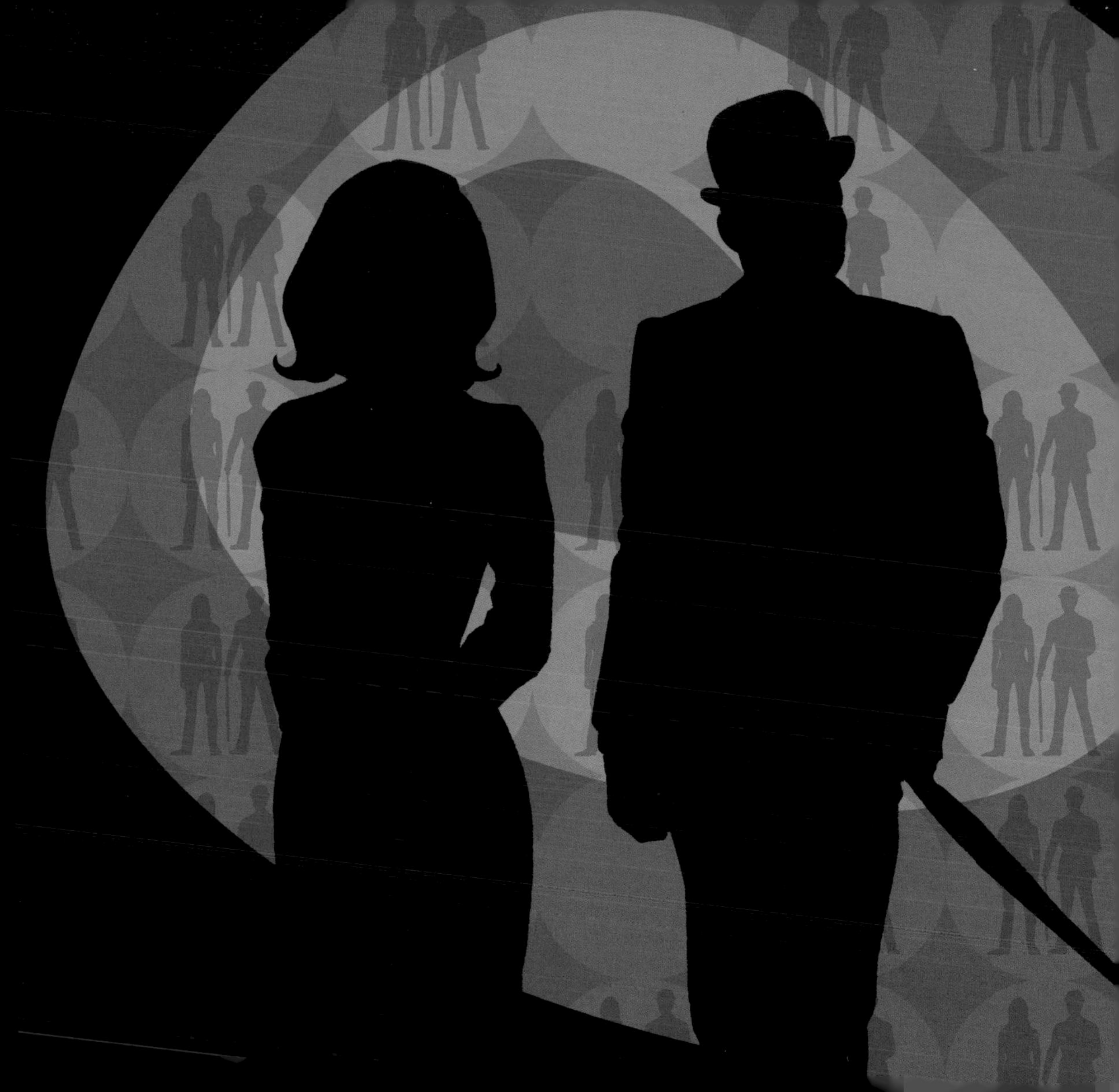

CHAPTER TEN

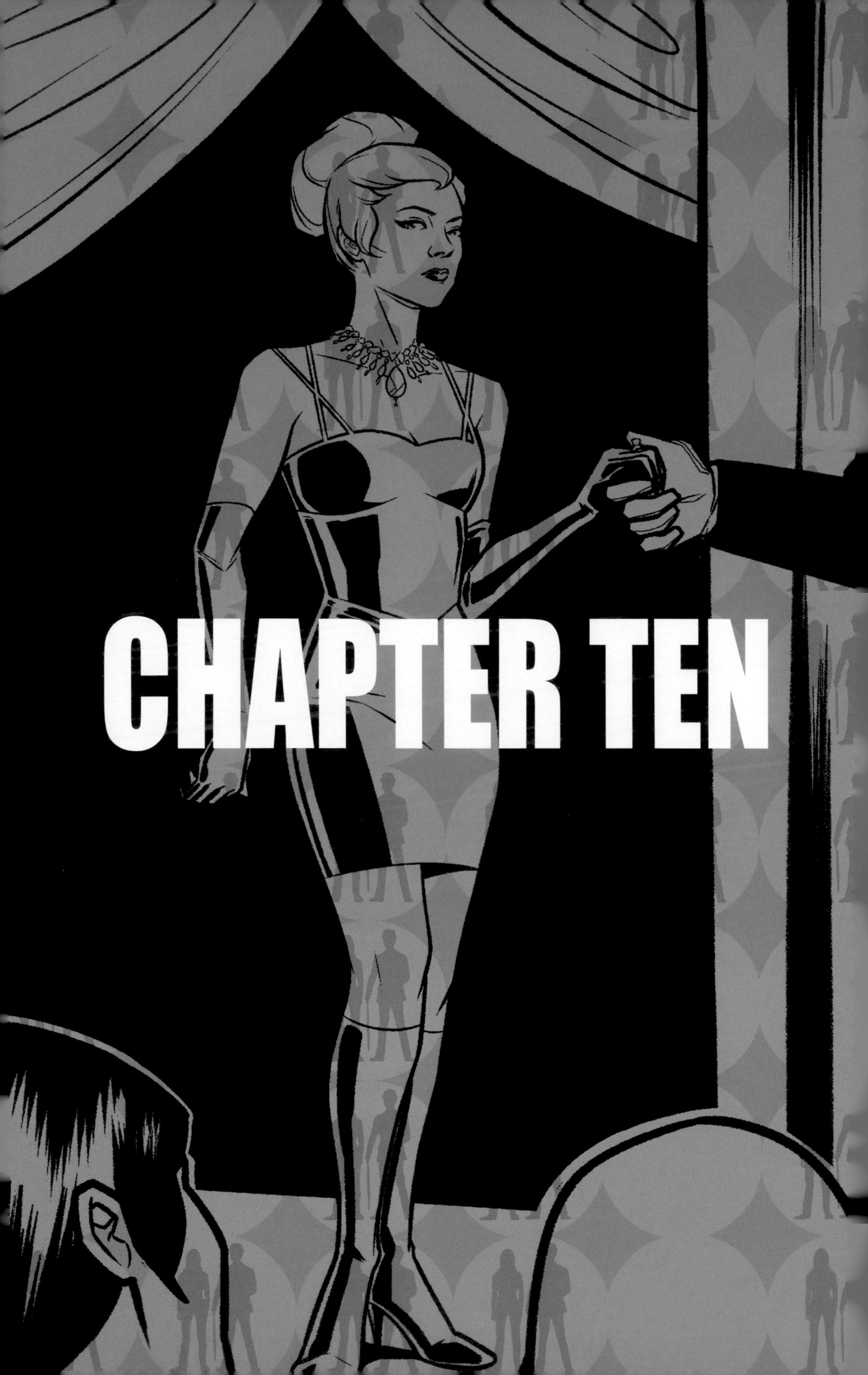

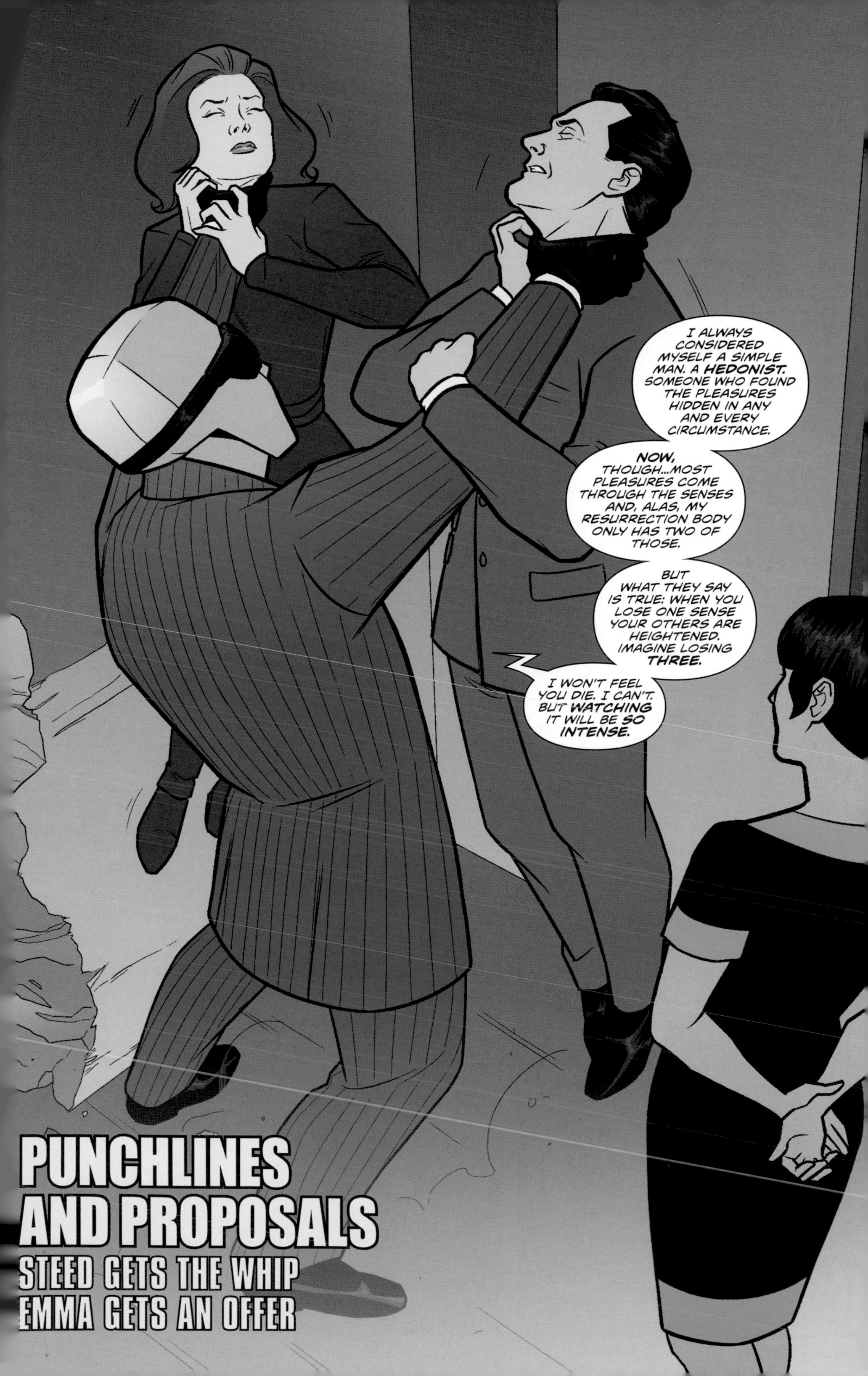
I ALWAYS CONSIDERED MYSELF A SIMPLE MAN. A HEDONIST. SOMEONE WHO FOUND THE PLEASURES HIDDEN IN ANY AND EVERY CIRCUMSTANCE.
NOW, THOUGH...MOST PLEASURES COME THROUGH THE SENSES AND, ALAS, MY RESURRECTION BODY ONLY HAS TWO OF THOSE.
BUT WHAT THEY SAY IS TRUE: WHEN YOU LOSE ONE SENSE YOUR OTHERS ARE HEIGHTENED. IMAGINE LOSING THREE.
I WON'T FEEL YOU DIE. I CAN'T. BUT WATCHING IT WILL BE SO INTENSE.
PUNCHLINES AND PROPOSALS
STEED GETS THE WHIP
EMMA GETS AN OFFER

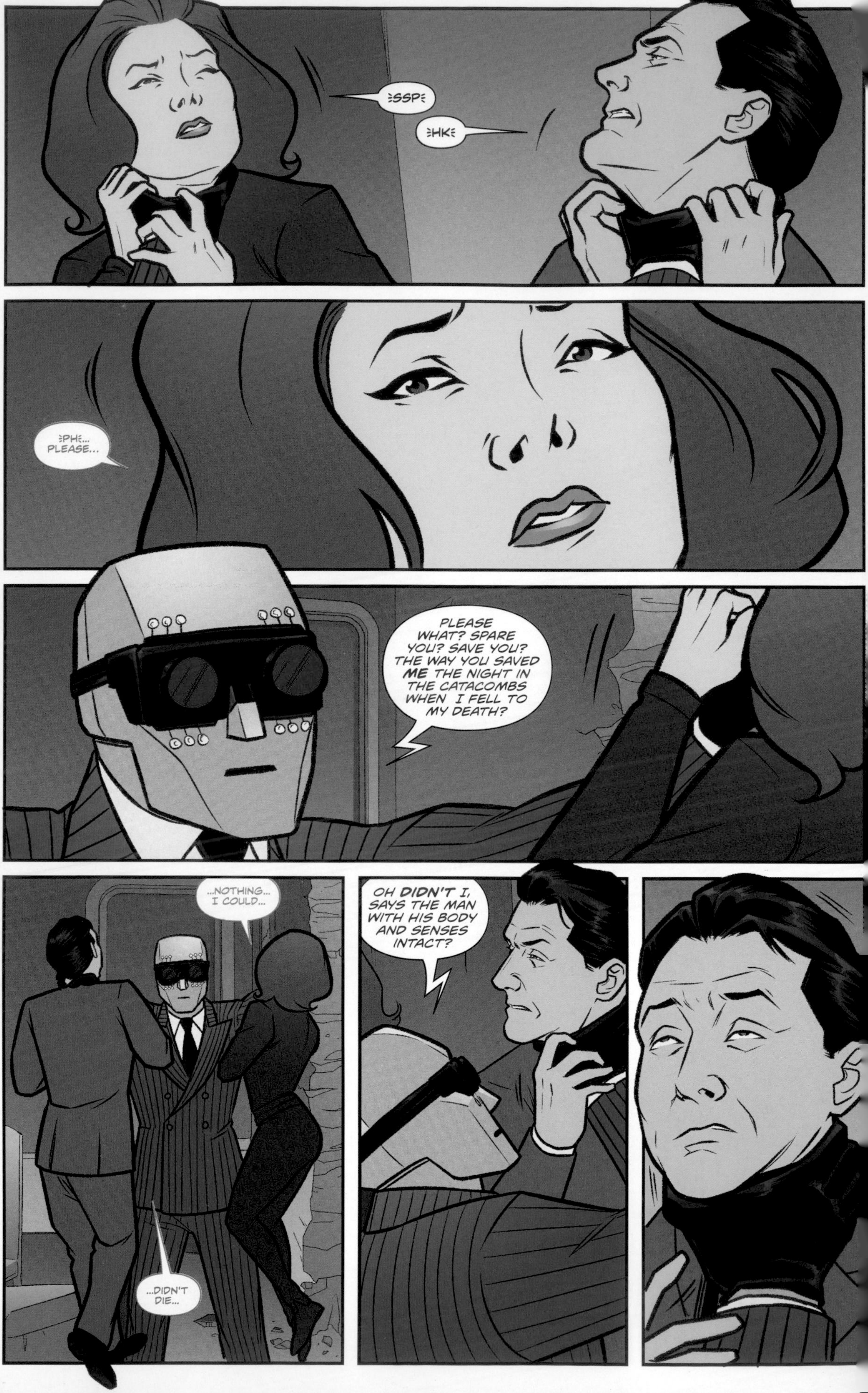
SSP
HK
PH... PLEASE...
PLEASE WHAT? SPARE YOU? SAVE YOU? THE WAY YOU SAVED ME THE NIGHT IN THE CATACOMBS WHEN I FELL TO MY DEATH?
...NOTHING... I COULD...
...DIDN'T DIE...
OH DIDN'T I, SAYS THE MAN WITH HIS BODY AND SENSES INTACT?

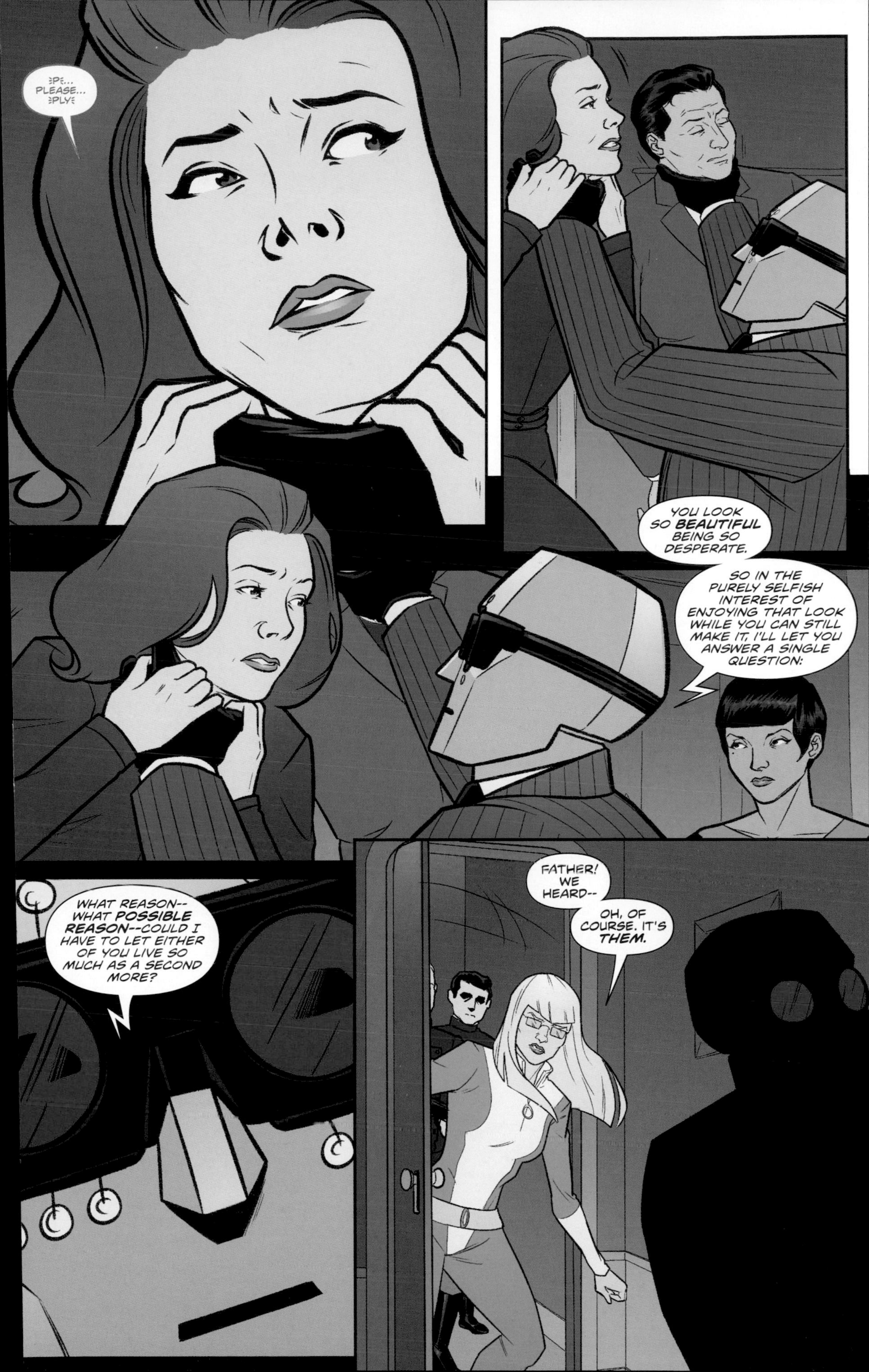

ΞPΞ... PLEASE... ΞPLYΞ
YOU LOOK SO BEAUTIFUL BEING SO DESPERATE.
SO IN THE PURELY SELFISH INTEREST OF ENJOYING THAT LOOK WHILE YOU CAN STILL MAKE IT, I'LL LET YOU ANSWER A SINGLE QUESTION:
WHAT REASON-- WHAT POSSIBLE REASON--COULD I HAVE TO LET EITHER OF YOU LIVE SO MUCH AS A SECOND MORE?
FATHER! WE HEARD--
OH, OF COURSE. IT'S THEM.

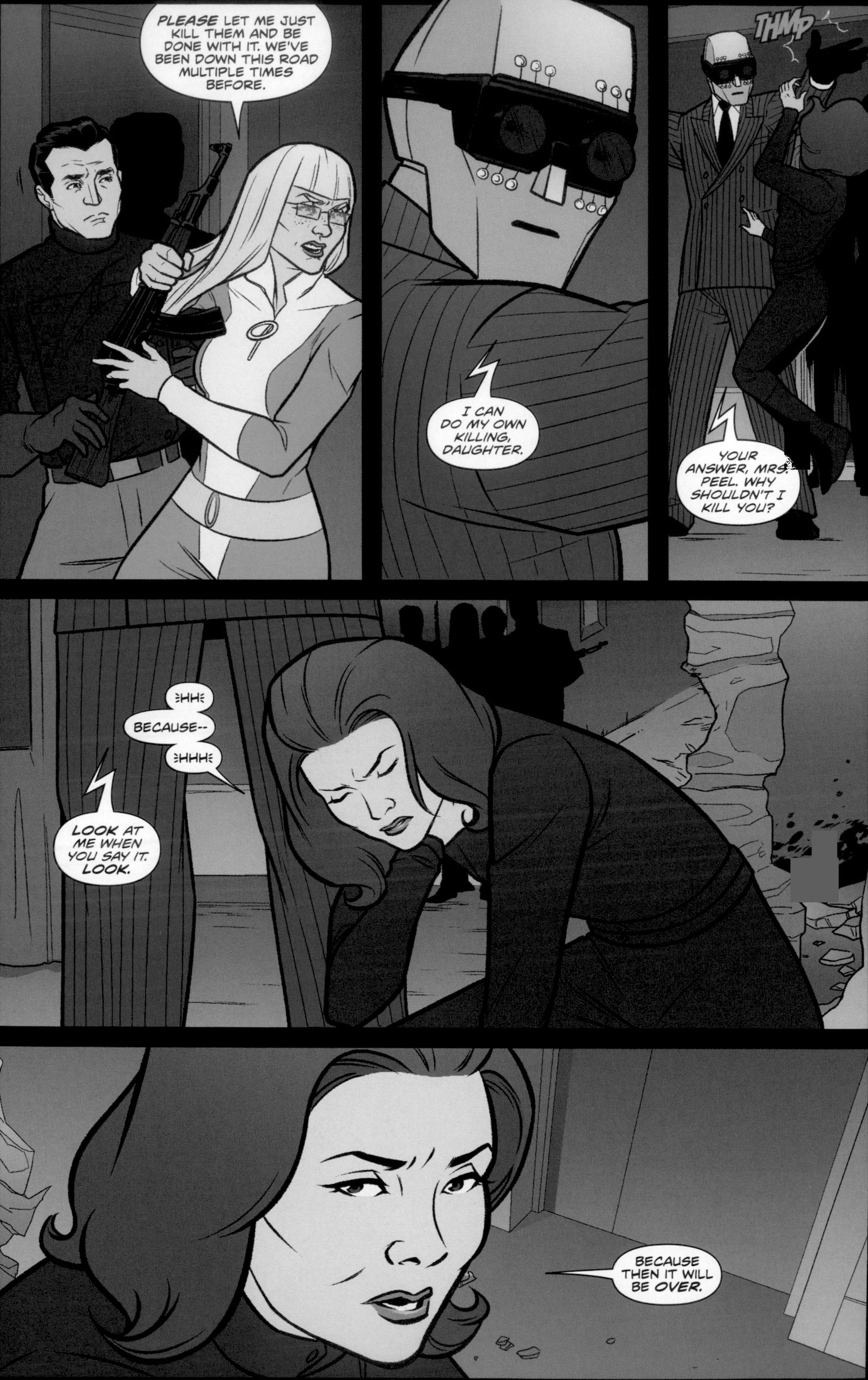

PLEASE LET ME JUST KILL THEM AND BE DONE WITH IT. WE'VE BEEN DOWN THIS ROAD MULTIPLE TIMES BEFORE.
I CAN DO MY OWN KILLING, DAUGHTER.
THMP
YOUR ANSWER, MRS. PEEL. WHY SHOULDN'T I KILL YOU?
HH
BECAUSE--
HHH
LOOK AT ME WHEN YOU SAY IT. LOOK.
BECAUSE THEN IT WILL BE OVER.

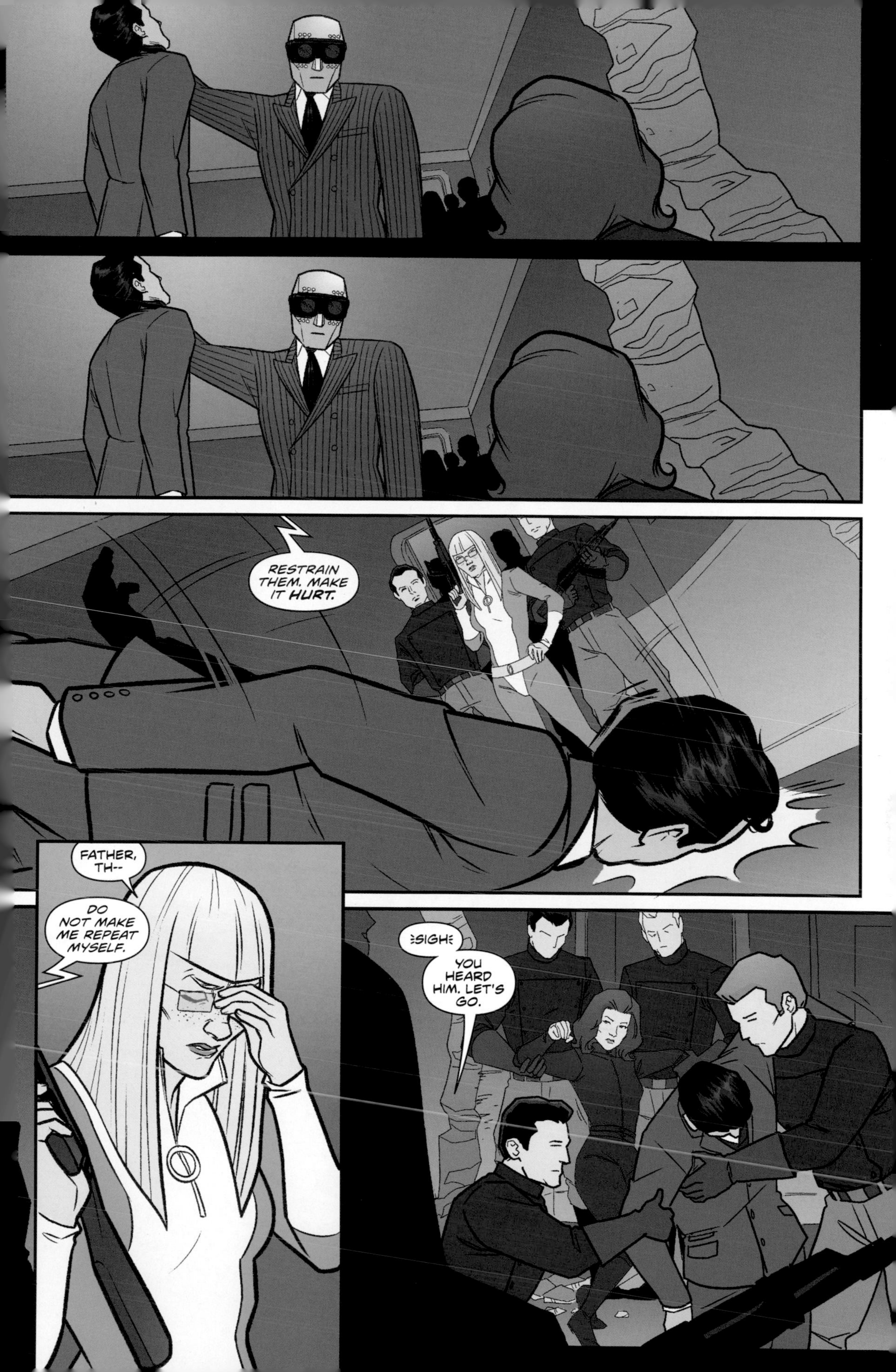
RESTRAIN THEM. MAKE IT HURT.
FATHER, TH--
DO NOT MAKE ME REPEAT MYSELF.
SIGH
YOU HEARD HIM. LET'S GO.

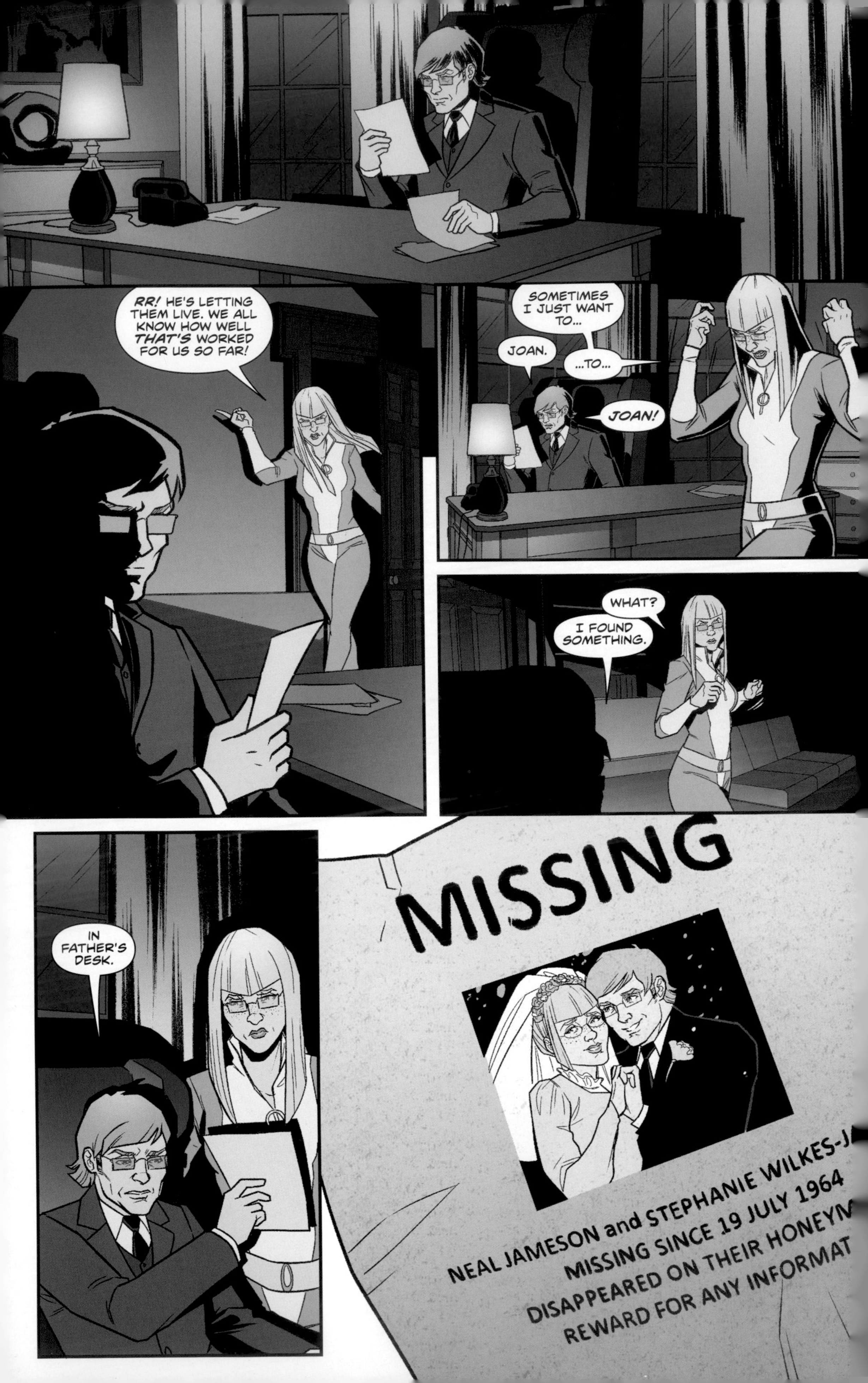

RR! HE'S LETTING THEM LIVE. WE ALL KNOW HOW WELL THAT'S WORKED FOR US SO FAR!
SOMETIMES I JUST WANT TO...
JOAN.
...TO...
JOAN!
WHAT?
I FOUND SOMETHING.
IN FATHER'S DESK.
MISSING
NEAL JAMESON and STEPHANIE WILKES-J
MISSING SINCE 19 JULY 1964
DISAPPEARED ON THEIR HONEYM
REWARD FOR ANY INFORMAT

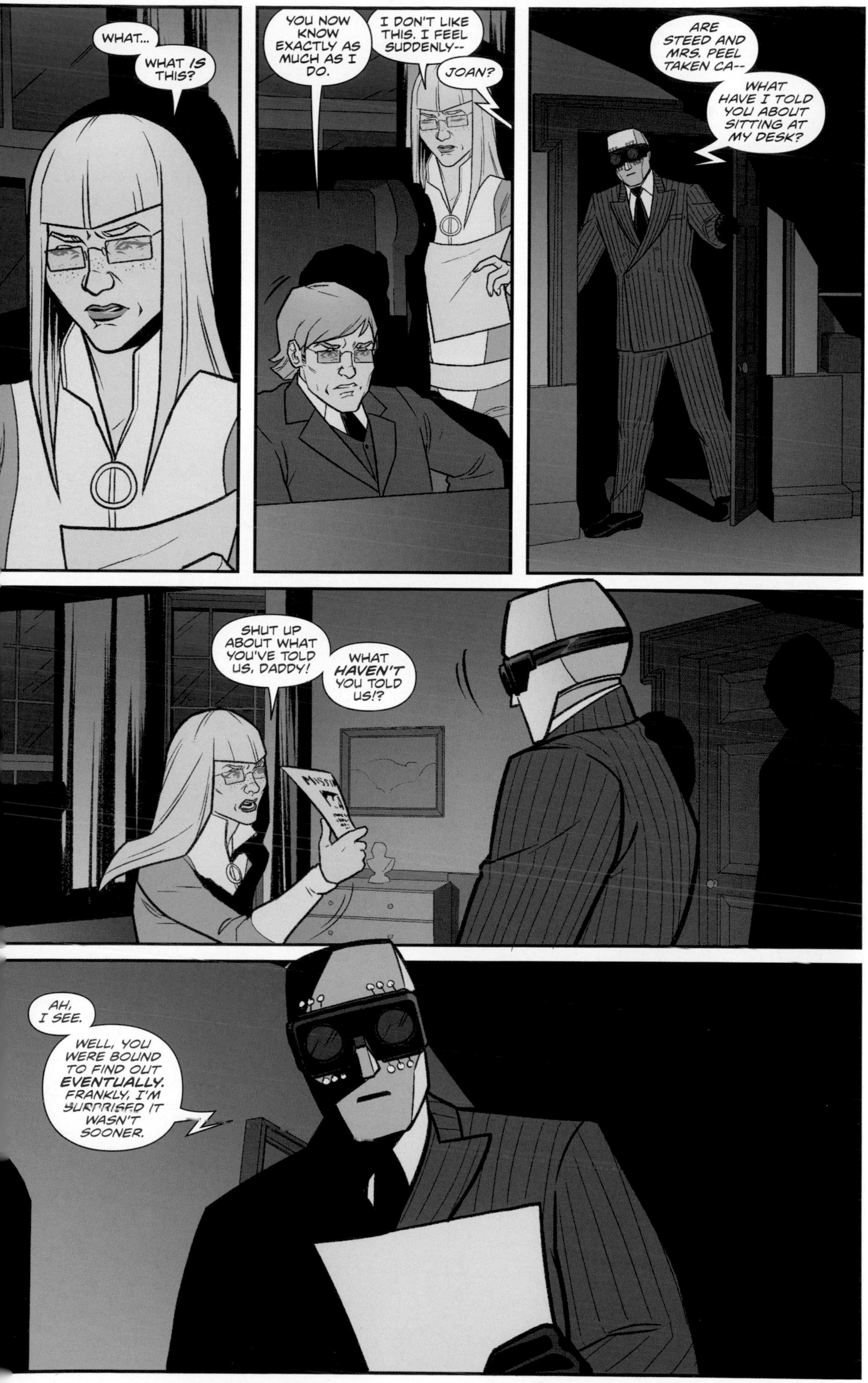
WHAT...
WHAT IS THIS?
YOU NOW KNOW EXACTLY AS MUCH AS I DO.
I DON'T LIKE THIS. I FEEL SUDDENLY--
JOAN?
ARE STEED AND MRS. PEEL TAKEN CA--
WHAT HAVE I TOLD YOU ABOUT SITTING AT MY DESK?
SHUT UP ABOUT WHAT YOU'VE TOLD US, DADDY!
WHAT HAVEN'T YOU TOLD US!?
AH, I SEE.
WELL, YOU WERE BOUND TO FIND OUT EVENTUALLY. FRANKLY, I'M SURPRISED IT WASN'T SOONER.

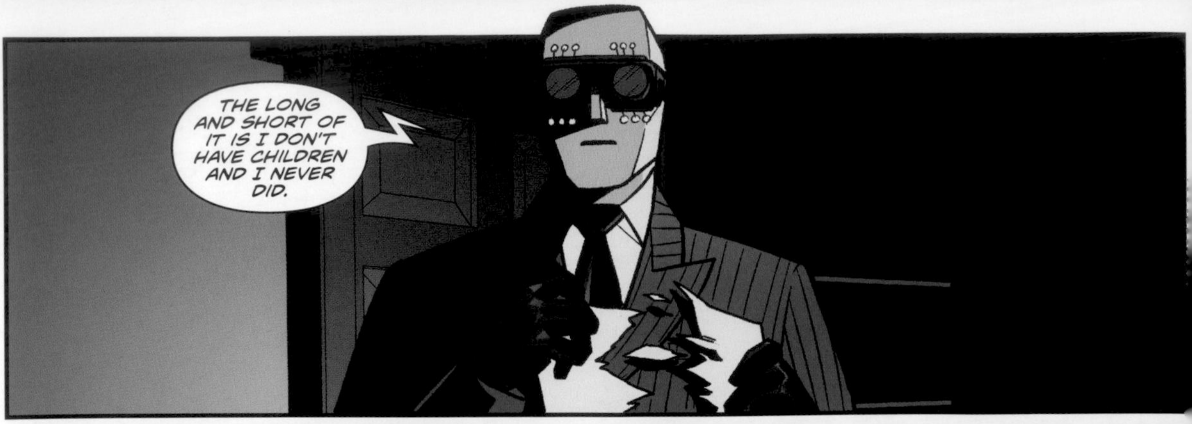
THE LONG AND SHORT OF IT IS I DON'T HAVE CHILDREN AND I NEVER DID.

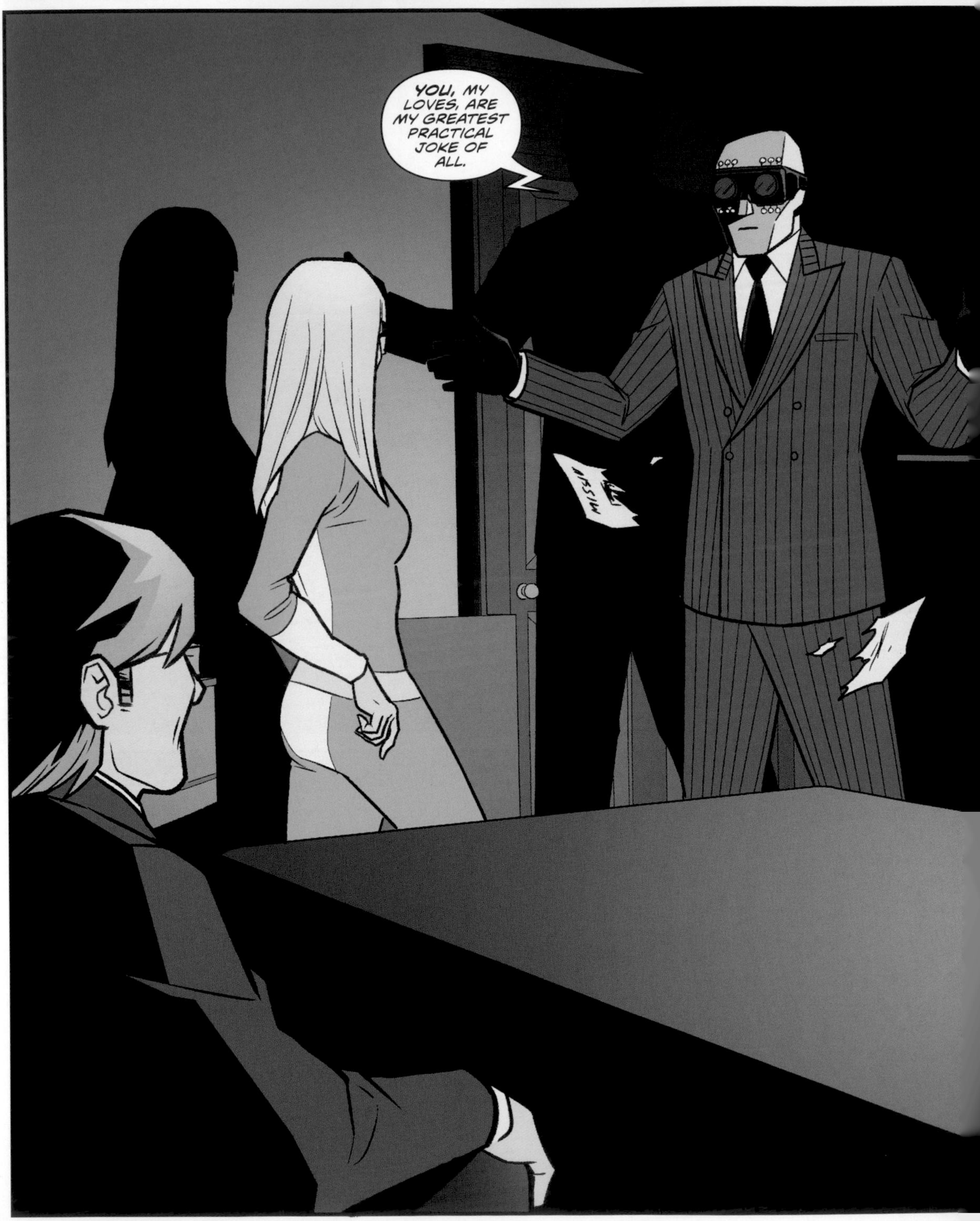
YOU, MY LOVES, ARE MY GREATEST PRACTICAL JOKE OF ALL.

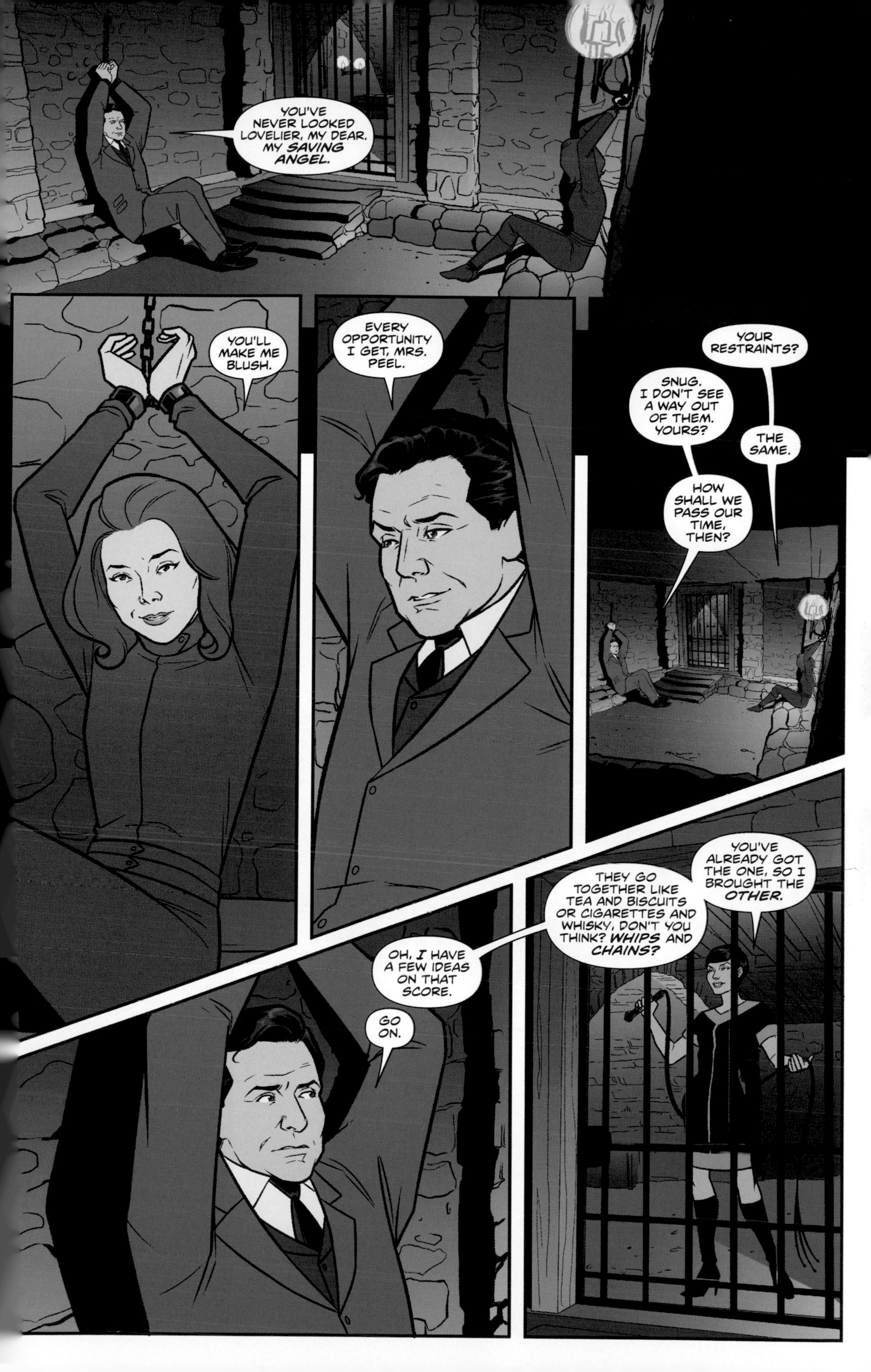

YOU'VE NEVER LOOKED LOVELIER, MY DEAR. MY SAVING ANGEL.
YOU'LL MAKE ME BLUSH.
EVERY OPPORTUNITY I GET, MRS. PEEL.
YOUR RESTRAINTS?
SNUG. I DON'T SEE A WAY OUT OF THEM. YOURS?
THE SAME.
HOW SHALL WE PASS OUR TIME, THEN?
OH, I HAVE A FEW IDEAS ON THAT SCORE.
GO ON.
THEY GO TOGETHER LIKE TEA AND BISCUITS OR CIGARETTES AND WHISKY, DON'T YOU THINK? WHIPS AND CHAINS?
YOU'VE ALREADY GOT THE ONE, SO I BROUGHT THE OTHER.

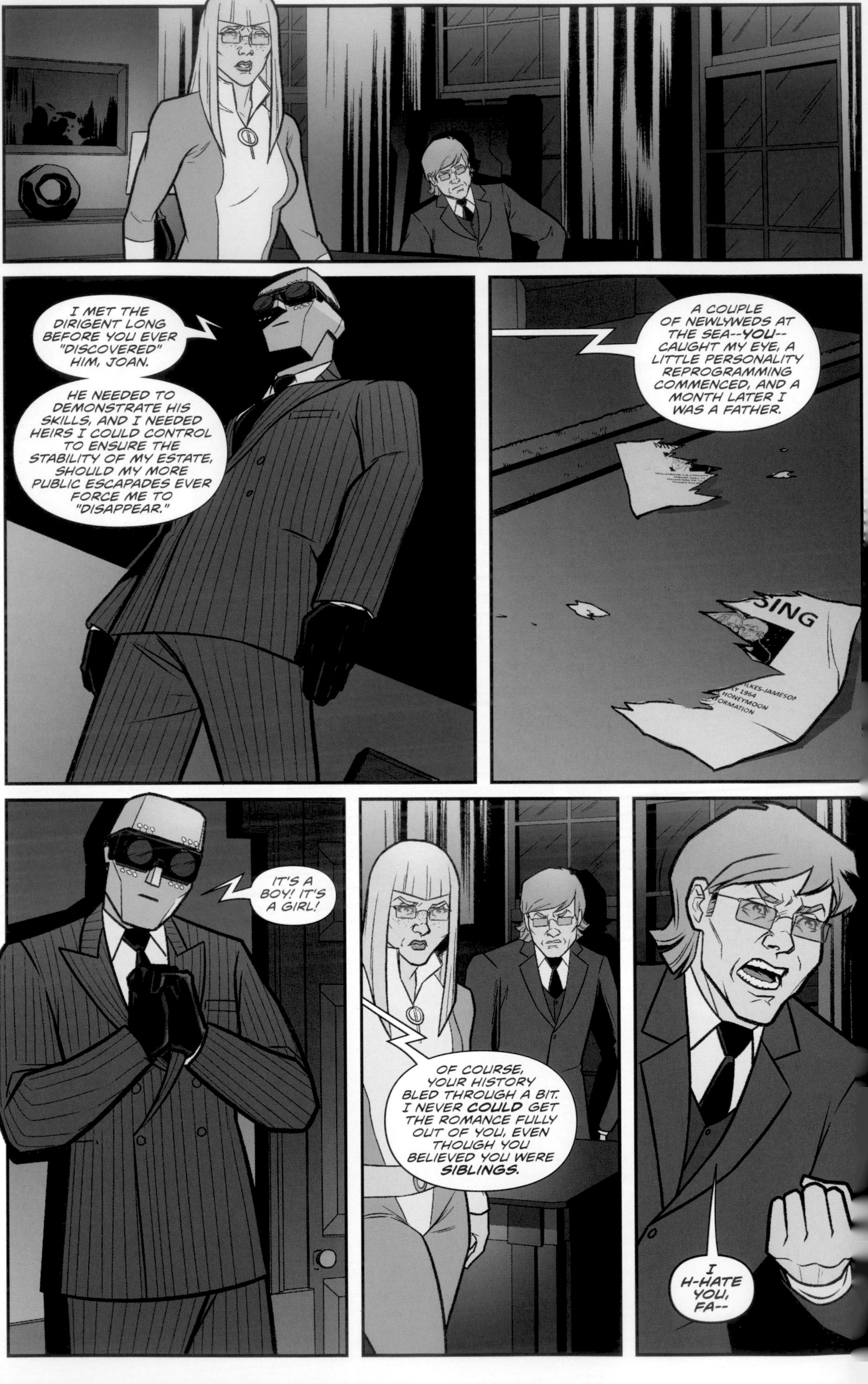
I MET THE DIRIGENT LONG BEFORE YOU EVER "DISCOVERED" HIM, JOAN.
HE NEEDED TO DEMONSTRATE HIS SKILLS, AND I NEEDED HEIRS I COULD CONTROL TO ENSURE THE STABILITY OF MY ESTATE, SHOULD MY MORE PUBLIC ESCAPADES EVER FORCE ME TO "DISAPPEAR."
A COUPLE OF NEWLYWEDS AT THE SEA--**YOU**--CAUGHT MY EYE, A LITTLE PERSONALITY REPROGRAMMING COMMENCED, AND A MONTH LATER I WAS A FATHER.
SING
HONEYMOON
IT'S A BOY! IT'S A GIRL!
OF COURSE, YOUR HISTORY BLED THROUGH A BIT. I NEVER **COULD** GET THE ROMANCE FULLY OUT OF YOU, EVEN THOUGH YOU BELIEVED YOU WERE **SIBLINGS.**
I H-HATE YOU, FA--

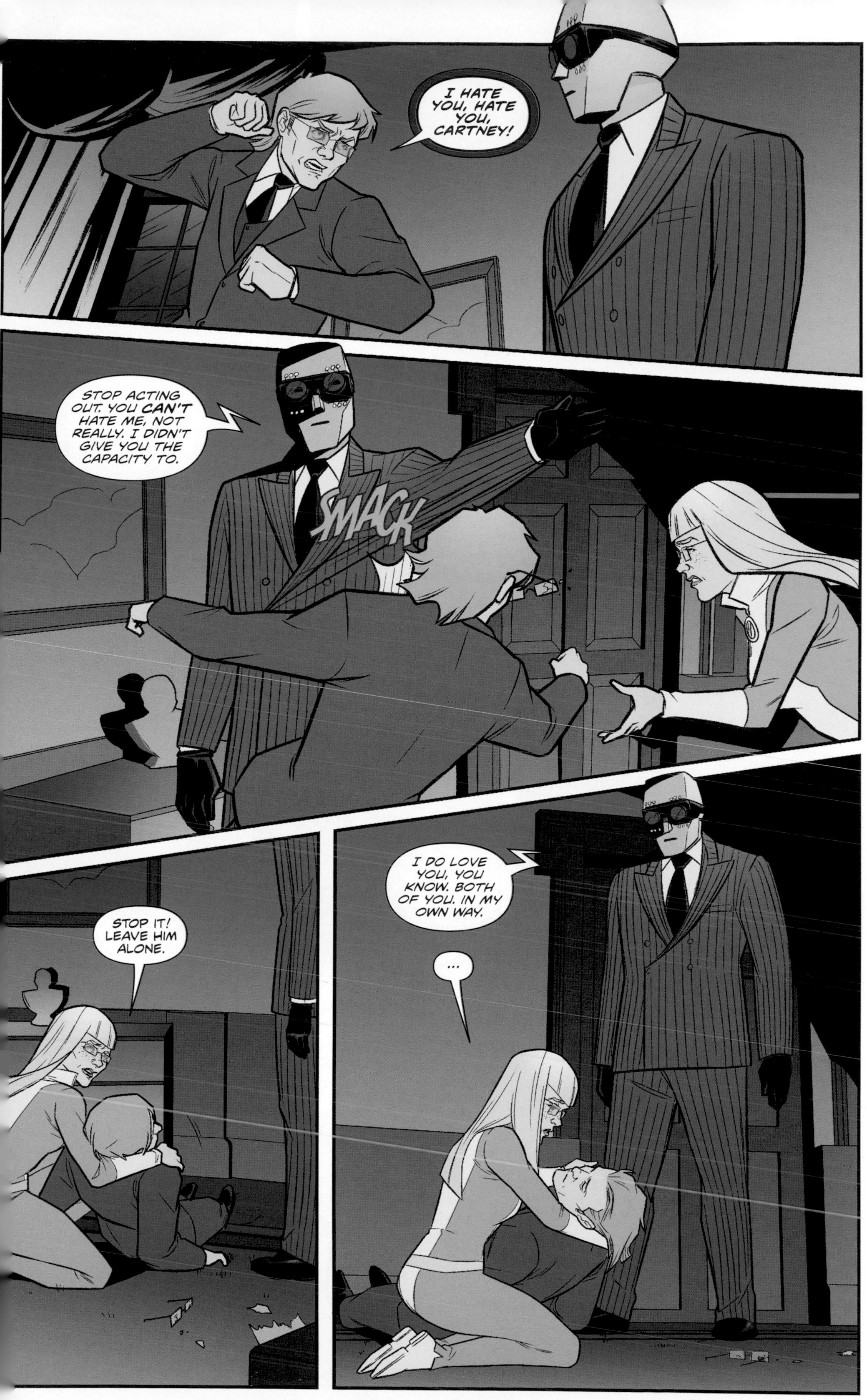
I HATE YOU, HATE YOU, CARTNEY!
STOP ACTING OUT. YOU CAN'T HATE ME, NOT REALLY. I DIDN'T GIVE YOU THE CAPACITY TO.
SMACK
STOP IT! LEAVE HIM ALONE.
I DO LOVE YOU, YOU KNOW. BOTH OF YOU. IN MY OWN WAY.
...

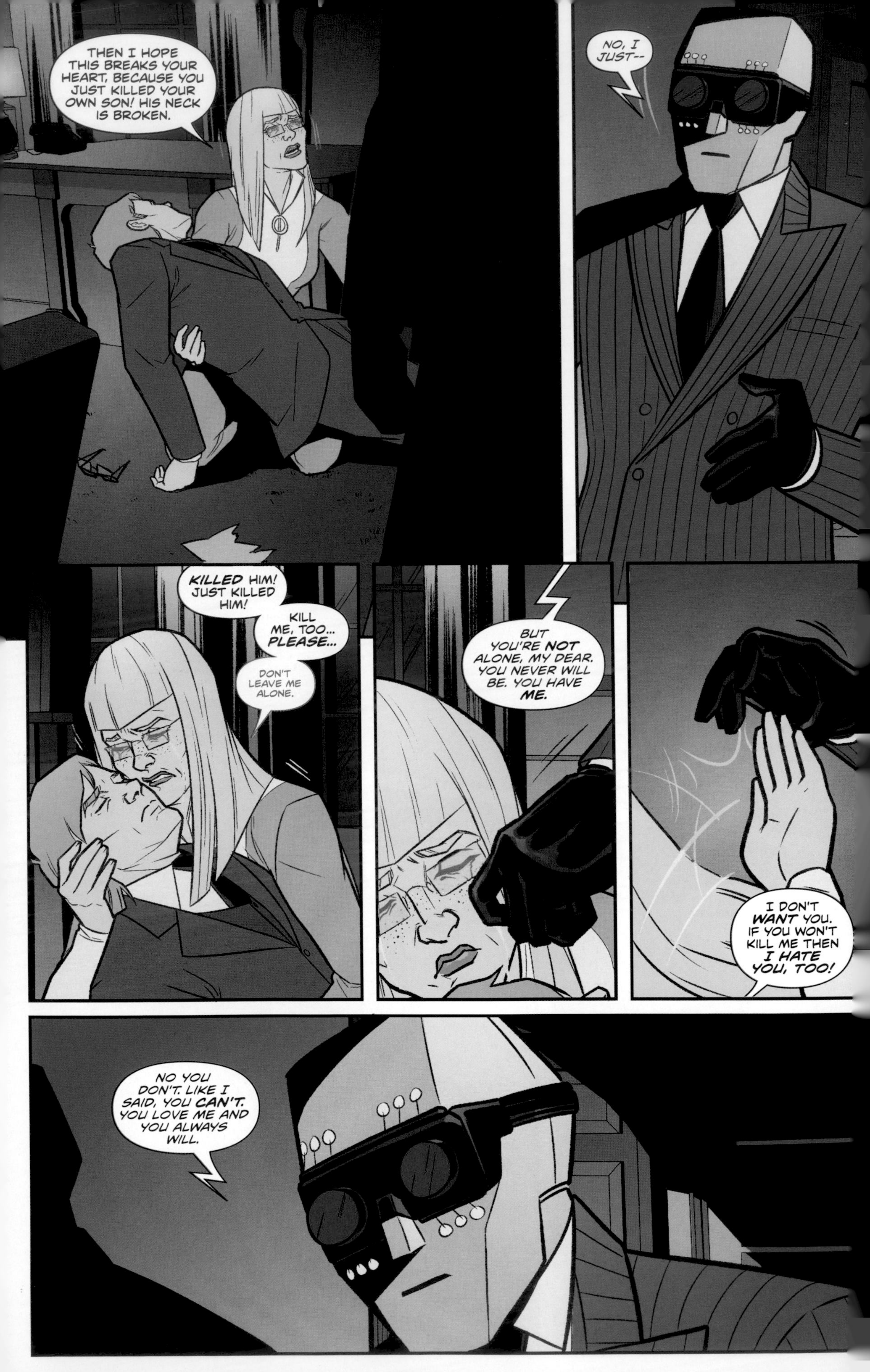
THEN I HOPE THIS BREAKS YOUR HEART, BECAUSE YOU JUST KILLED YOUR OWN SON! HIS NECK IS BROKEN.
NO, I JUST--
KILLED HIM! JUST KILLED HIM!
KILL ME, TOO... PLEASE...
DON'T LEAVE ME ALONE.
BUT YOU'RE NOT ALONE, MY DEAR. YOU NEVER WILL BE. YOU HAVE ME.
I DON'T WANT YOU. IF YOU WON'T KILL ME THEN I HATE YOU, TOO!
NO YOU DON'T. LIKE I SAID, YOU CAN'T. YOU LOVE ME AND YOU ALWAYS WILL.

... I KNOW. I DO.

GOD HELP ME, I STILL DO.

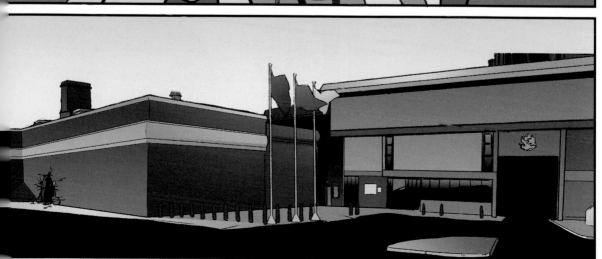

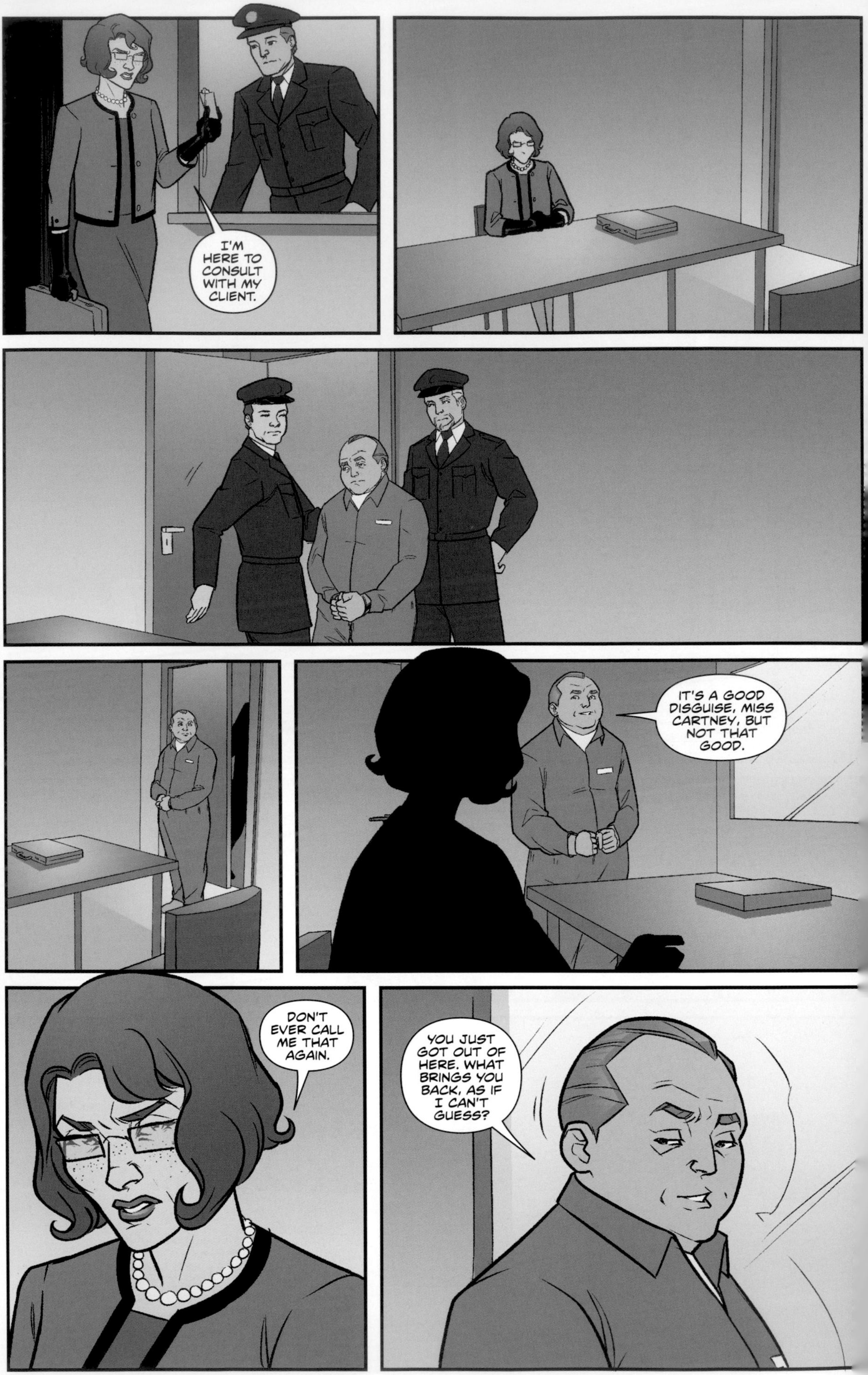
I'M HERE TO CONSULT WITH MY CLIENT.
IT'S A GOOD DISGUISE, MISS CARTNEY, BUT NOT THAT GOOD.
DON'T EVER CALL ME THAT AGAIN.
YOU JUST GOT OUT OF HERE. WHAT BRINGS YOU BACK, AS IF I CAN'T GUESS?

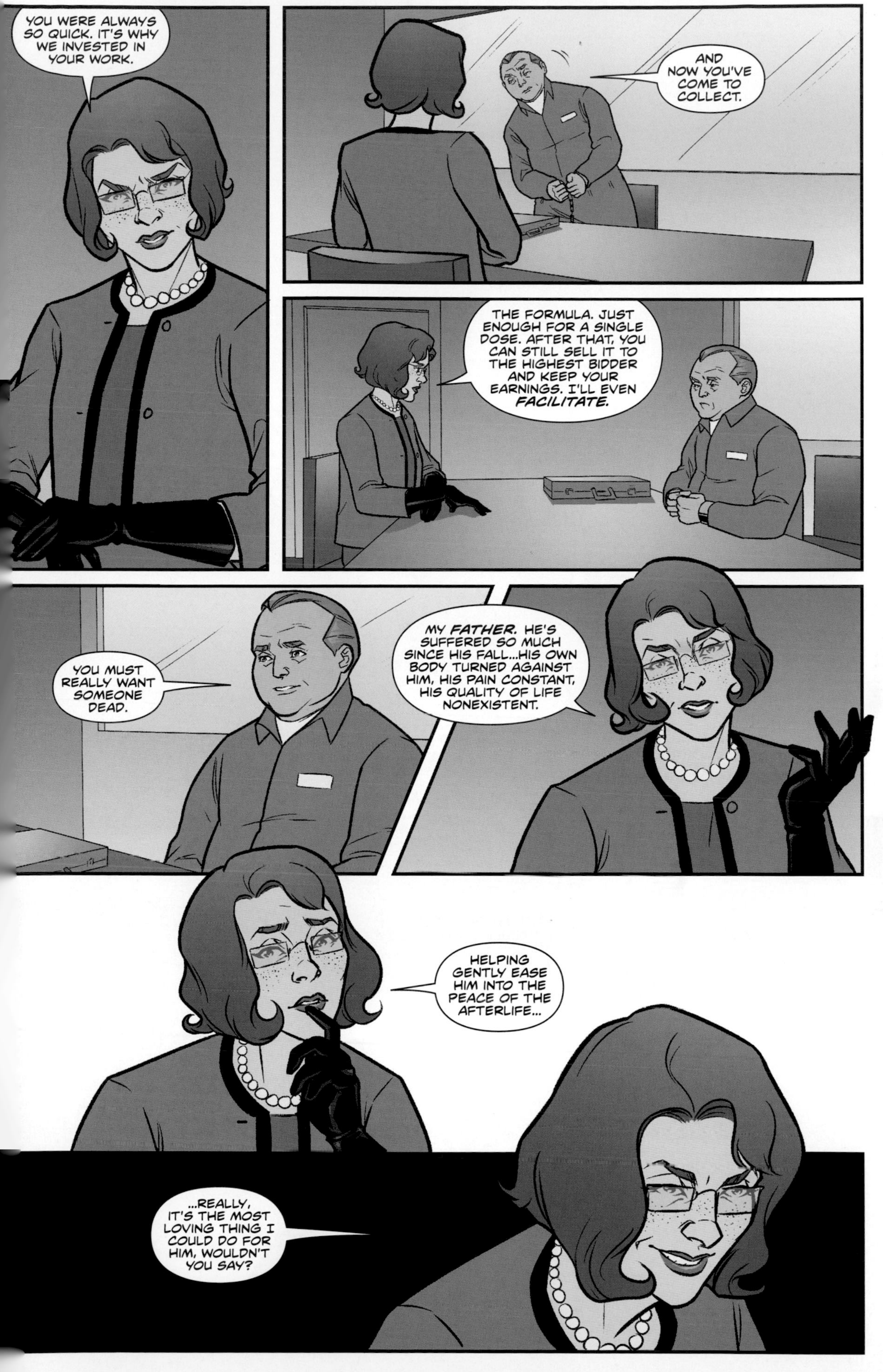
YOU WERE ALWAYS SO QUICK. IT'S WHY WE INVESTED IN YOUR WORK.
AND NOW YOU'VE COME TO COLLECT.
THE FORMULA. JUST ENOUGH FOR A SINGLE DOSE. AFTER THAT, YOU CAN STILL SELL IT TO THE HIGHEST BIDDER AND KEEP YOUR EARNINGS. I'LL EVEN FACILITATE.
YOU MUST REALLY WANT SOMEONE DEAD.
MY FATHER. HE'S SUFFERED SO MUCH SINCE HIS FALL...HIS OWN BODY TURNED AGAINST HIM, HIS PAIN CONSTANT, HIS QUALITY OF LIFE NONEXISTENT.
HELPING GENTLY EASE HIM INTO THE PEACE OF THE AFTERLIFE...
...REALLY, IT'S THE MOST LOVING THING I COULD DO FOR HIM, WOULDN'T YOU SAY?

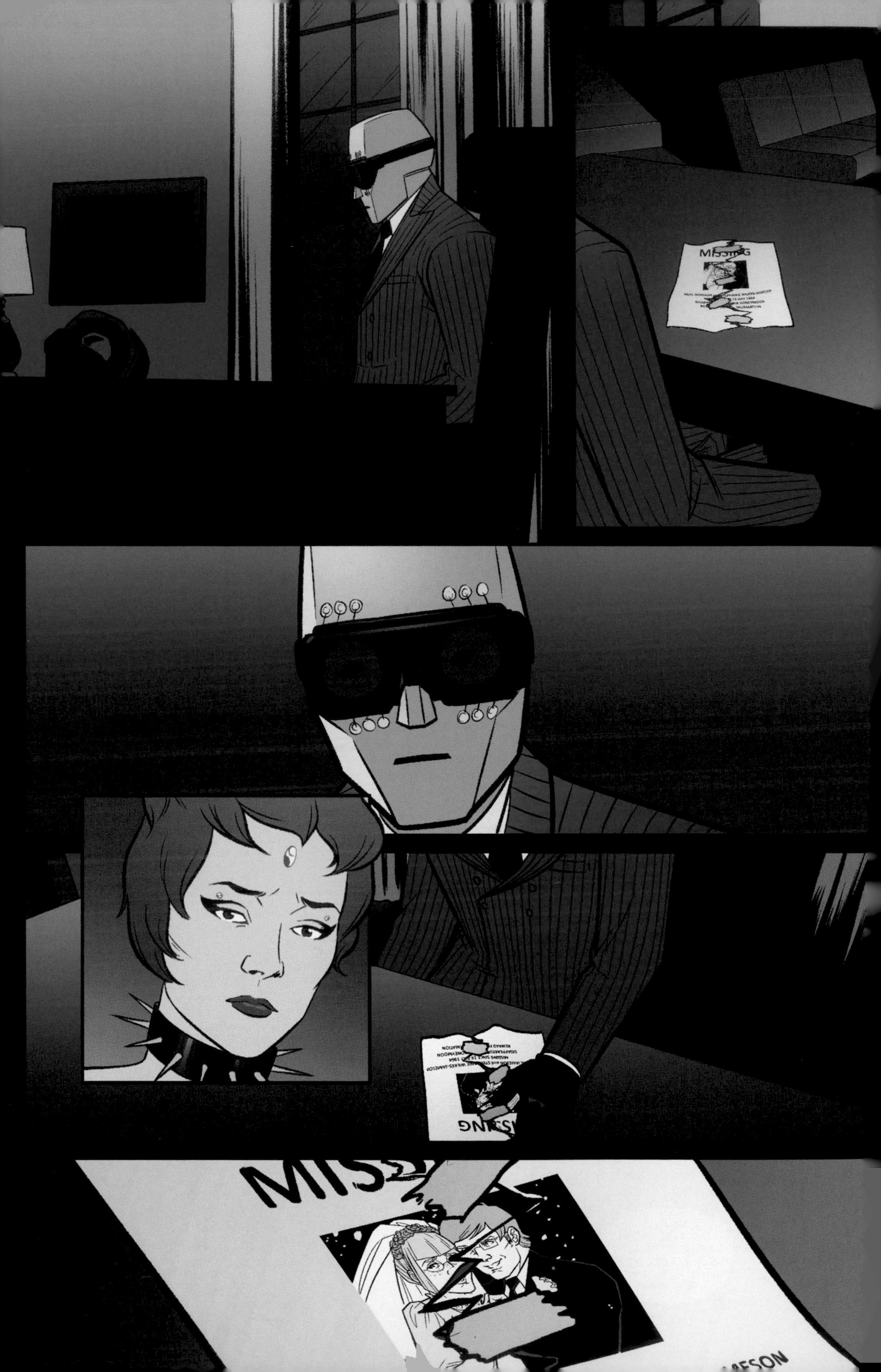
MISSING

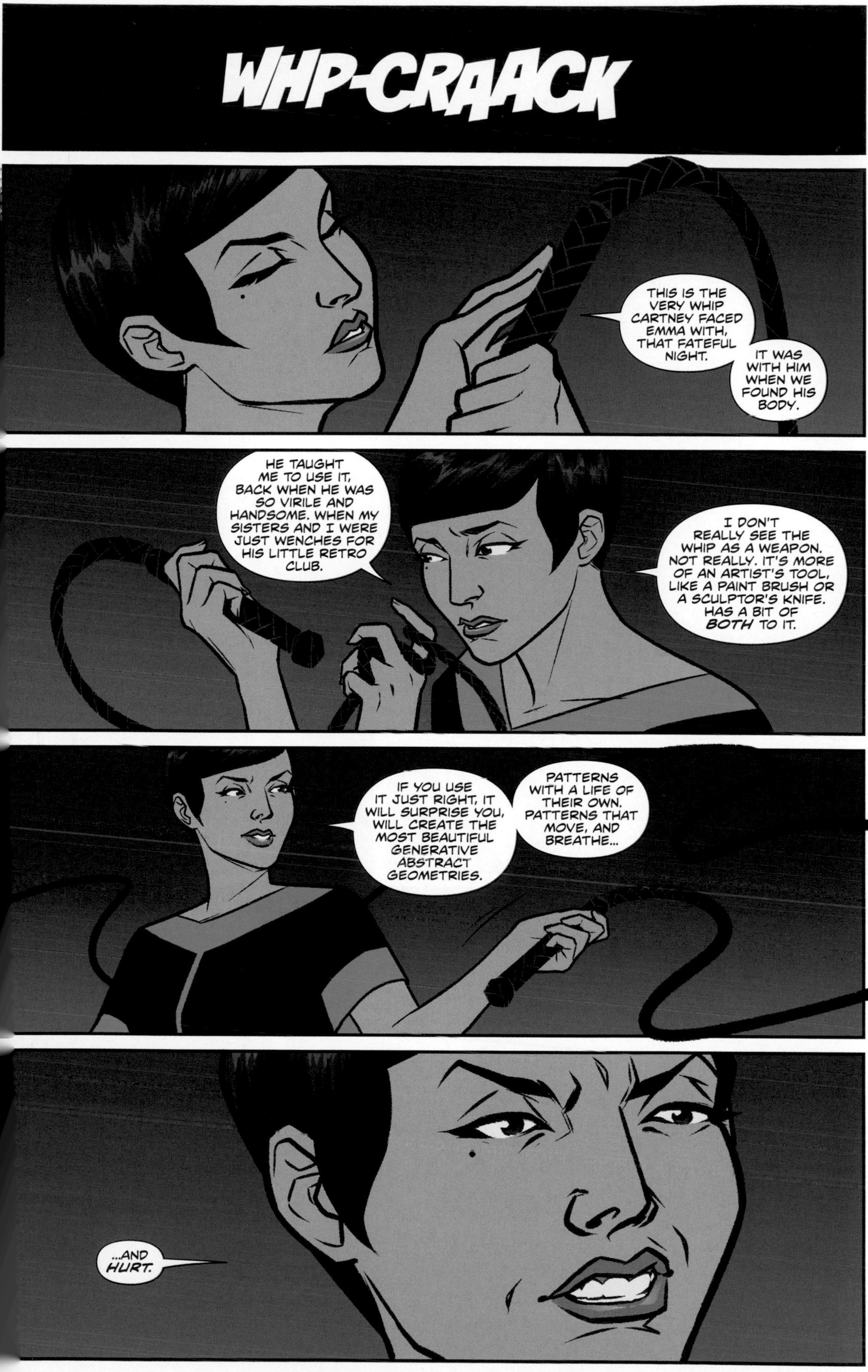
WHP-CRAACK
THIS IS THE VERY WHIP CARTNEY FACED EMMA WITH, THAT FATEFUL NIGHT.
IT WAS WITH HIM WHEN WE FOUND HIS BODY.
HE TAUGHT ME TO USE IT, BACK WHEN HE WAS SO VIRILE AND HANDSOME. WHEN MY SISTERS AND I WERE JUST WENCHES FOR HIS LITTLE RETRO CLUB.
I DON'T REALLY SEE THE WHIP AS A WEAPON. NOT REALLY. IT'S MORE OF AN ARTIST'S TOOL, LIKE A PAINT BRUSH OR A SCULPTOR'S KNIFE. HAS A BIT OF BOTH TO IT.
IF YOU USE IT JUST RIGHT, IT WILL SURPRISE YOU, WILL CREATE THE MOST BEAUTIFUL GENERATIVE ABSTRACT GEOMETRIES.
PATTERNS WITH A LIFE OF THEIR OWN. PATTERNS THAT MOVE, AND BREATHE...
...AND HURT.

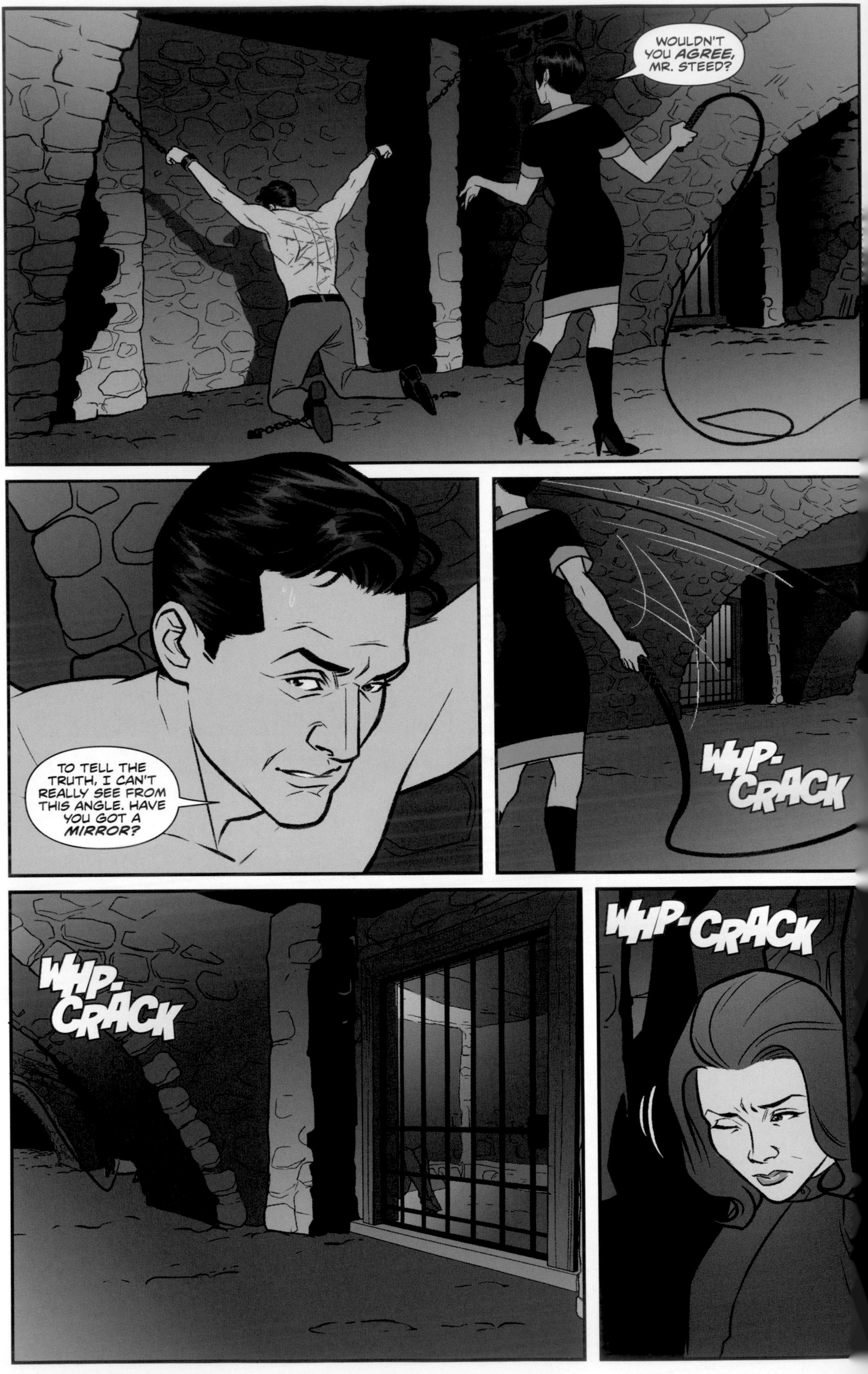
WOULDN'T YOU AGREE, MR. STEED?
TO TELL THE TRUTH, I CAN'T REALLY SEE FROM THIS ANGLE. HAVE YOU GOT A MIRROR?
WHP-CRACK
WHP-CRACK
WHP-CRACK

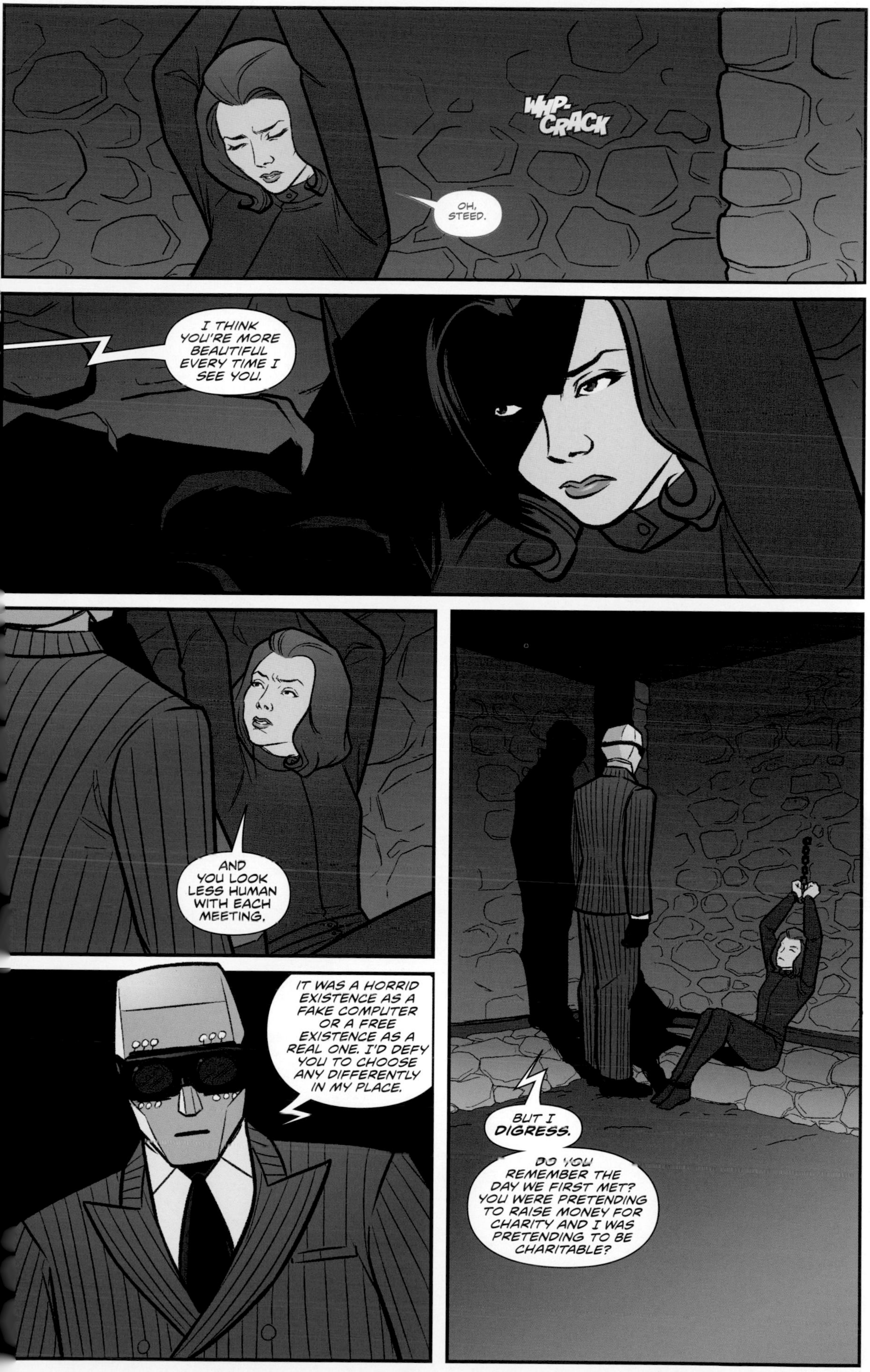
WHP-CRACK
OH, STEED.
I THINK YOU'RE MORE BEAUTIFUL EVERY TIME I SEE YOU.
AND YOU LOOK LESS HUMAN WITH EACH MEETING.
IT WAS A HORRID EXISTENCE AS A FAKE COMPUTER OR A FREE EXISTENCE AS A REAL ONE. I'D DEFY YOU TO CHOOSE ANY DIFFERENTLY IN MY PLACE.
BUT I DIGRESS.
DO YOU REMEMBER THE DAY WE FIRST MET? YOU WERE PRETENDING TO RAISE MONEY FOR CHARITY AND I WAS PRETENDING TO BE CHARITABLE?

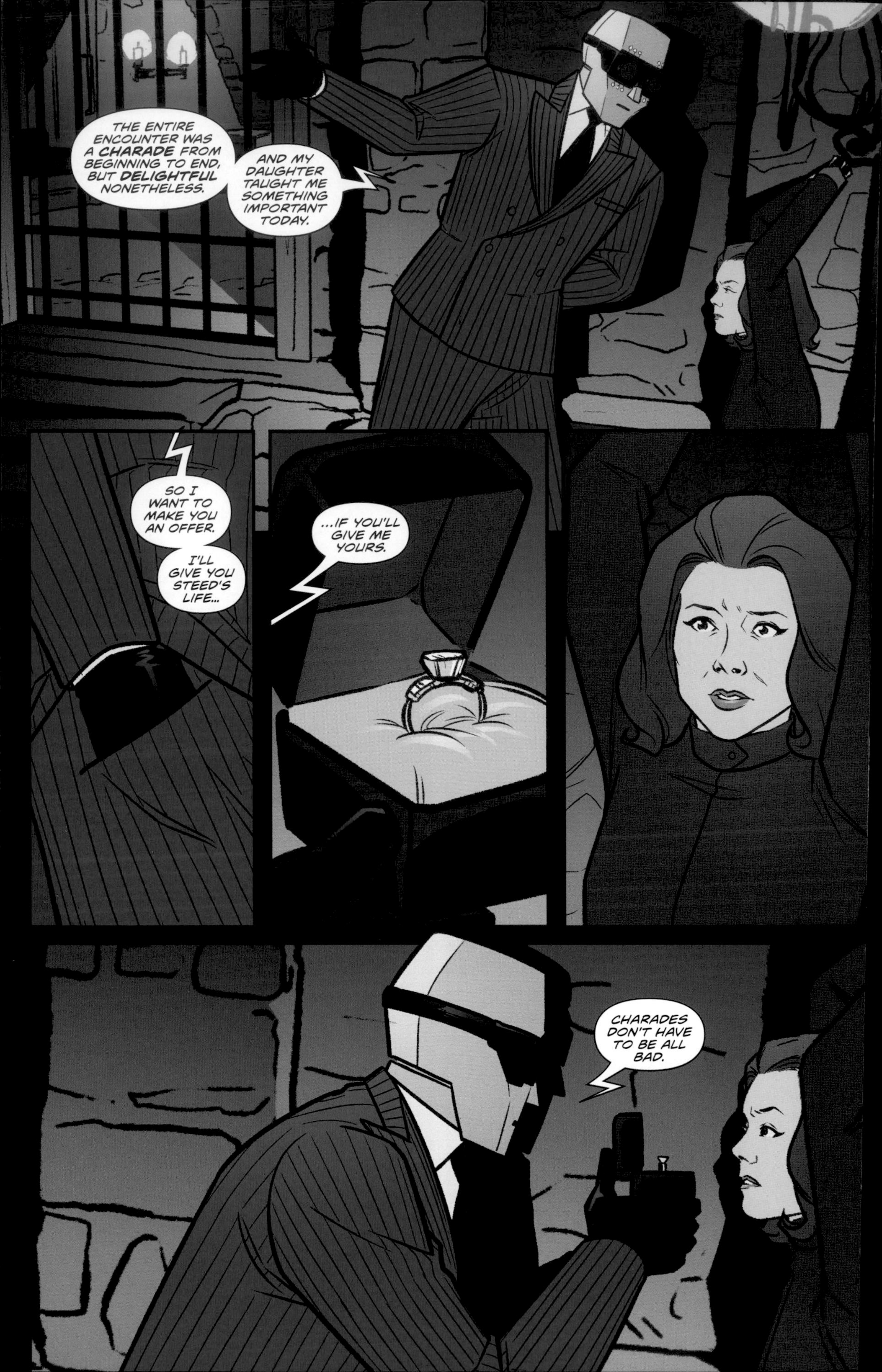
THE ENTIRE ENCOUNTER WAS A **CHARADE** FROM BEGINNING TO END, BUT **DELIGHTFUL** NONETHELESS.
AND MY DAUGHTER TAUGHT ME SOMETHING IMPORTANT TODAY.
SO I WANT TO MAKE YOU AN OFFER.
I'LL GIVE YOU STEED'S LIFE...
...IF YOU'LL GIVE ME YOURS.
CHARADES DON'T HAVE TO BE ALL BAD.

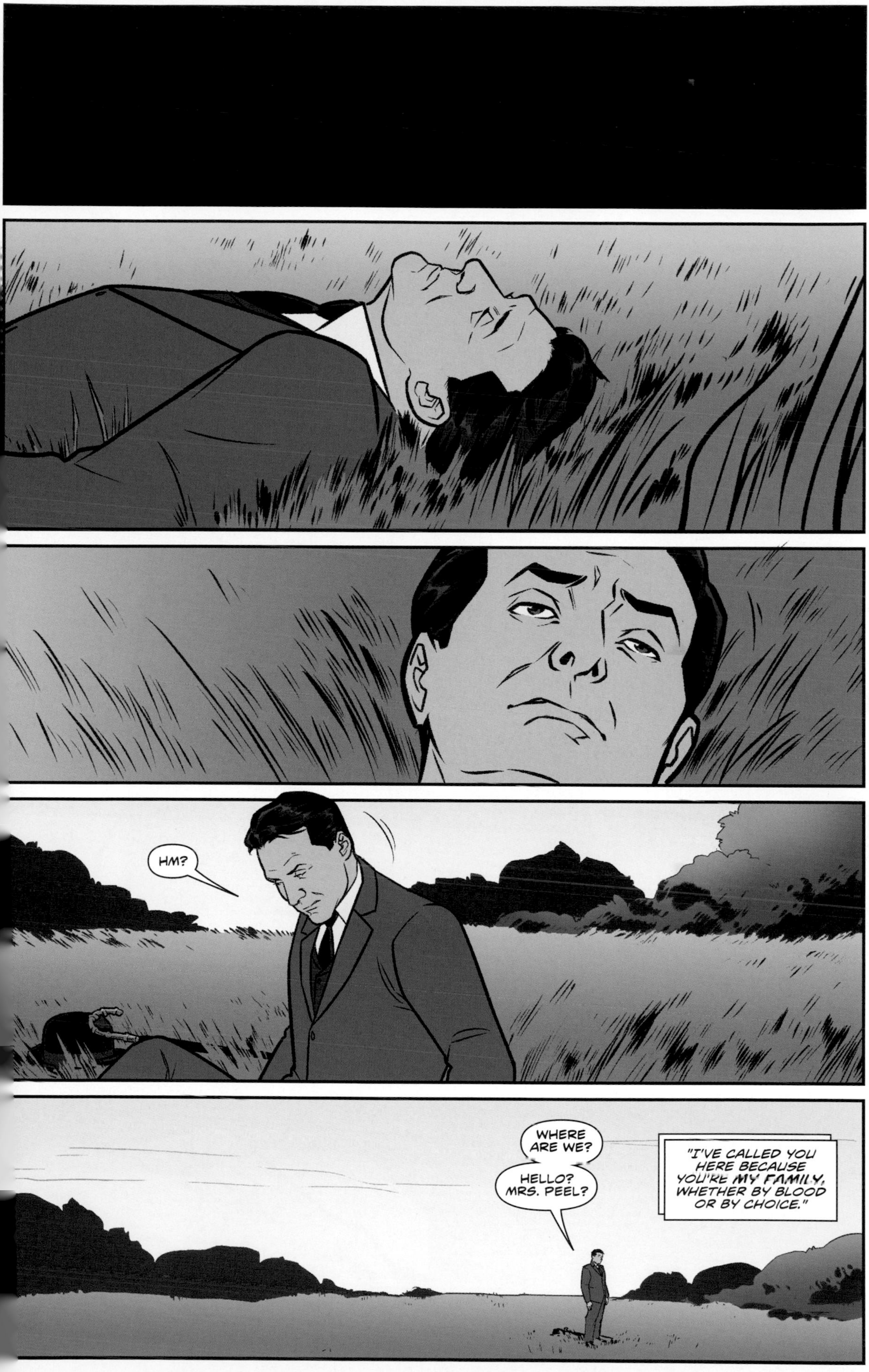
HM?
WHERE ARE WE?
HELLO? MRS. PEEL?
"I'VE CALLED YOU HERE BECAUSE YOU'RE MY FAMILY, WHETHER BY BLOOD OR BY CHOICE."

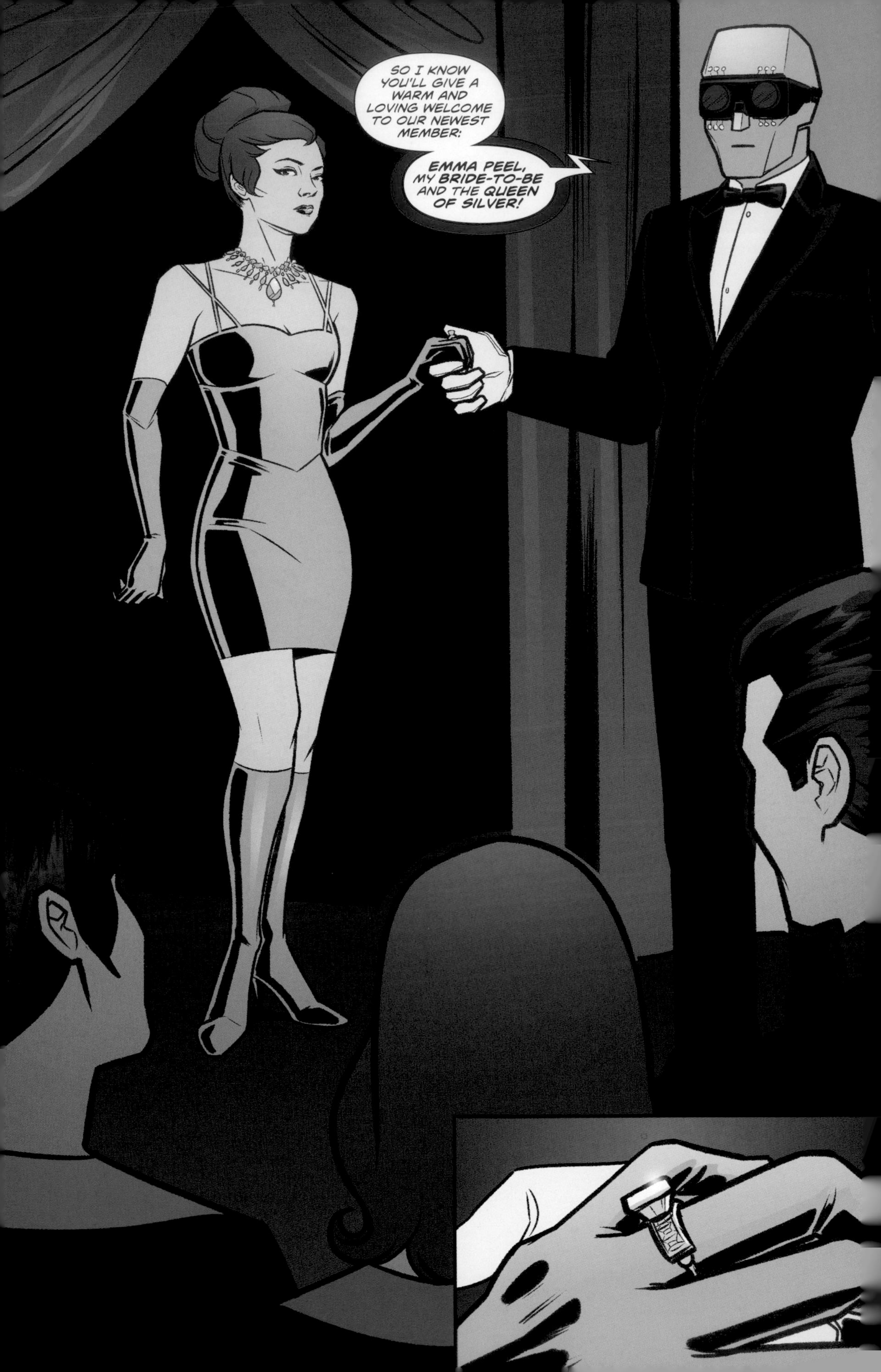
SO I KNOW YOU'LL GIVE A WARM AND LOVING WELCOME TO OUR NEWEST MEMBER:
EMMA PEEL, MY BRIDE-TO-BE AND THE QUEEN OF SILVER!

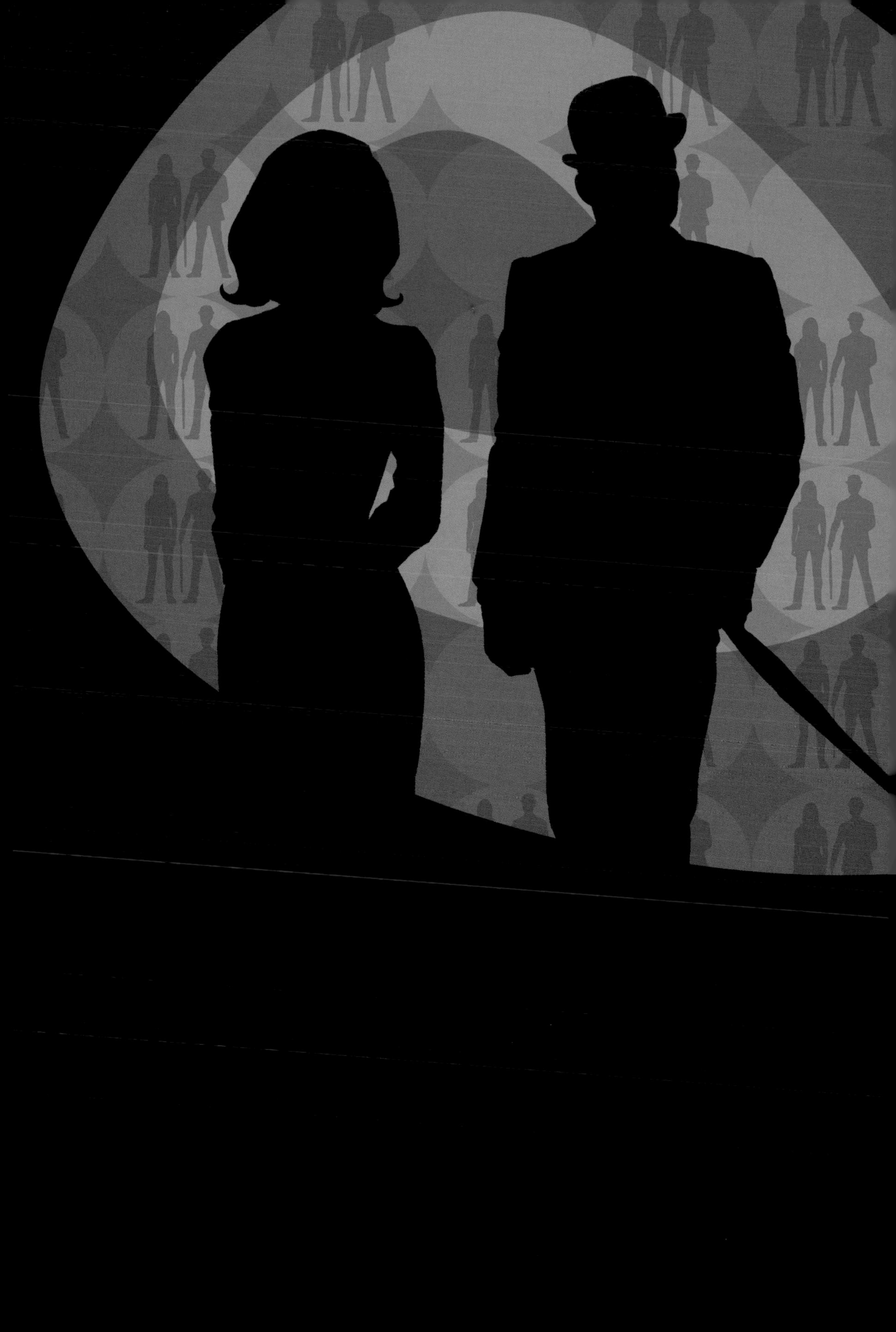

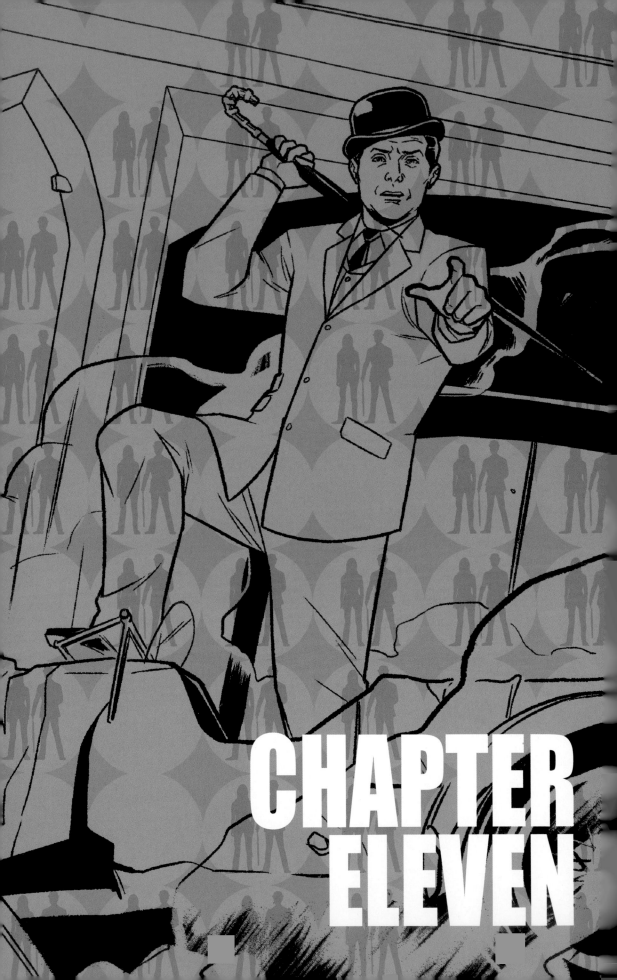

CHAPTER ELEVEN

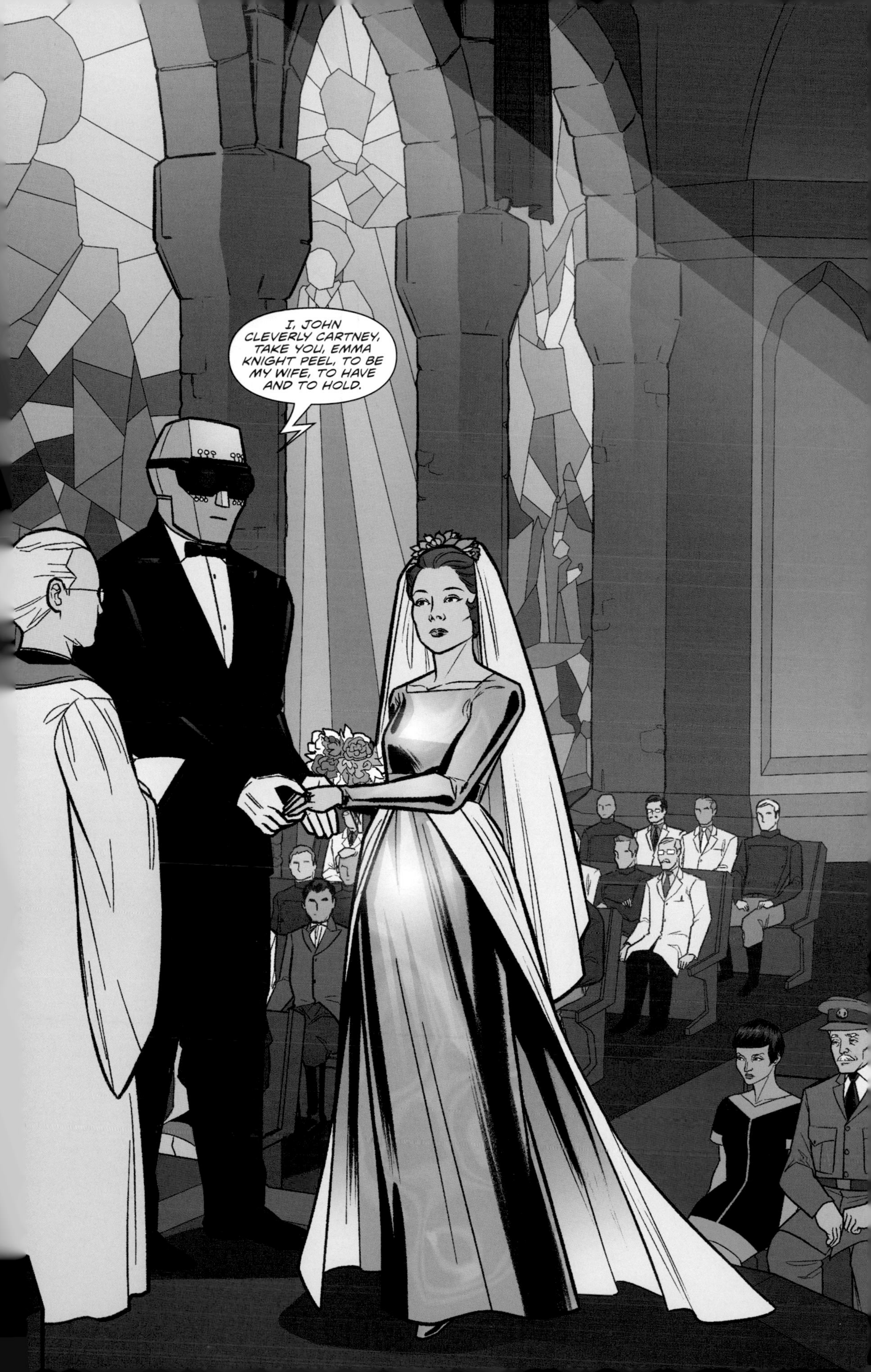
I, JOHN CLEVERLY CARTNEY, TAKE YOU, EMMA KNIGHT PEEL, TO BE MY WIFE, TO HAVE AND TO HOLD.

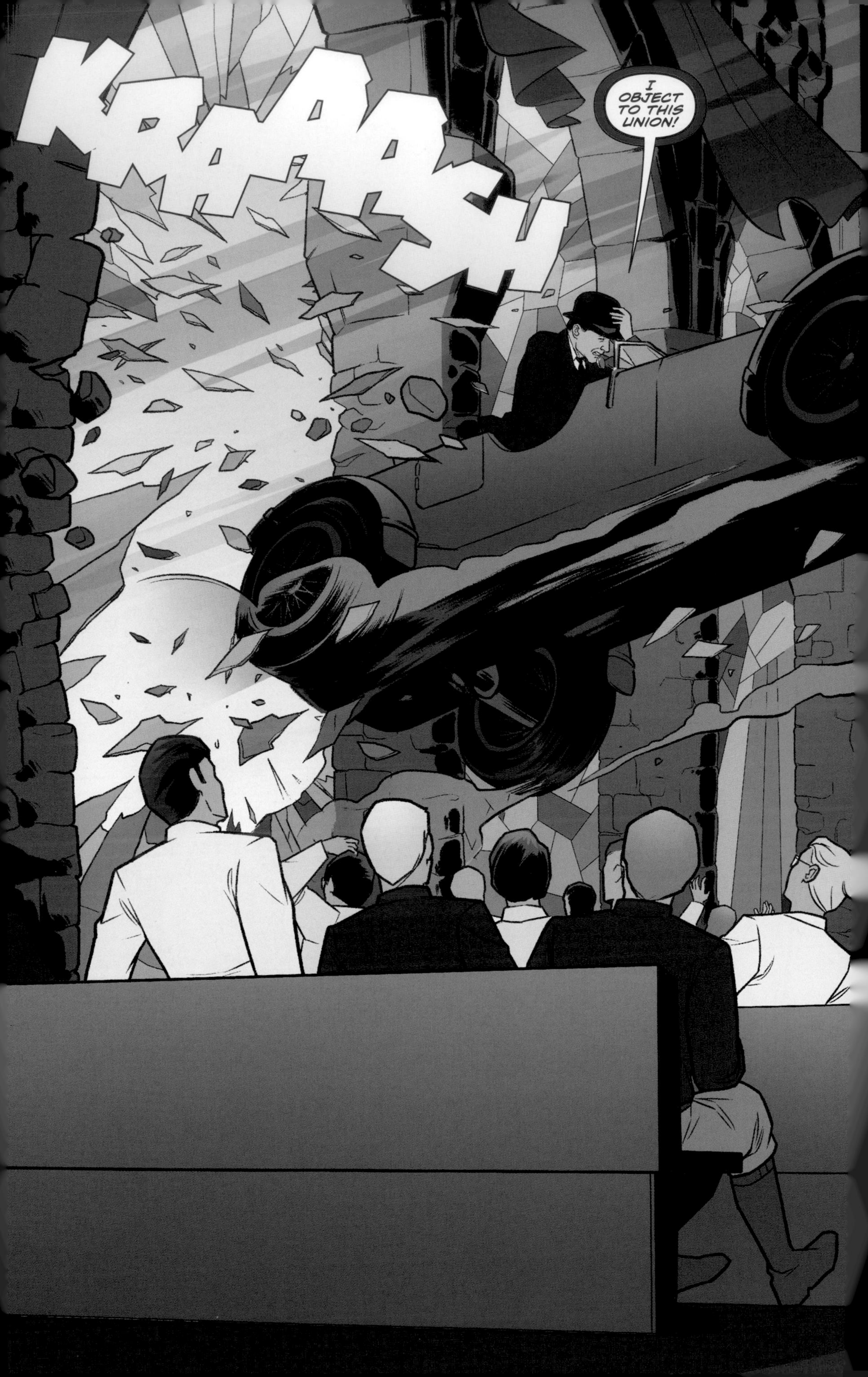
KRAAASH
I OBJECT TO THIS UNION!

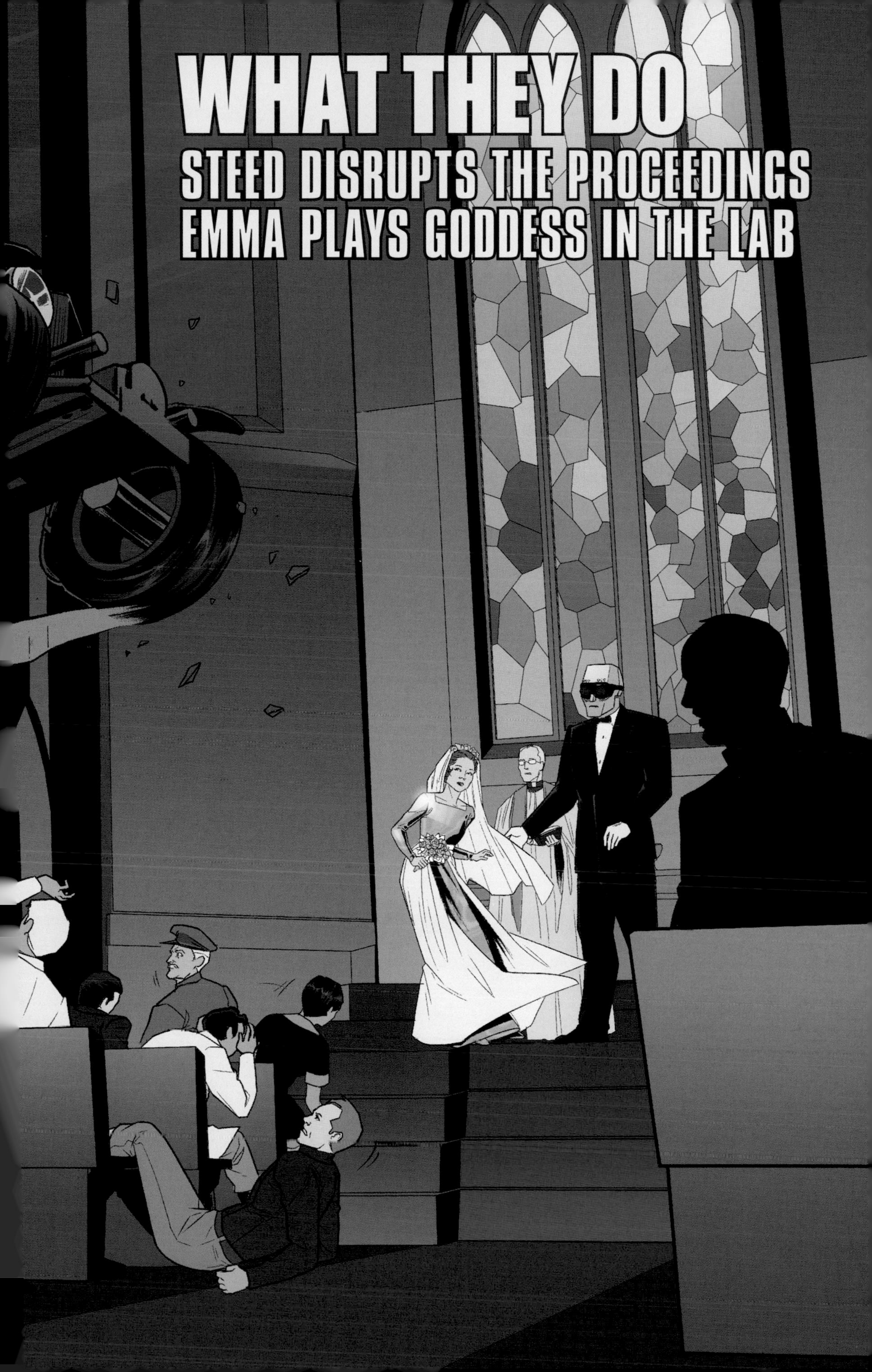
WHAT THEY DO
STEED DISRUPTS THE PROCEEDINGS
EMMA PLAYS GODDESS IN THE LAB

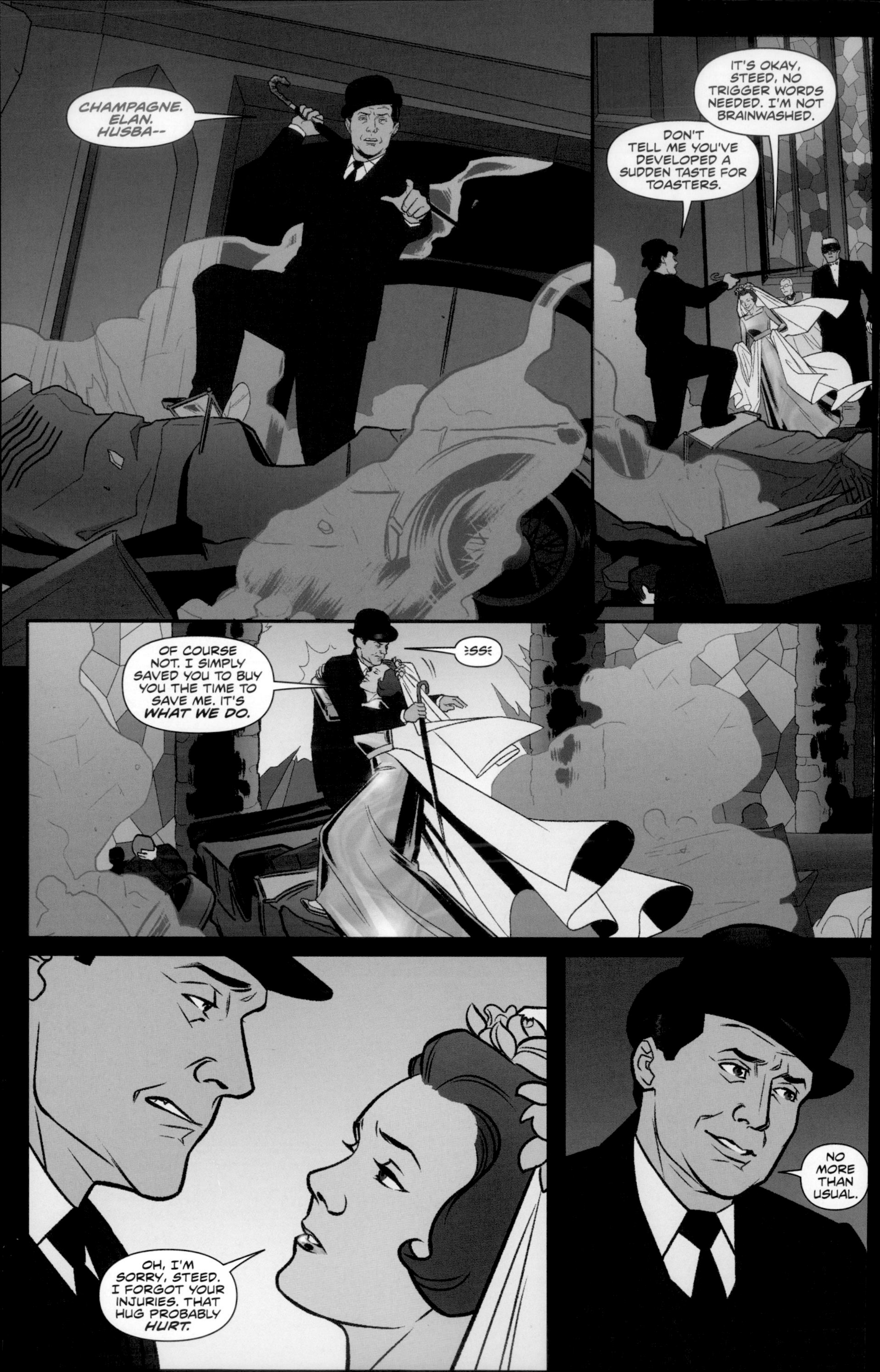

CHAMPAGNE. ELAN. HUSBA--
DON'T TELL ME YOU'VE DEVELOPED A SUDDEN TASTE FOR TOASTERS.
IT'S OKAY, STEED, NO TRIGGER WORDS NEEDED. I'M NOT BRAINWASHED.
OF COURSE NOT. I SIMPLY SAVED YOU TO BUY YOU THE TIME TO SAVE ME. IT'S *WHAT WE DO.*
SS
OH, I'M SORRY, STEED. I FORGOT YOUR INJURIES. THAT HUG PROBABLY *HURT.*
NO MORE THAN USUAL.

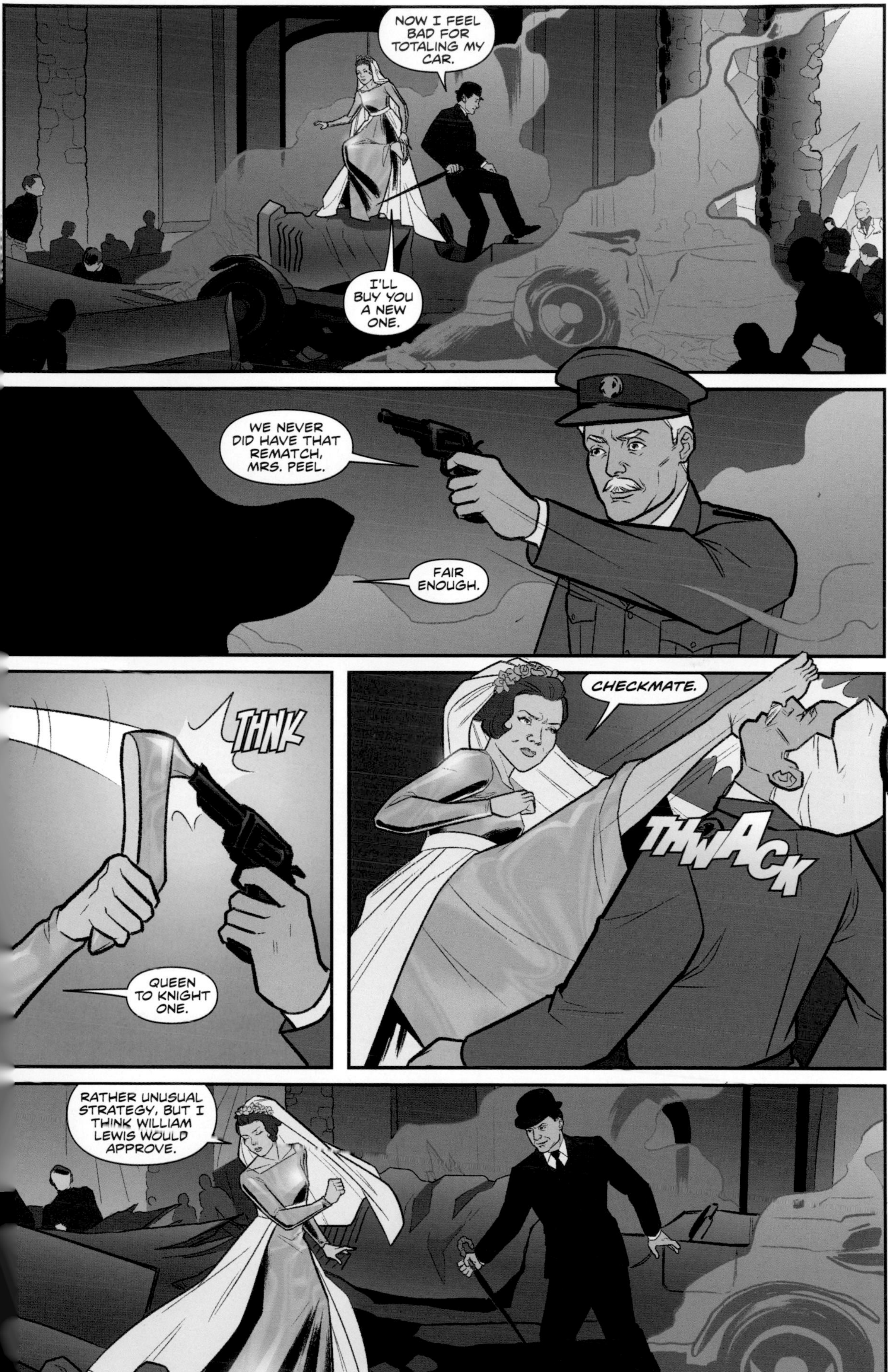
NOW I FEEL BAD FOR TOTALING MY CAR.
I'LL BUY YOU A NEW ONE.
WE NEVER DID HAVE THAT REMATCH, MRS. PEEL.
FAIR ENOUGH.
THNK
QUEEN TO KNIGHT ONE.
CHECKMATE.
THWACK
RATHER UNUSUAL STRATEGY, BUT I THINK WILLIAM LEWIS WOULD APPROVE.

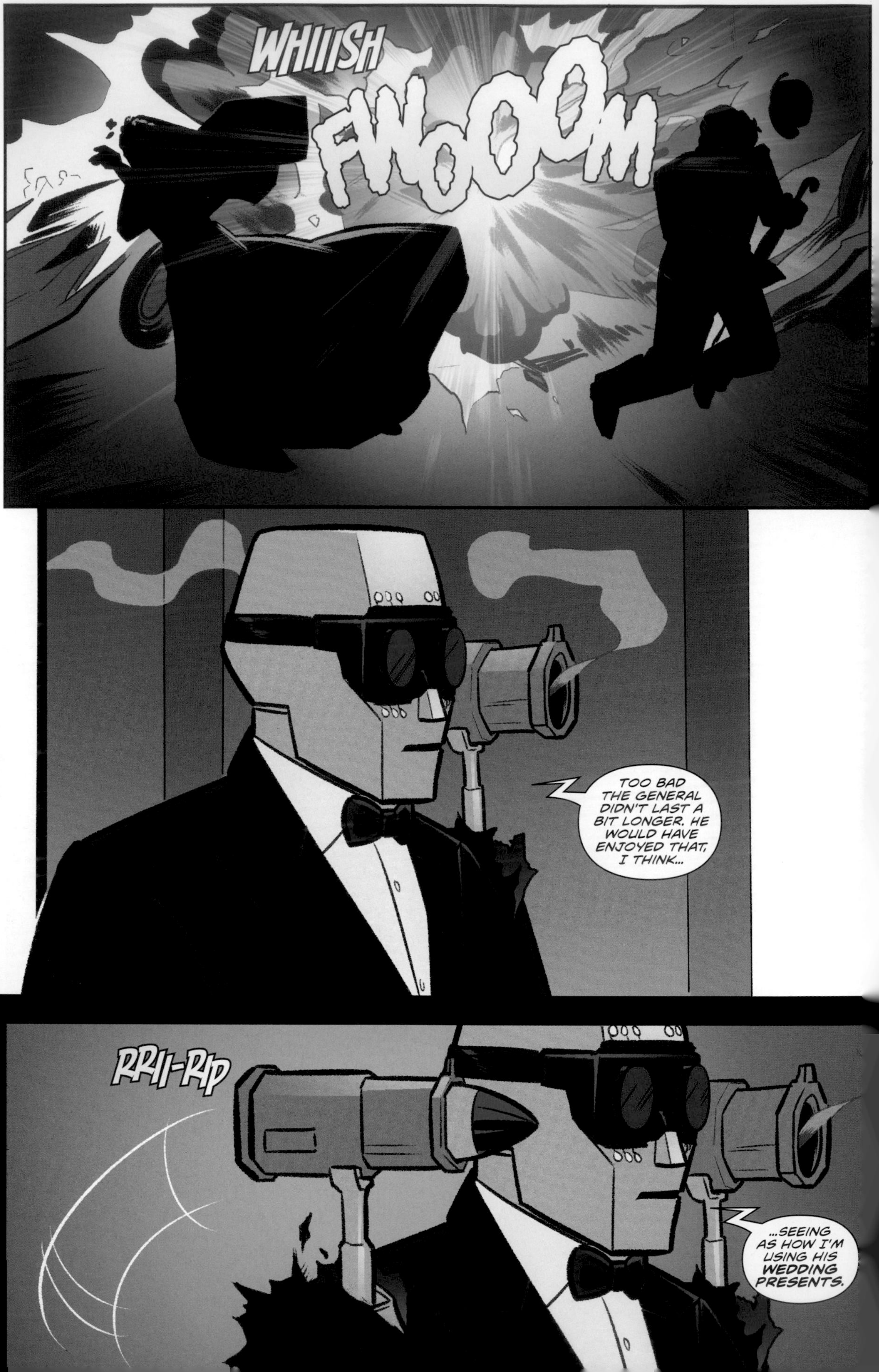
WHIIISH
FWOOOM
TOO BAD THE GENERAL DIDN'T LAST A BIT LONGER. HE WOULD HAVE ENJOYED THAT, I THINK...
RRII-RIP
...SEEING AS HOW I'M USING HIS WEDDING PRESENTS.

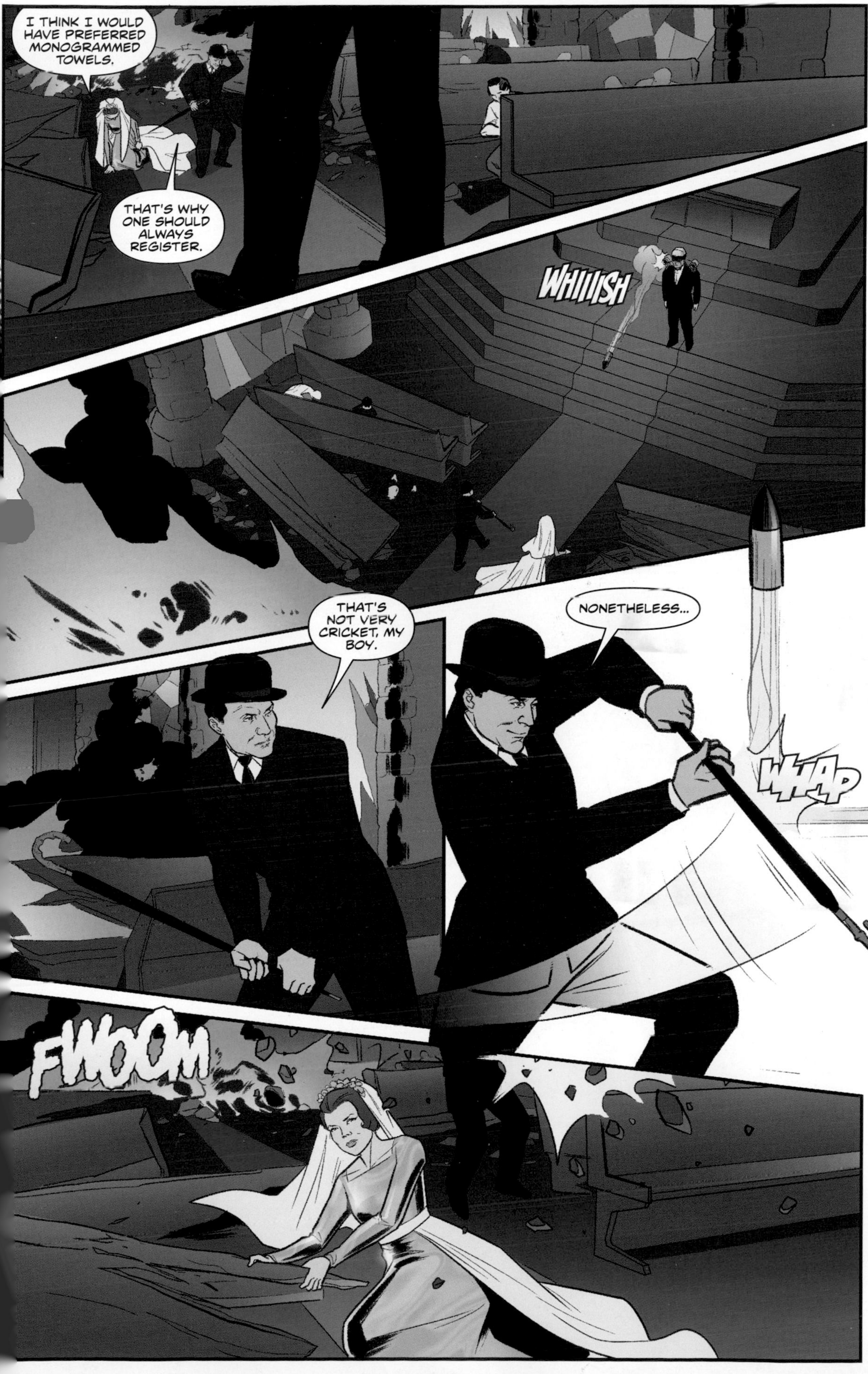
I THINK I WOULD HAVE PREFERRED MONOGRAMMED TOWELS.
THAT'S WHY ONE SHOULD ALWAYS REGISTER.
WHIIIISH
THAT'S NOT VERY CRICKET, MY BOY.
NONETHELESS...
WHAP
FWOOM

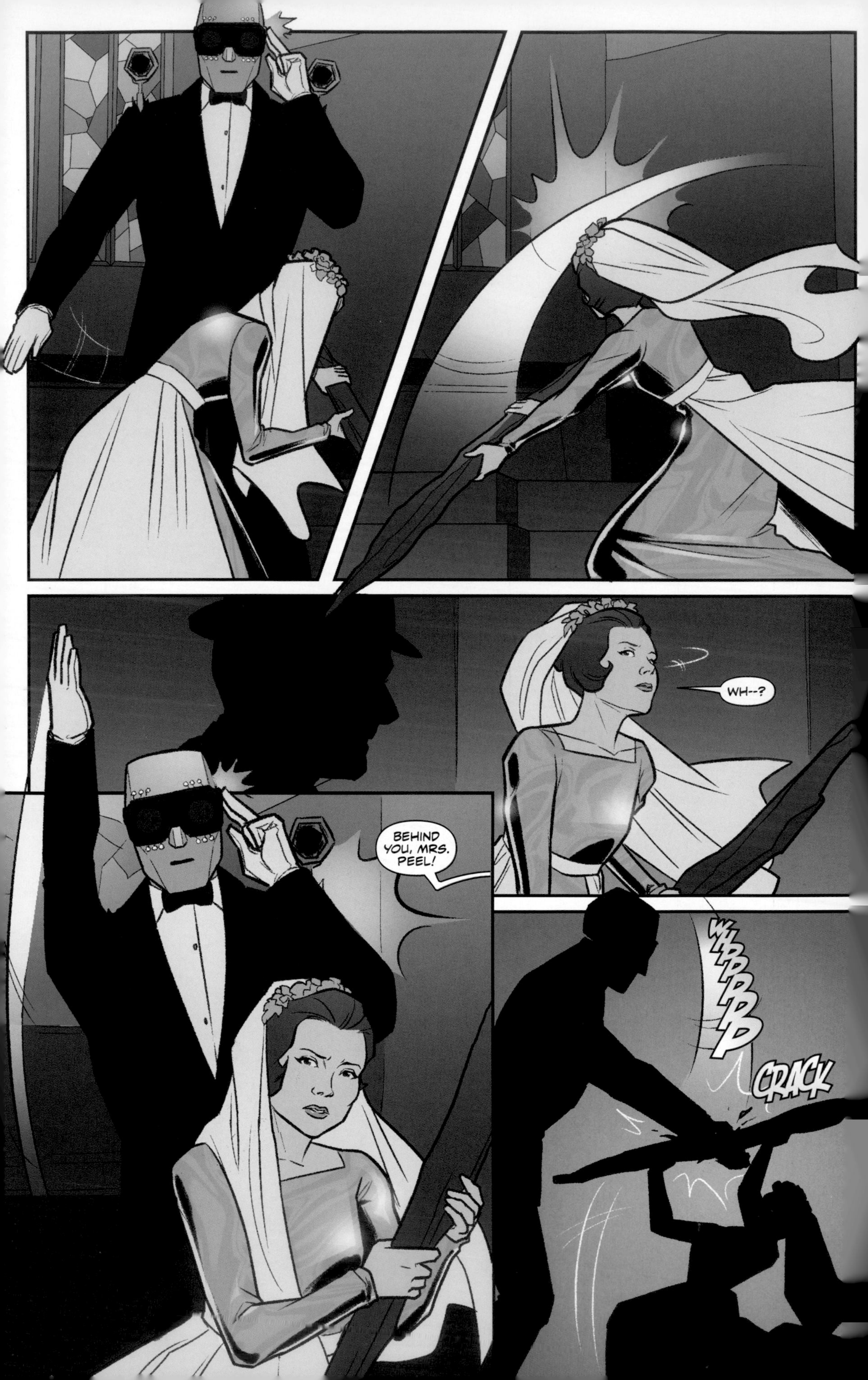
WH--?
BEHIND YOU, MRS. PEEL!
WHPPPP
CRACK

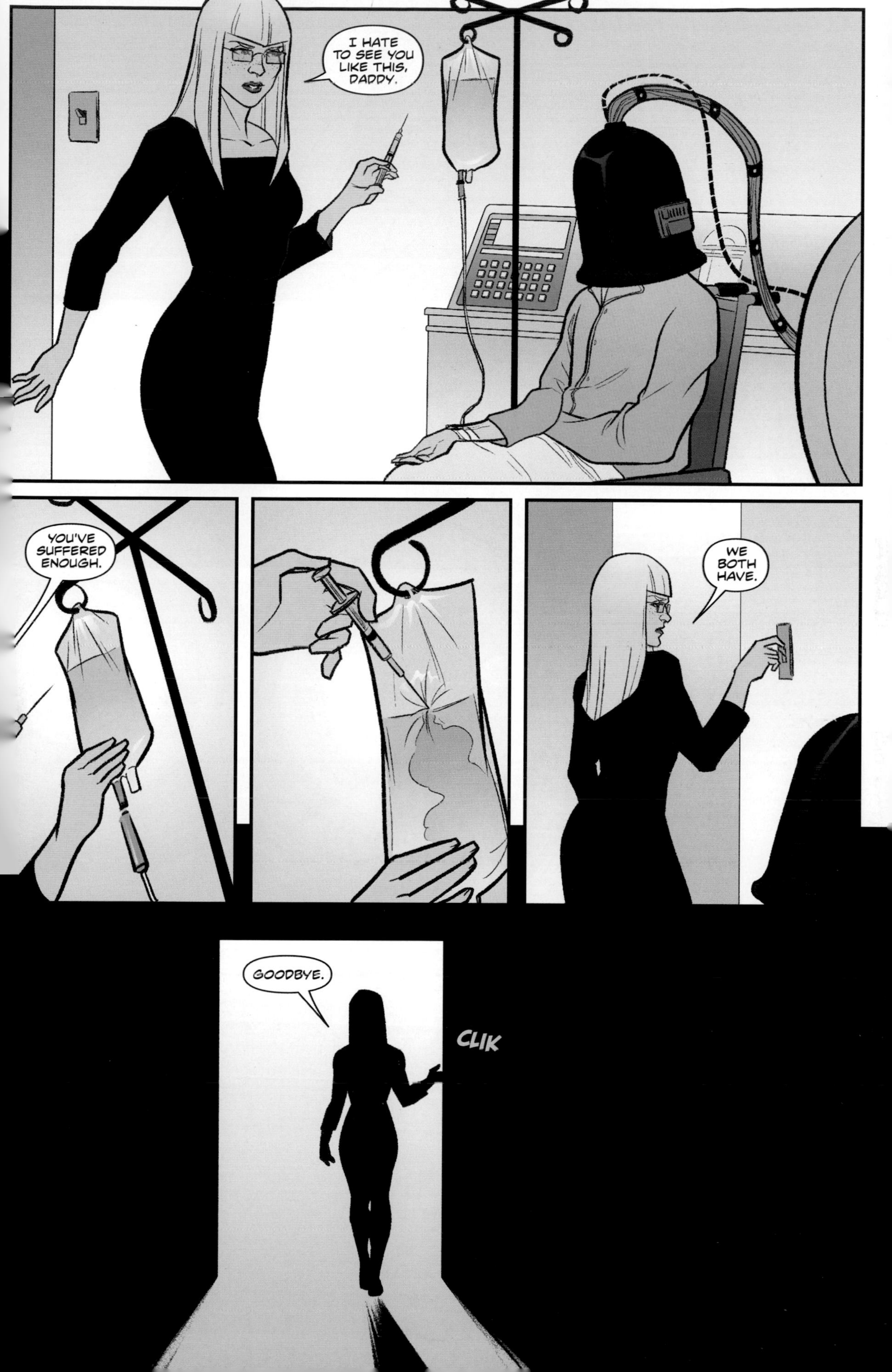
I HATE TO SEE YOU LIKE THIS, DADDY.
YOU'VE SUFFERED ENOUGH.
WE BOTH HAVE.
GOODBYE.
CLIK

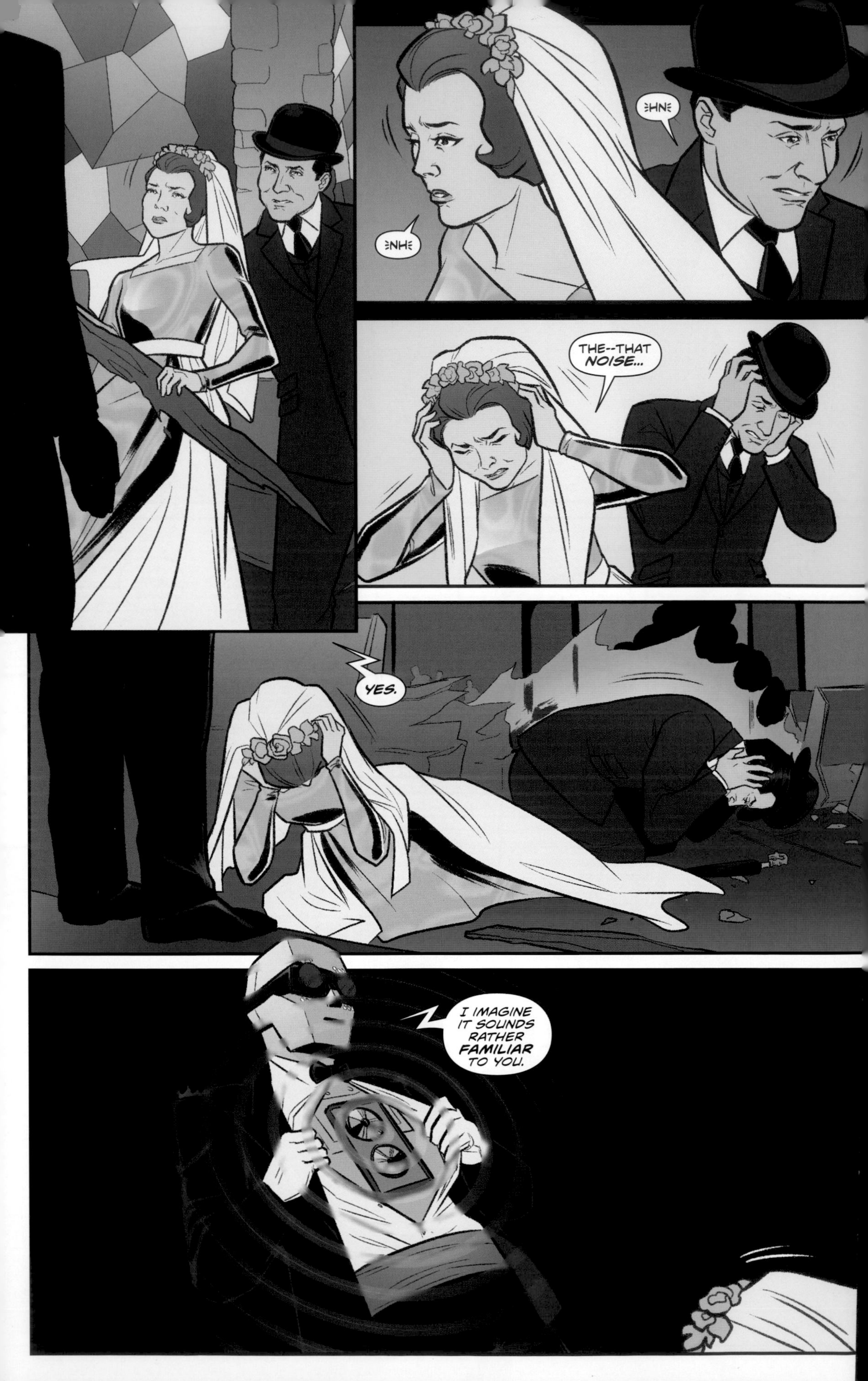
HN
NH
THE--THAT NOISE...
YES.
I IMAGINE IT SOUNDS RATHER FAMILIAR TO YOU.

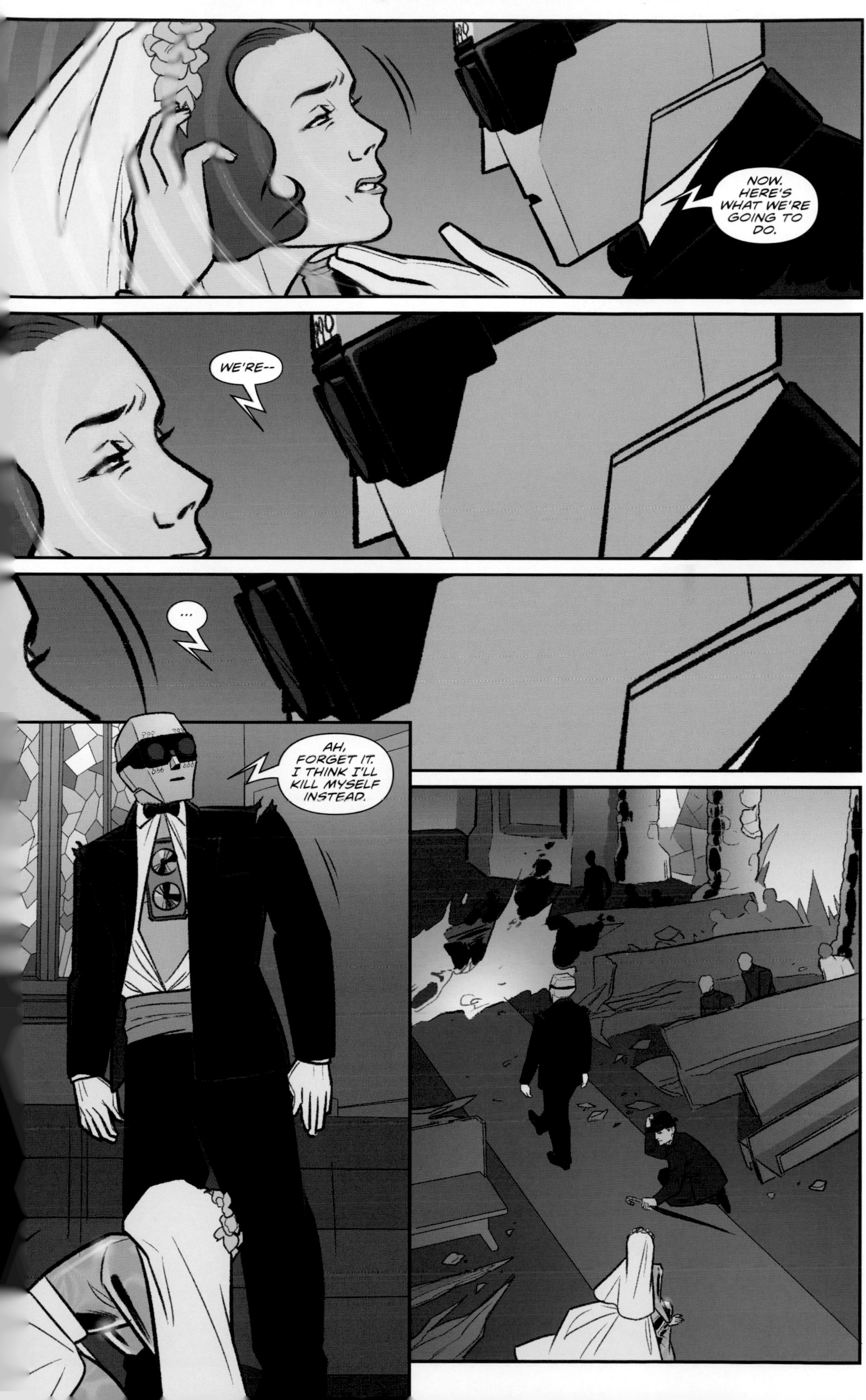
NOW. HERE'S WHAT WE'RE GOING TO DO.
WE'RE--
...
AH, FORGET IT. I THINK I'LL KILL MYSELF INSTEAD.

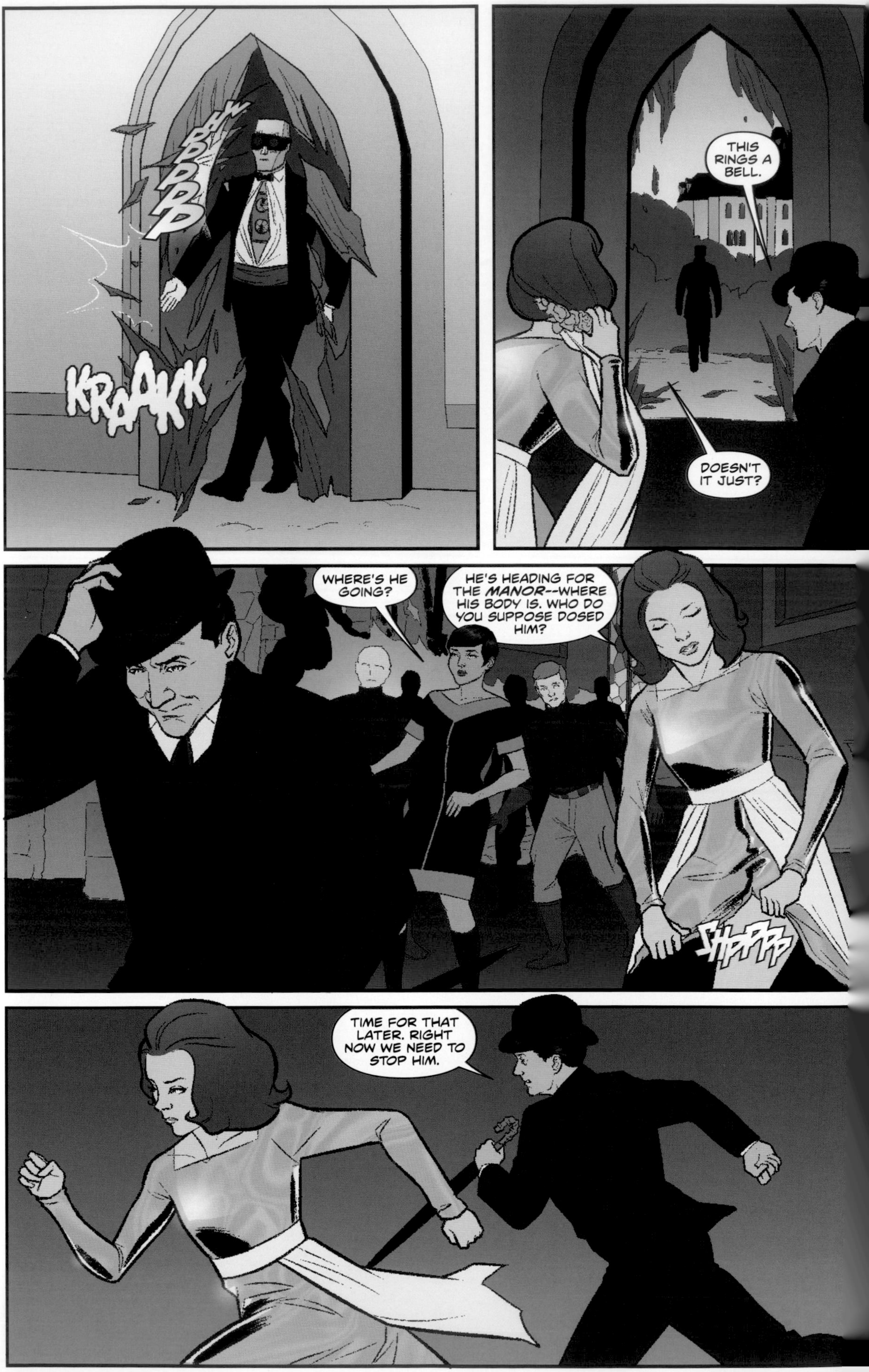
WHPPPP
KRAAKK
THIS RINGS A BELL.
DOESN'T IT JUST?
WHERE'S HE GOING?
HE'S HEADING FOR THE *MANOR*--WHERE HIS BODY IS. WHO DO YOU SUPPOSE DOSED HIM?
SHPPPP
TIME FOR THAT LATER. RIGHT NOW WE NEED TO STOP HIM.

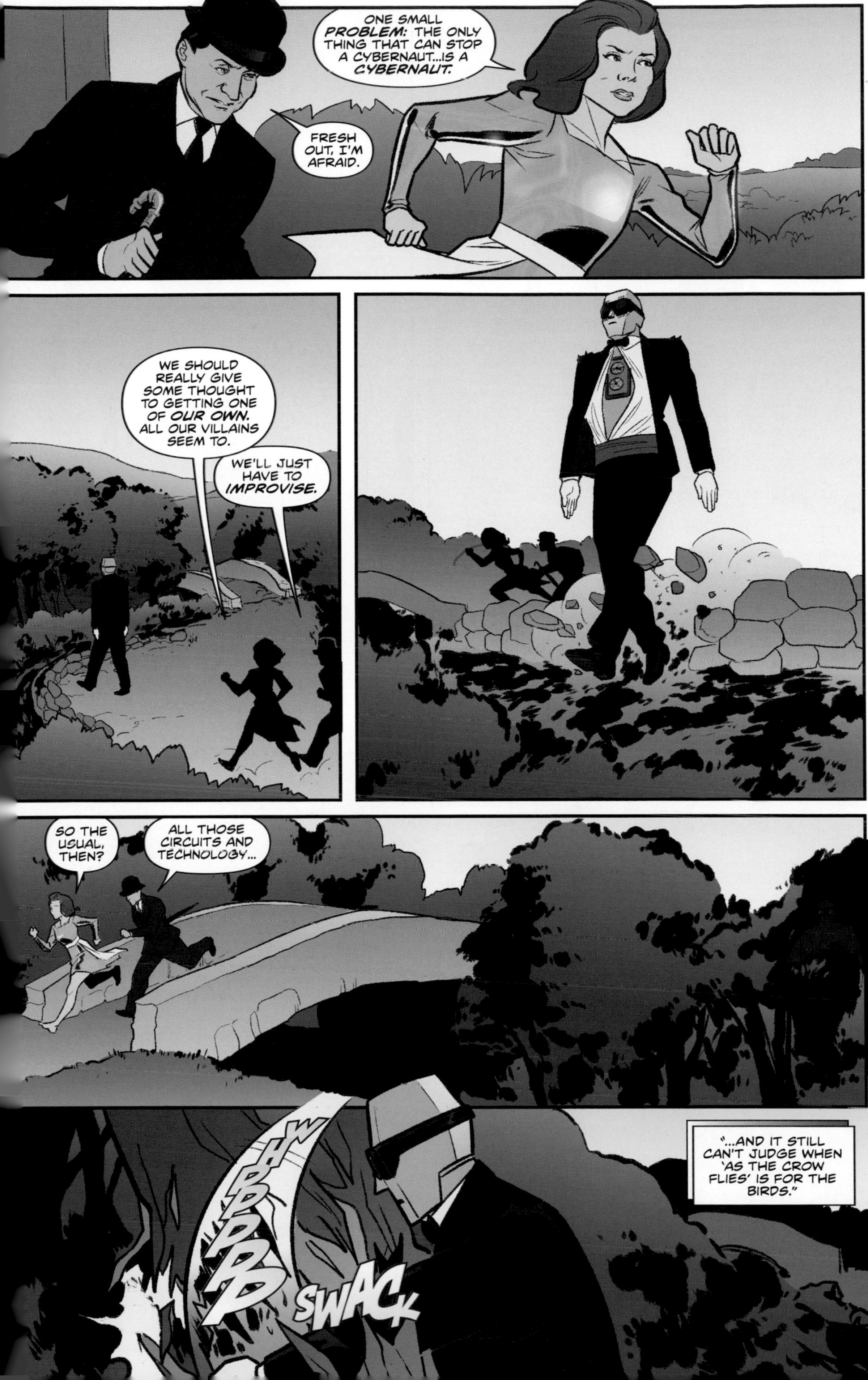
ONE SMALL PROBLEM: THE ONLY THING THAT CAN STOP A CYBERNAUT...IS A CYBERNAUT.
FRESH OUT, I'M AFRAID.
WE SHOULD REALLY GIVE SOME THOUGHT TO GETTING ONE OF OUR OWN. ALL OUR VILLAINS SEEM TO.
WE'LL JUST HAVE TO IMPROVISE.
SO THE USUAL, THEN?
ALL THOSE CIRCUITS AND TECHNOLOGY...
"...AND IT STILL CAN'T JUDGE WHEN 'AS THE CROW FLIES' IS FOR THE BIRDS."
WHPPPPPP
SWACK

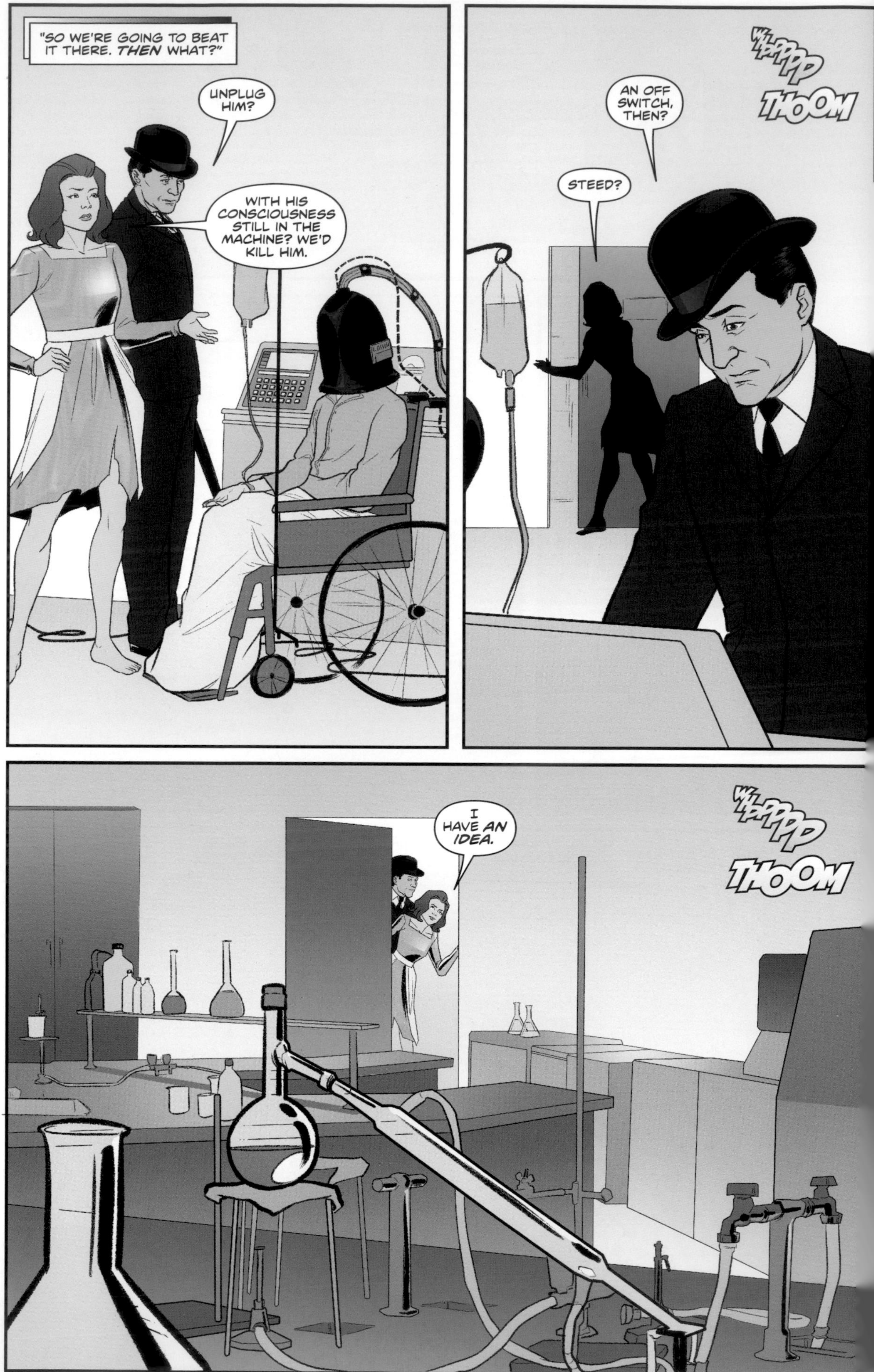
"SO WE'RE GOING TO BEAT IT THERE. *THEN* WHAT?"
UNPLUG HIM?
WITH HIS CONSCIOUSNESS STILL IN THE MACHINE? WE'D KILL HIM.
WHPPPP
THOOM
AN OFF SWITCH, THEN?
STEED?
WHPPPP
THOOM
I HAVE *AN IDEA.*

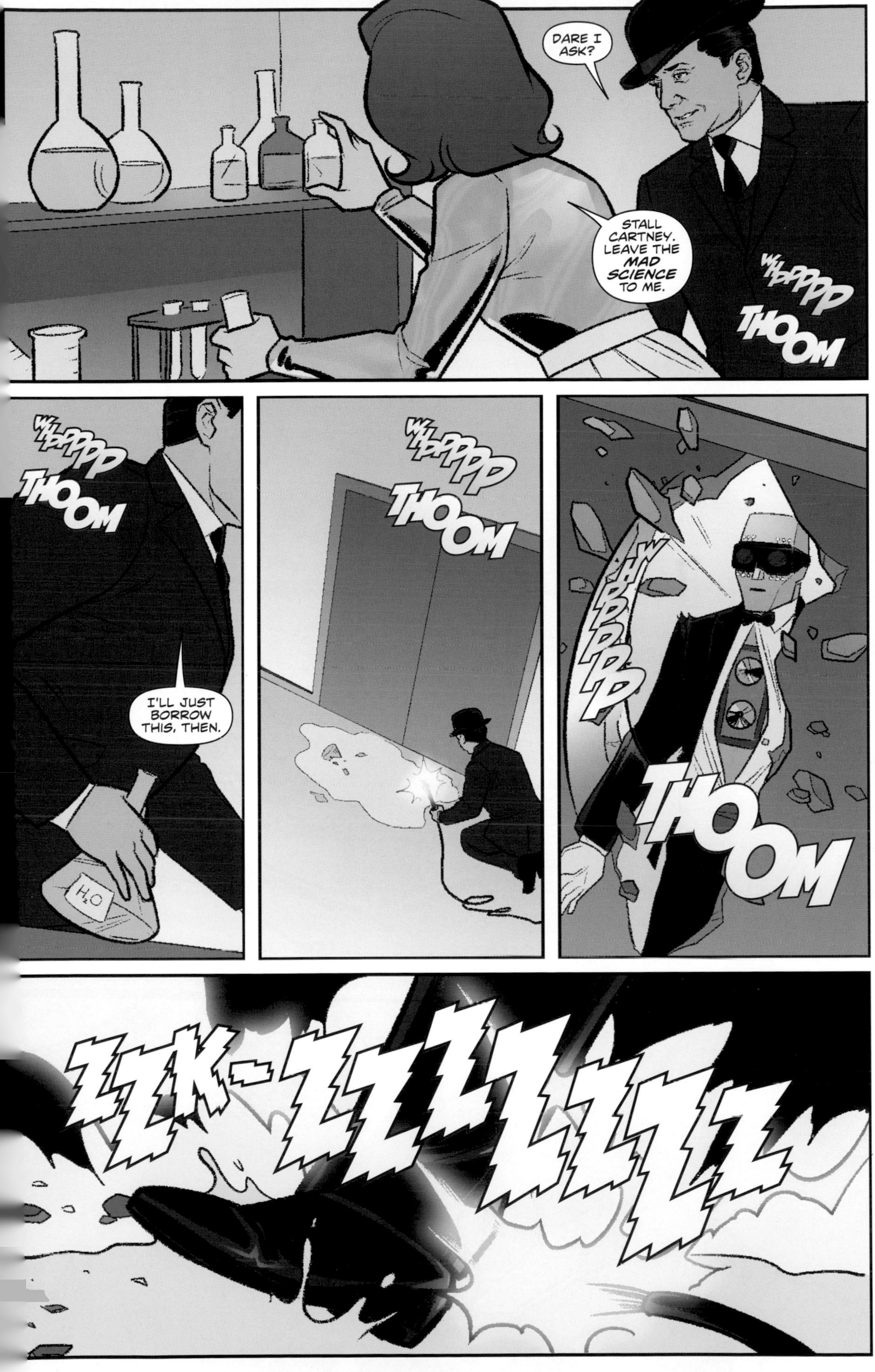
DARE I ASK?
STALL CARTNEY. LEAVE THE MAD SCIENCE TO ME.
WHIRPPPP
THOOM
WHIRPPPP
THOOM
I'LL JUST BORROW THIS, THEN.
H_2O
WHIRPPPP
THOOM
WHIRPPPP
THOOM
ZZK-ZZZZZZZZZ

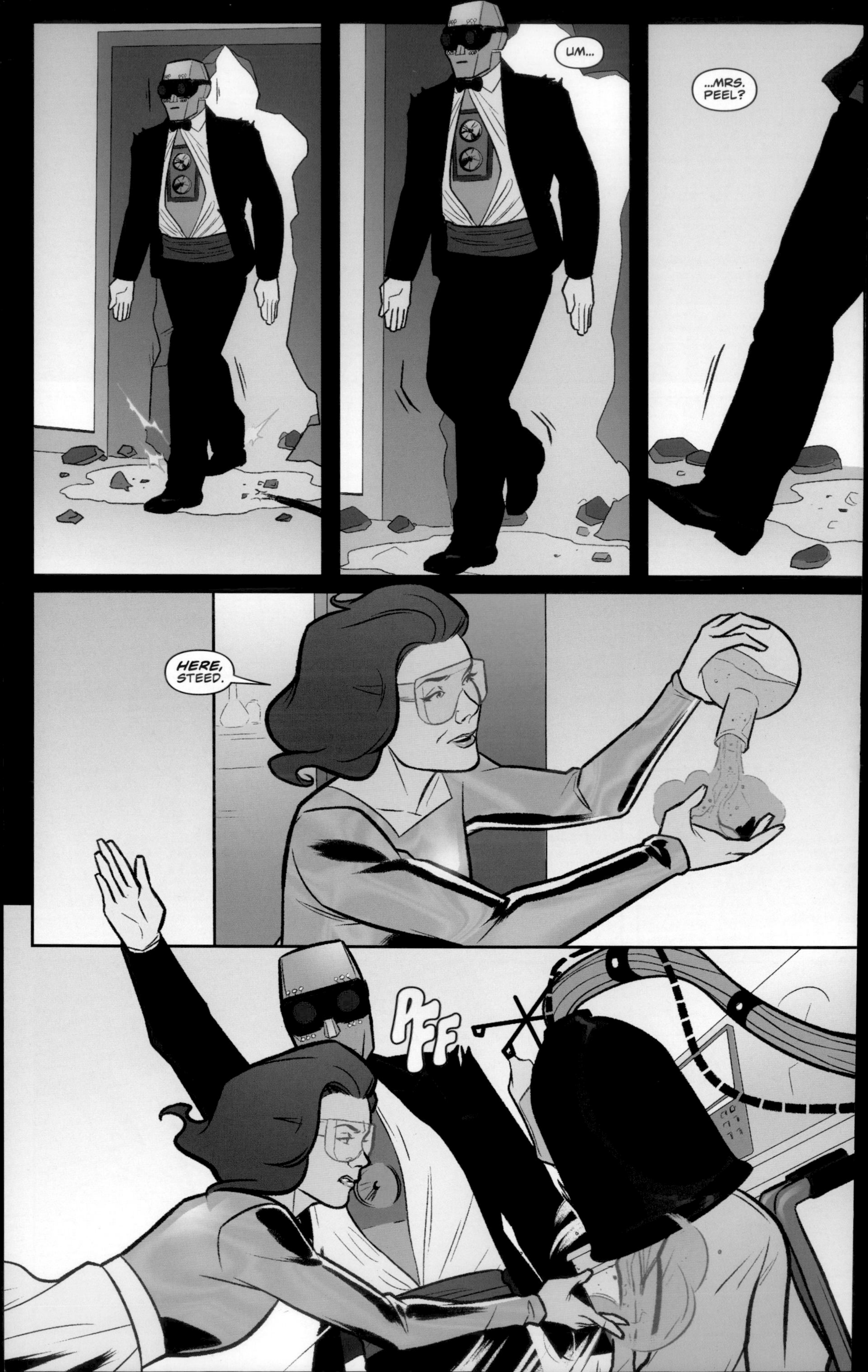
UM...
...MRS. PEEL?
HERE, STEED.
PFF

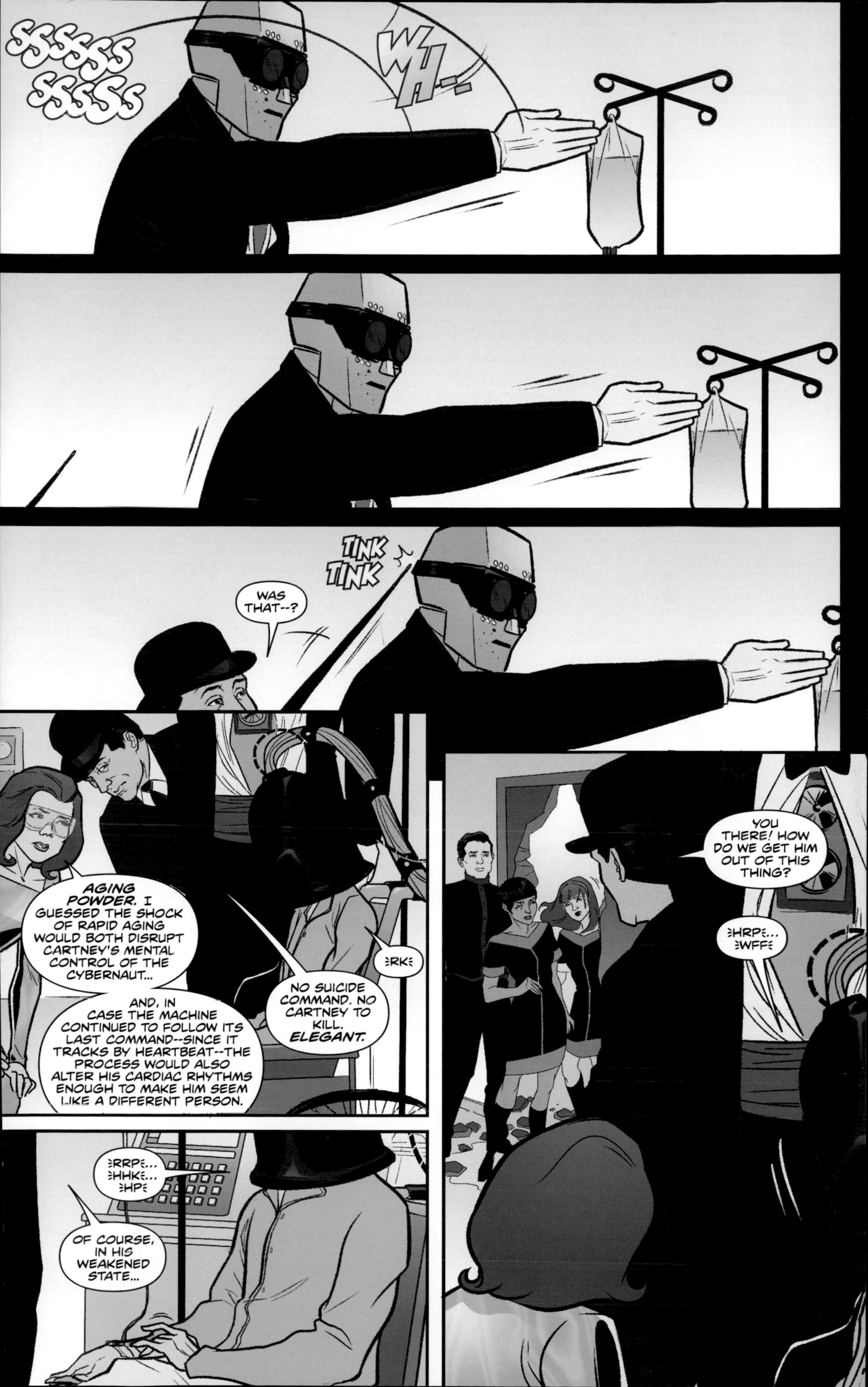
SSSSSS SSSSS
WH--
TINK TINK
WAS THAT--?
AGING POWDER. I GUESSED THE SHOCK OF RAPID AGING WOULD BOTH DISRUPT CARTNEY'S MENTAL CONTROL OF THE CYBERNAUT...
AND, IN CASE THE MACHINE CONTINUED TO FOLLOW ITS LAST COMMAND--SINCE IT TRACKS BY HEARTBEAT--THE PROCESS WOULD ALSO ALTER HIS CARDIAC RHYTHMS ENOUGH TO MAKE HIM SEEM LIKE A DIFFERENT PERSON.
RK
NO SUICIDE COMMAND. NO CARTNEY TO KILL. ELEGANT.
RRP... HHK... HP
OF COURSE, IN HIS WEAKENED STATE...
YOU THERE! HOW DO WE GET HIM OUT OF THIS THING?
HRP... WFF

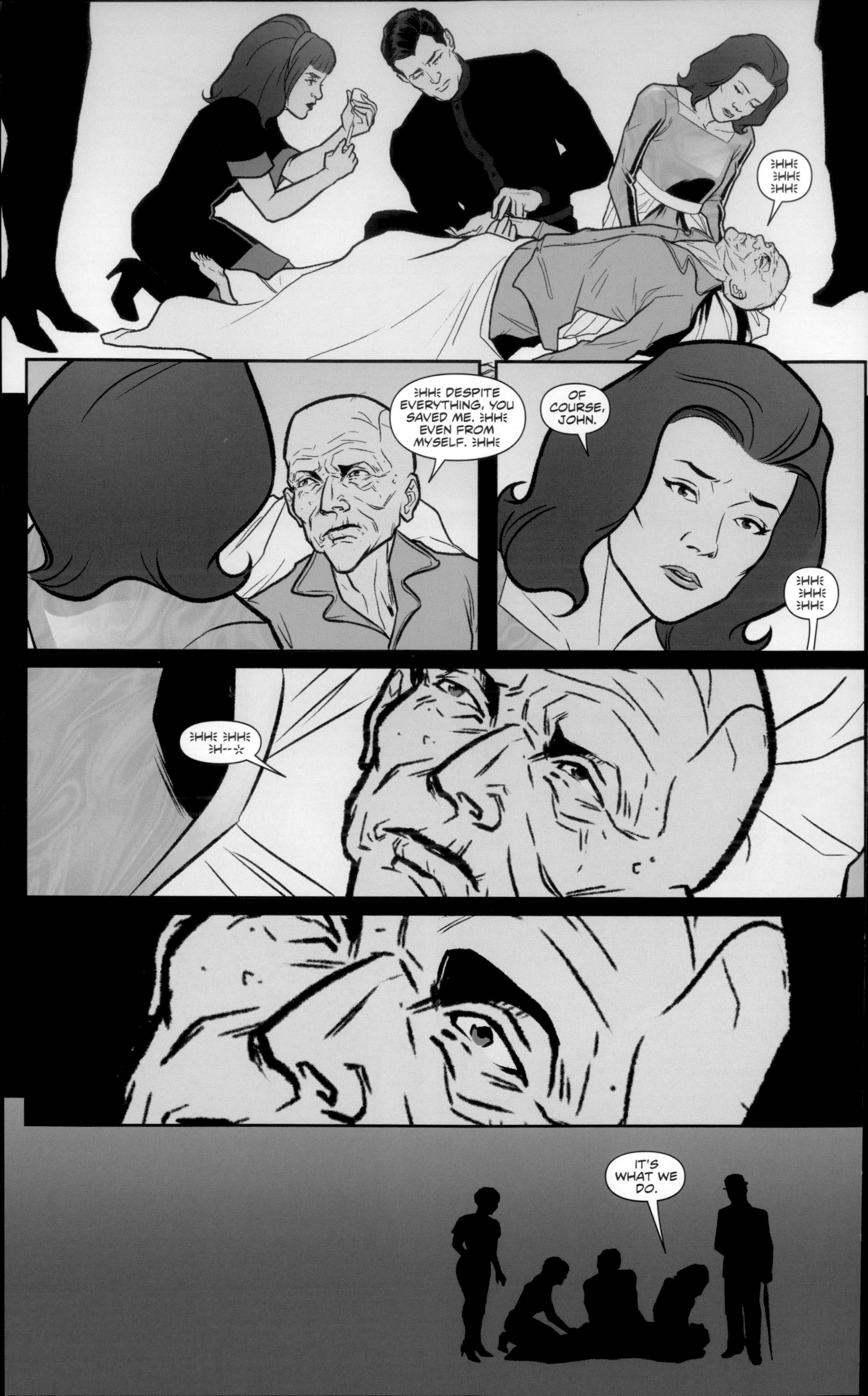
HH HH HH
HH DESPITE EVERYTHING, YOU SAVED ME. HH EVEN FROM MYSELF. HH
OF COURSE, JOHN.
HH HH HH
HH HH H--
IT'S WHAT WE DO.

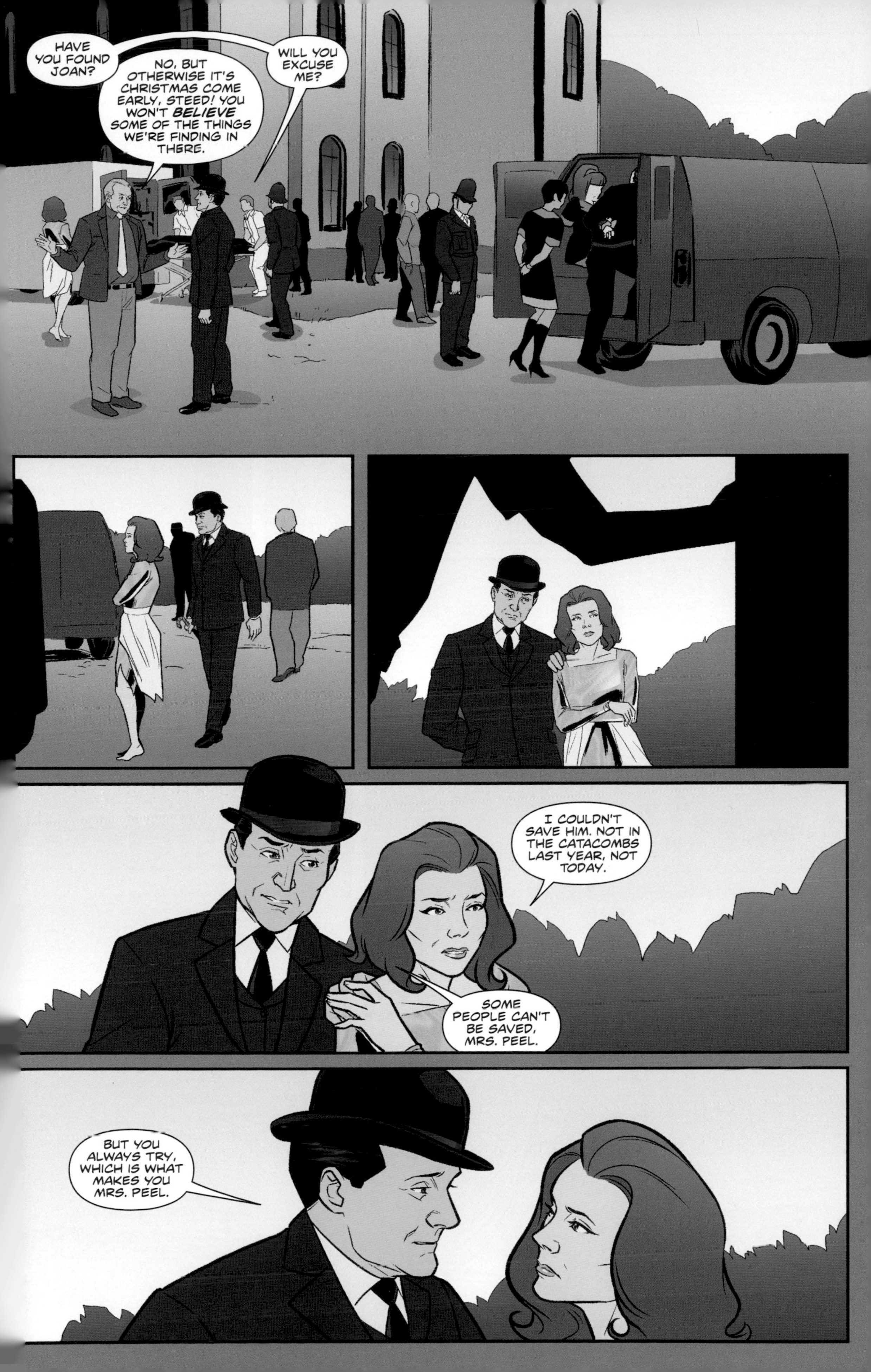
HAVE YOU FOUND JOAN?
NO, BUT OTHERWISE IT'S CHRISTMAS COME EARLY, STEED! YOU WON'T BELIEVE SOME OF THE THINGS WE'RE FINDING IN THERE.
WILL YOU EXCUSE ME?
I COULDN'T SAVE HIM. NOT IN THE CATACOMBS LAST YEAR, NOT TODAY.
SOME PEOPLE CAN'T BE SAVED, MRS. PEEL.
BUT YOU ALWAYS TRY, WHICH IS WHAT MAKES YOU MRS. PEEL.

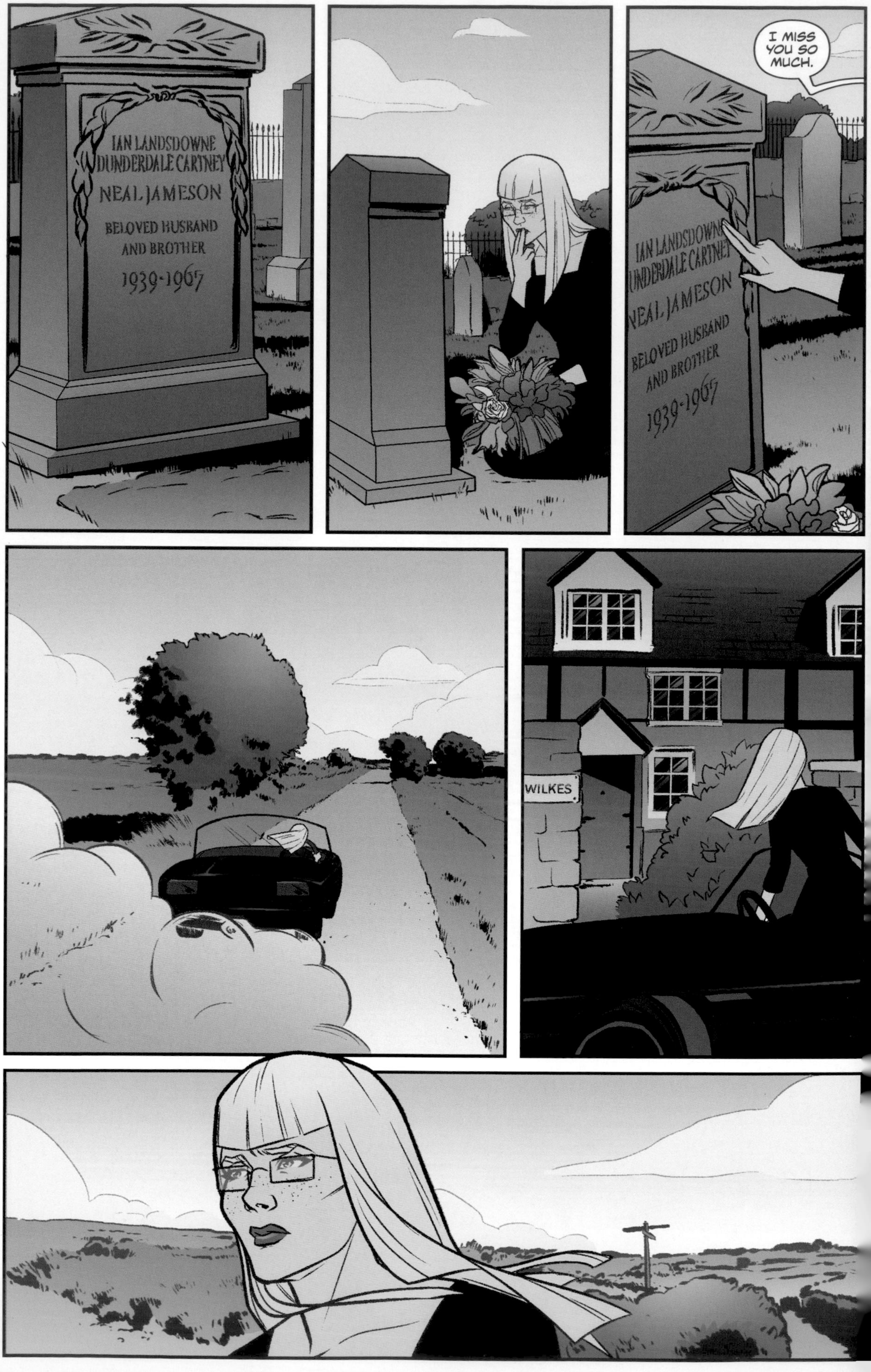
IAN LANDSDOWNE
DUNDERDALE CARTNEY
NEAL JAMESON
BELOVED HUSBAND
AND BROTHER
1939-1967
I MISS YOU SO MUCH.
WILKES

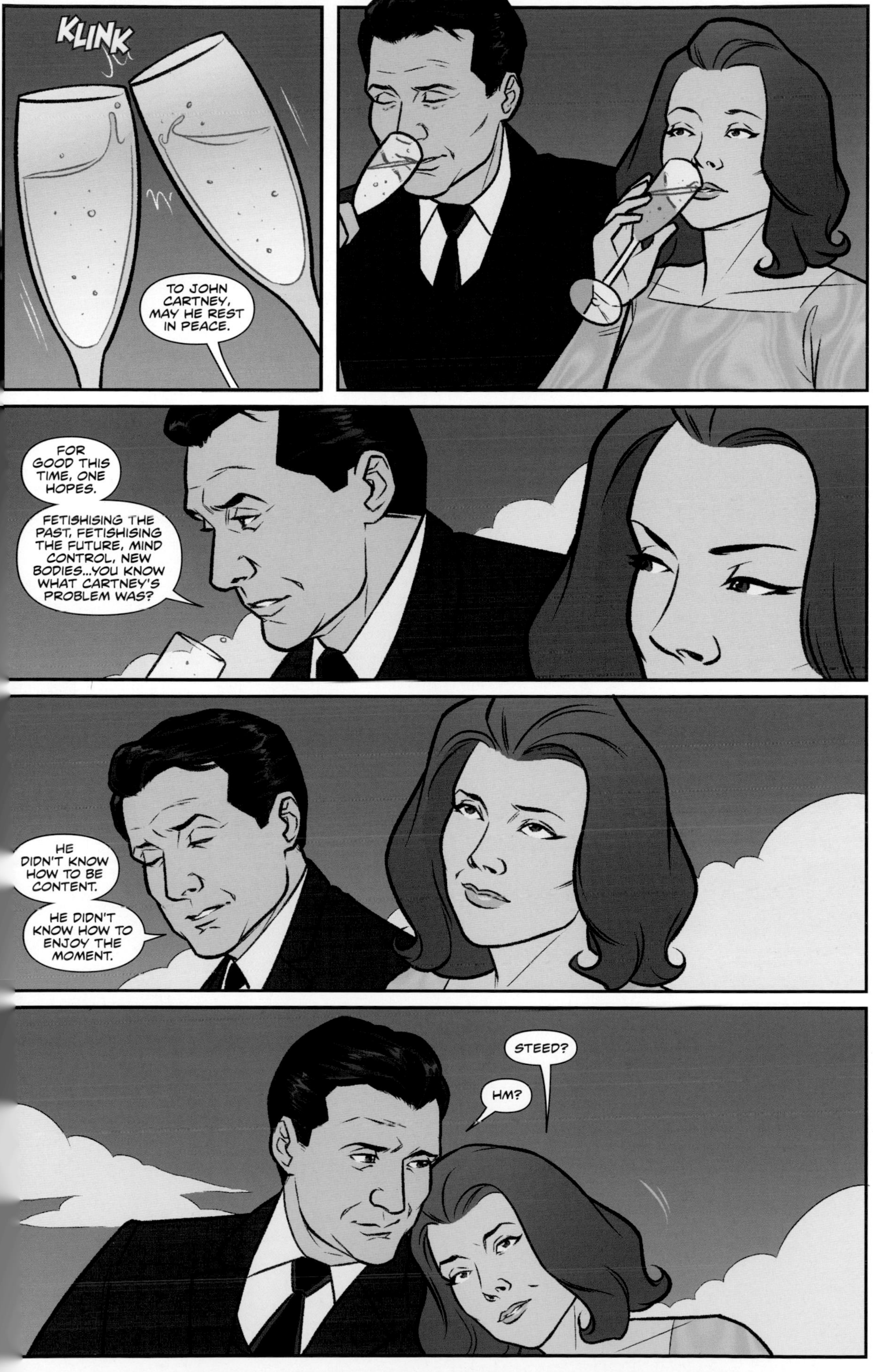
KLINK
TO JOHN CARTNEY, MAY HE REST IN PEACE.
FOR GOOD THIS TIME, ONE HOPES.
FETISHISING THE PAST, FETISHISING THE FUTURE, MIND CONTROL, NEW BODIES...YOU KNOW WHAT CARTNEY'S PROBLEM WAS?
HE DIDN'T KNOW HOW TO BE CONTENT.
HE DIDN'T KNOW HOW TO ENJOY THE MOMENT.
STEED?
HM?

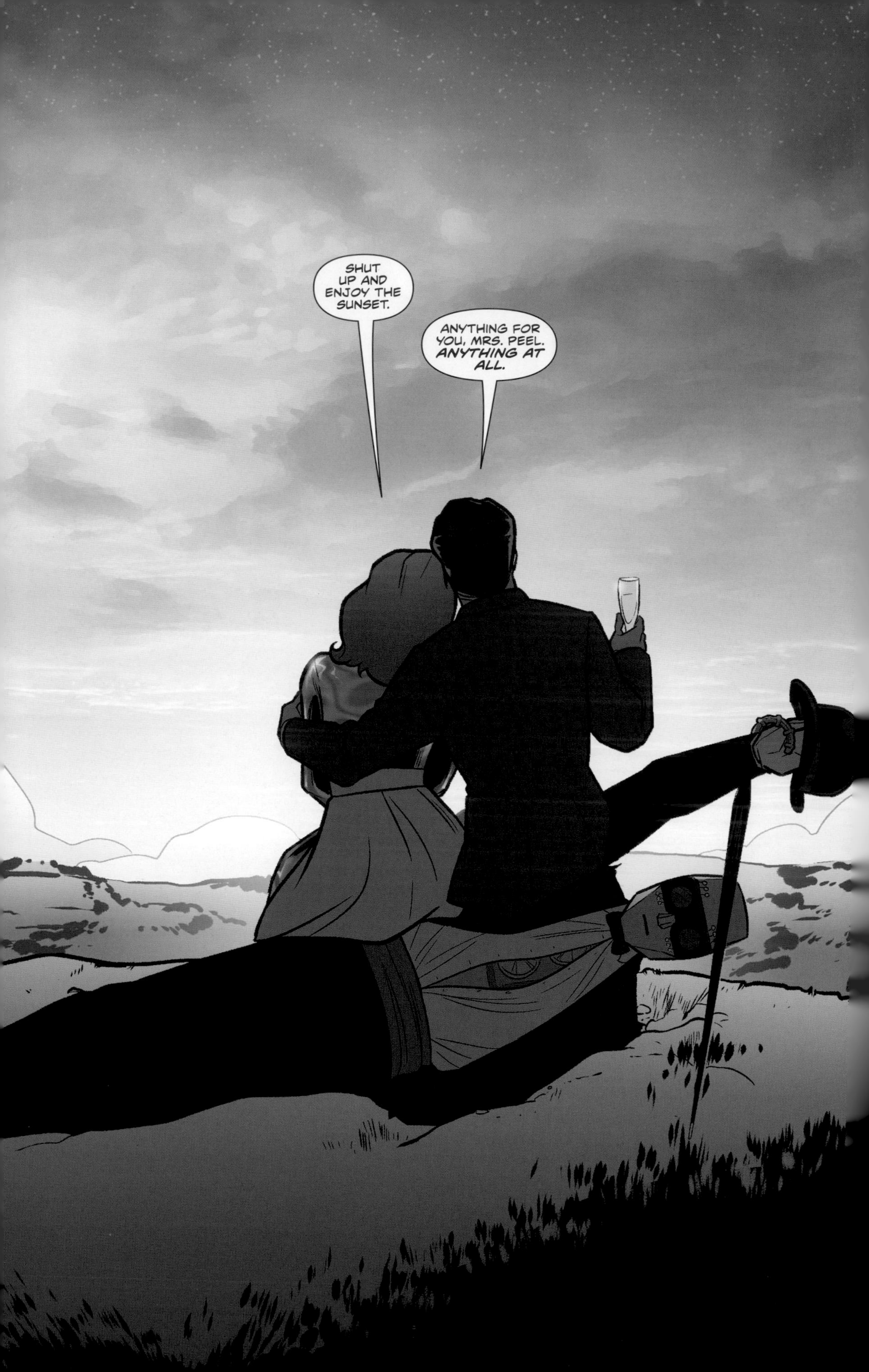
SHUT UP AND ENJOY THE SUNSET.
ANYTHING FOR YOU, MRS. PEEL. *ANYTHING AT ALL.*

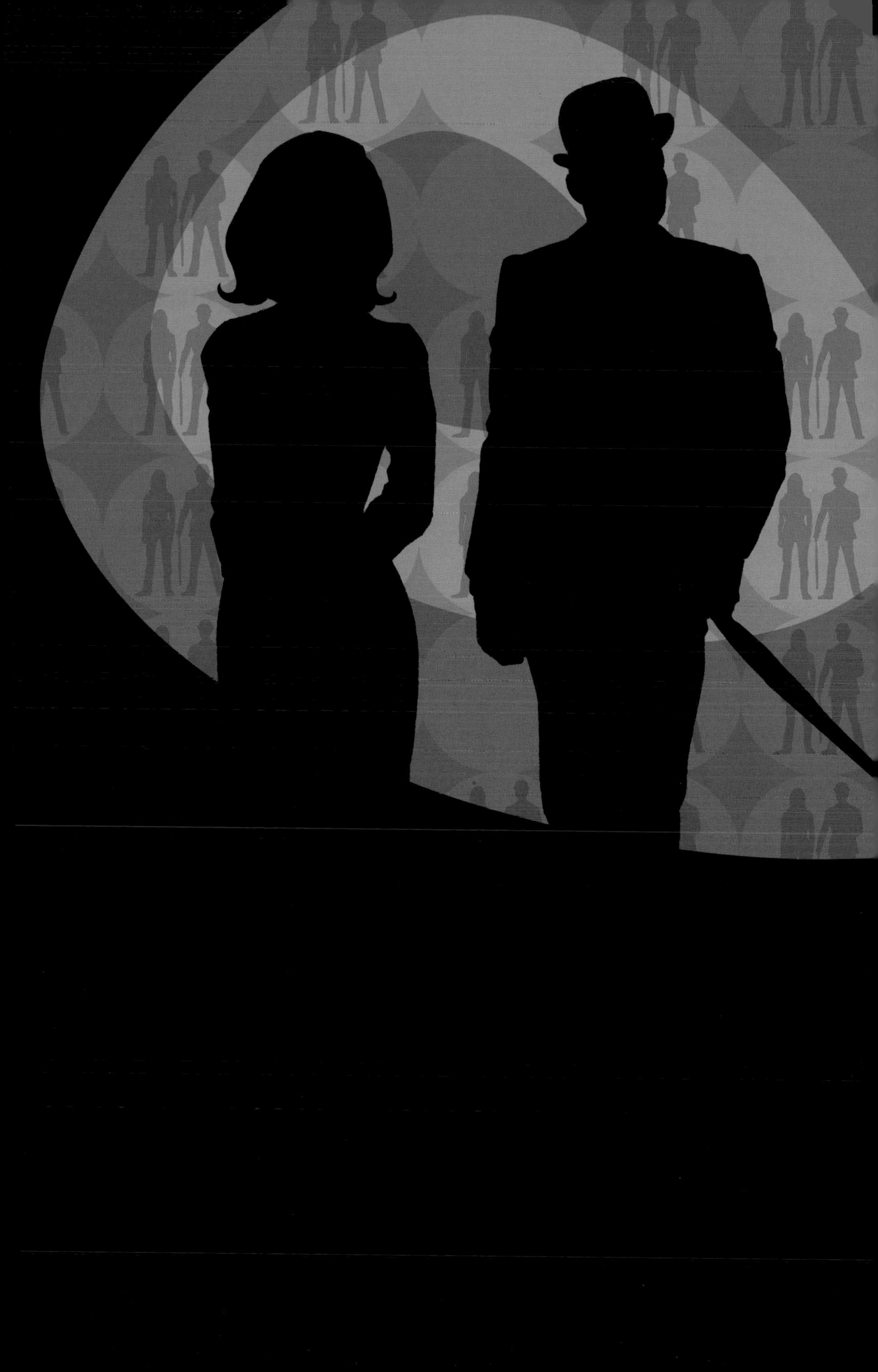

COVER GALLERY

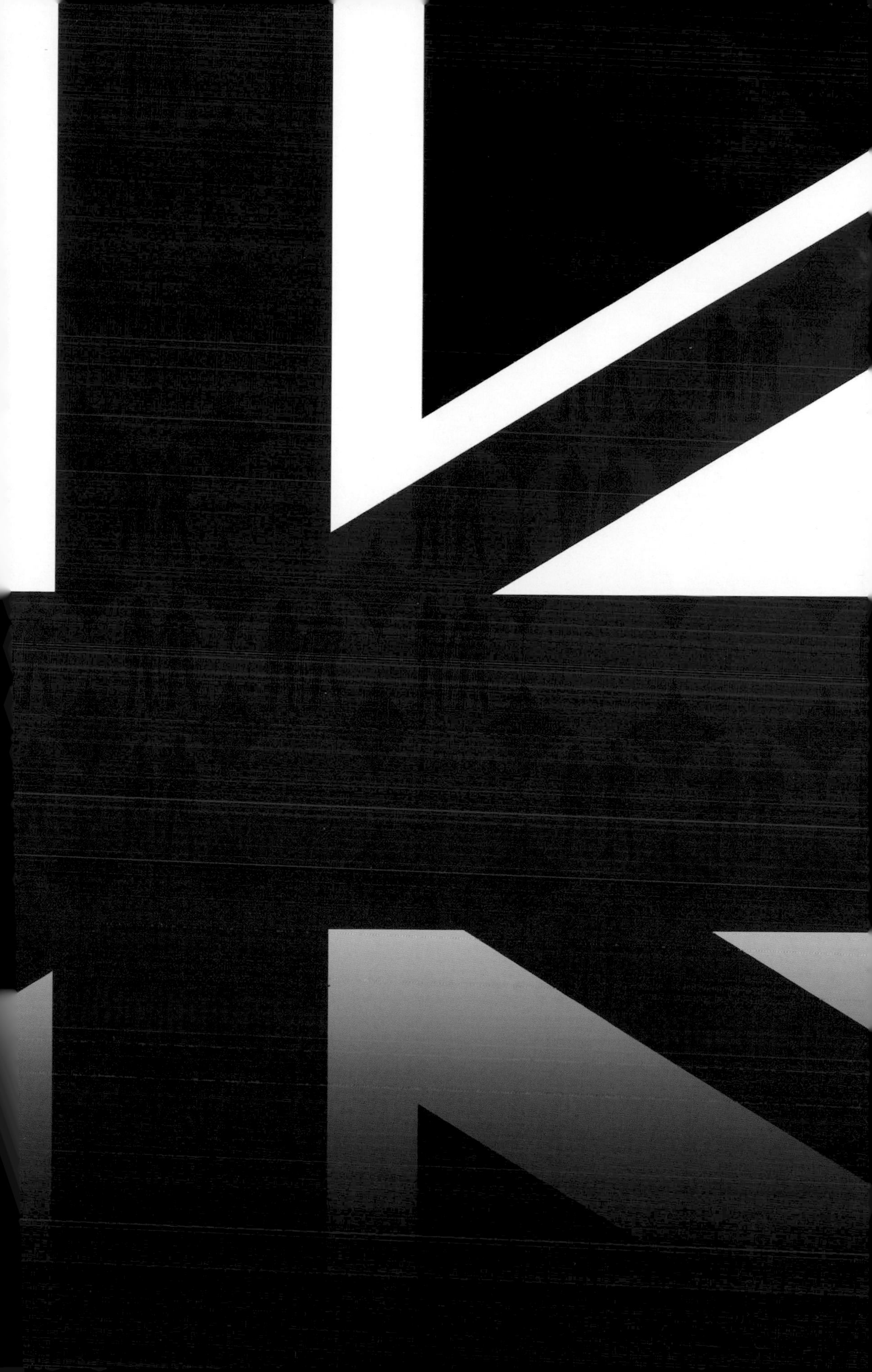

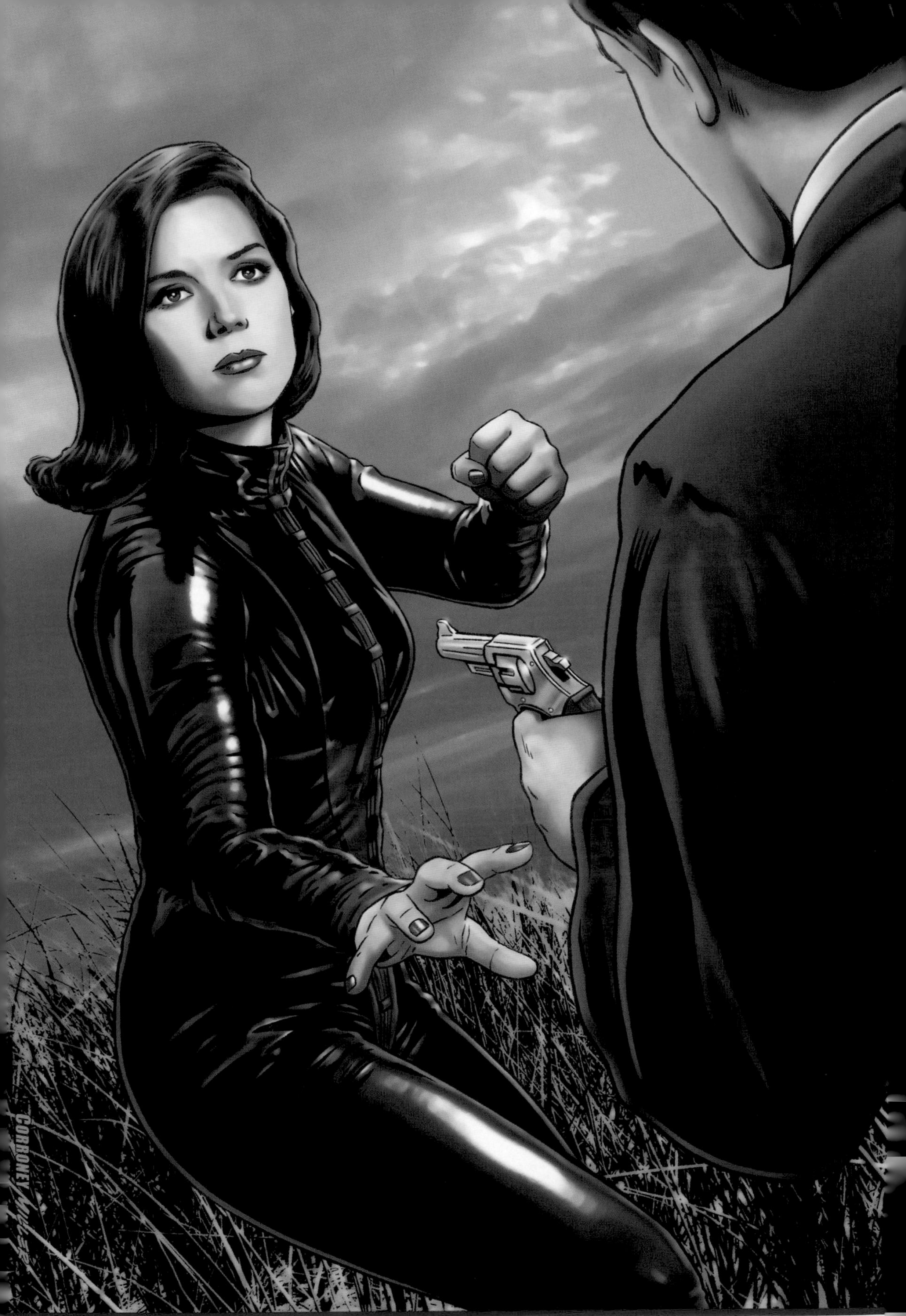
CORRONEY
MILLER

JOE CORRONEY
BRIAN MILLER

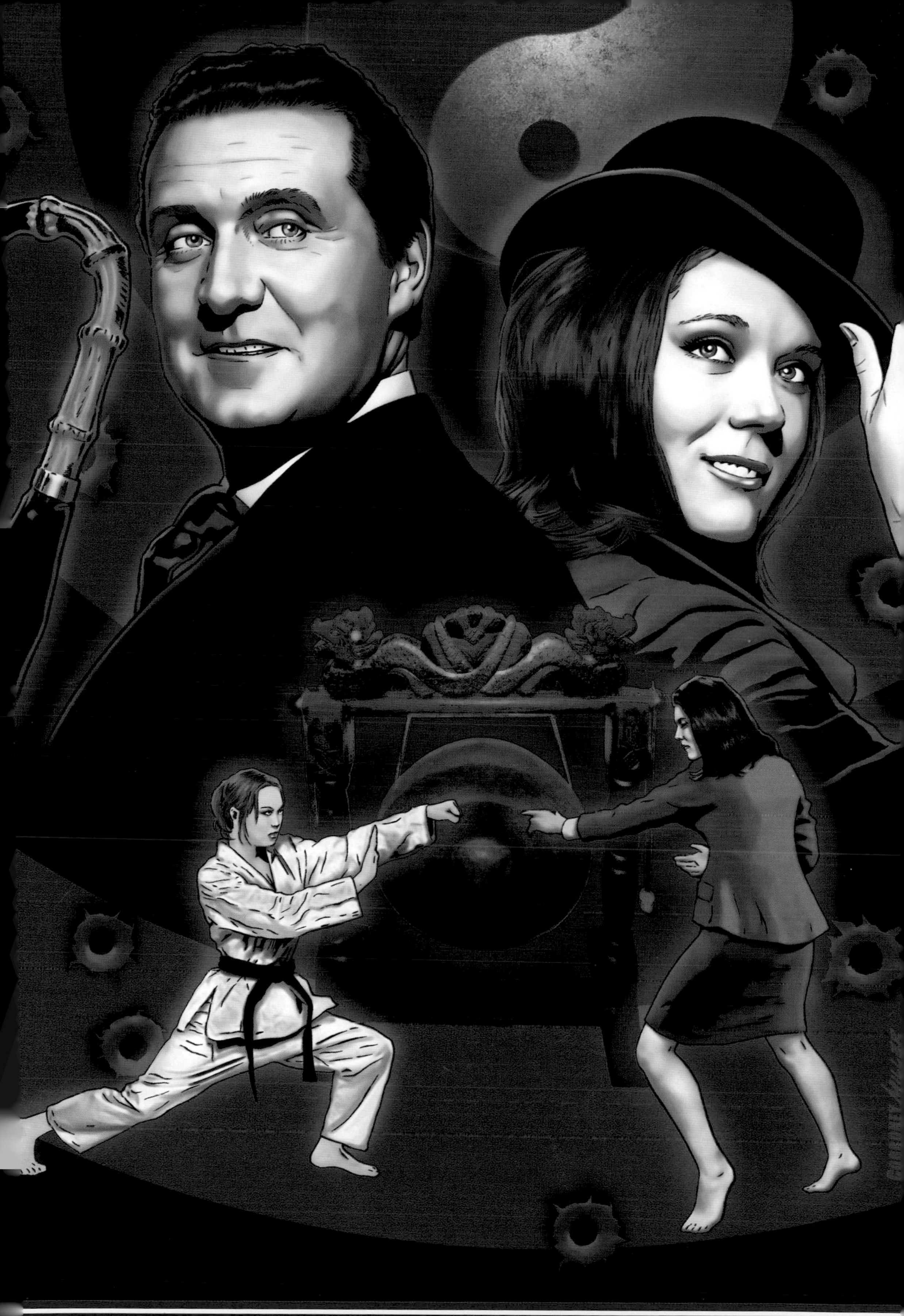

ISSUE 3 COVER: **JOE CORRONEY**
COLOURS BY: **BRIAN MILLER**

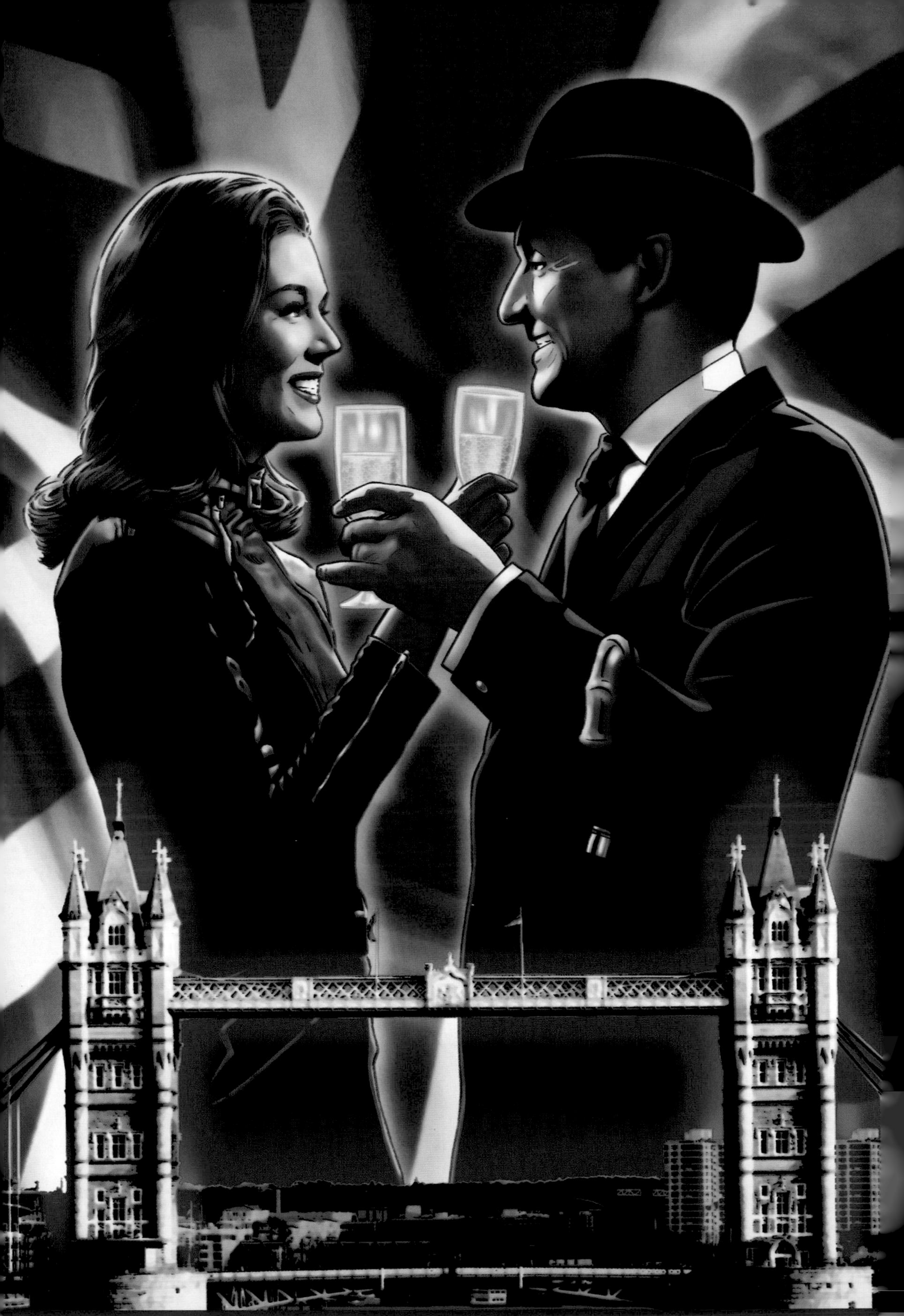

JOE CORRONEY
COLORS BY: BRIAN MILLER

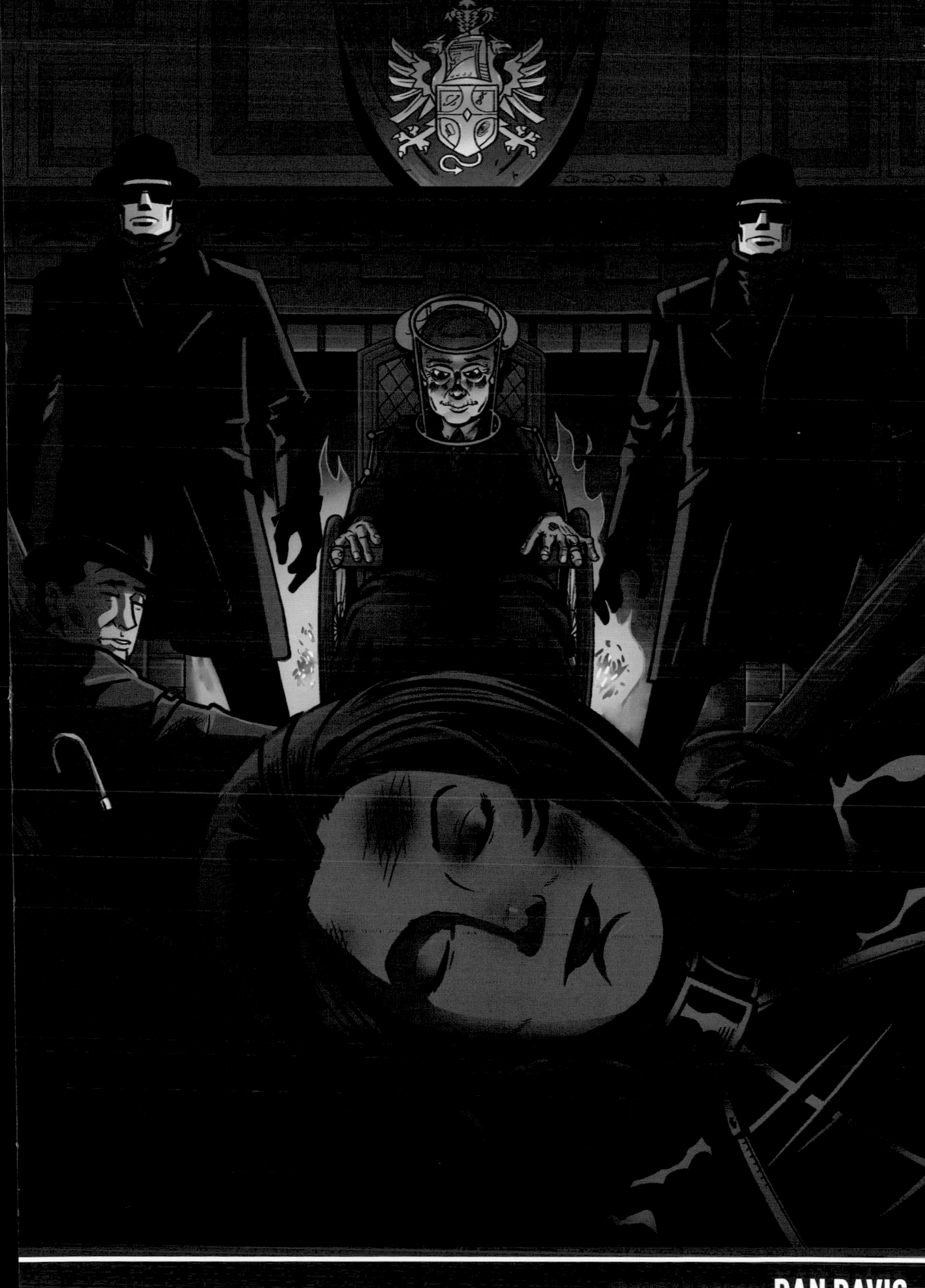

ISSUE 11 COVER: DAN DAVIS
COLORS BY: VLADIMIR POPOV

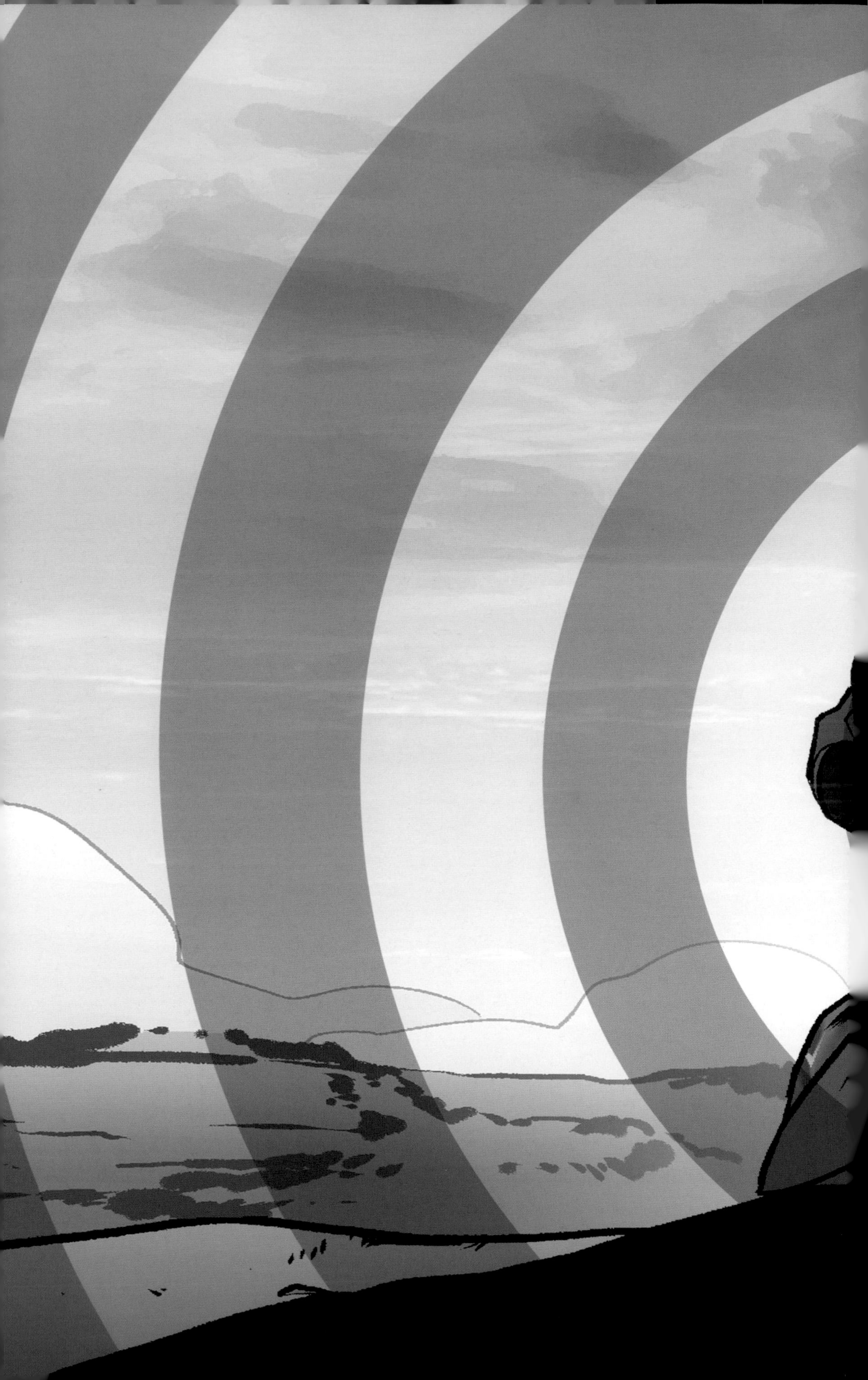

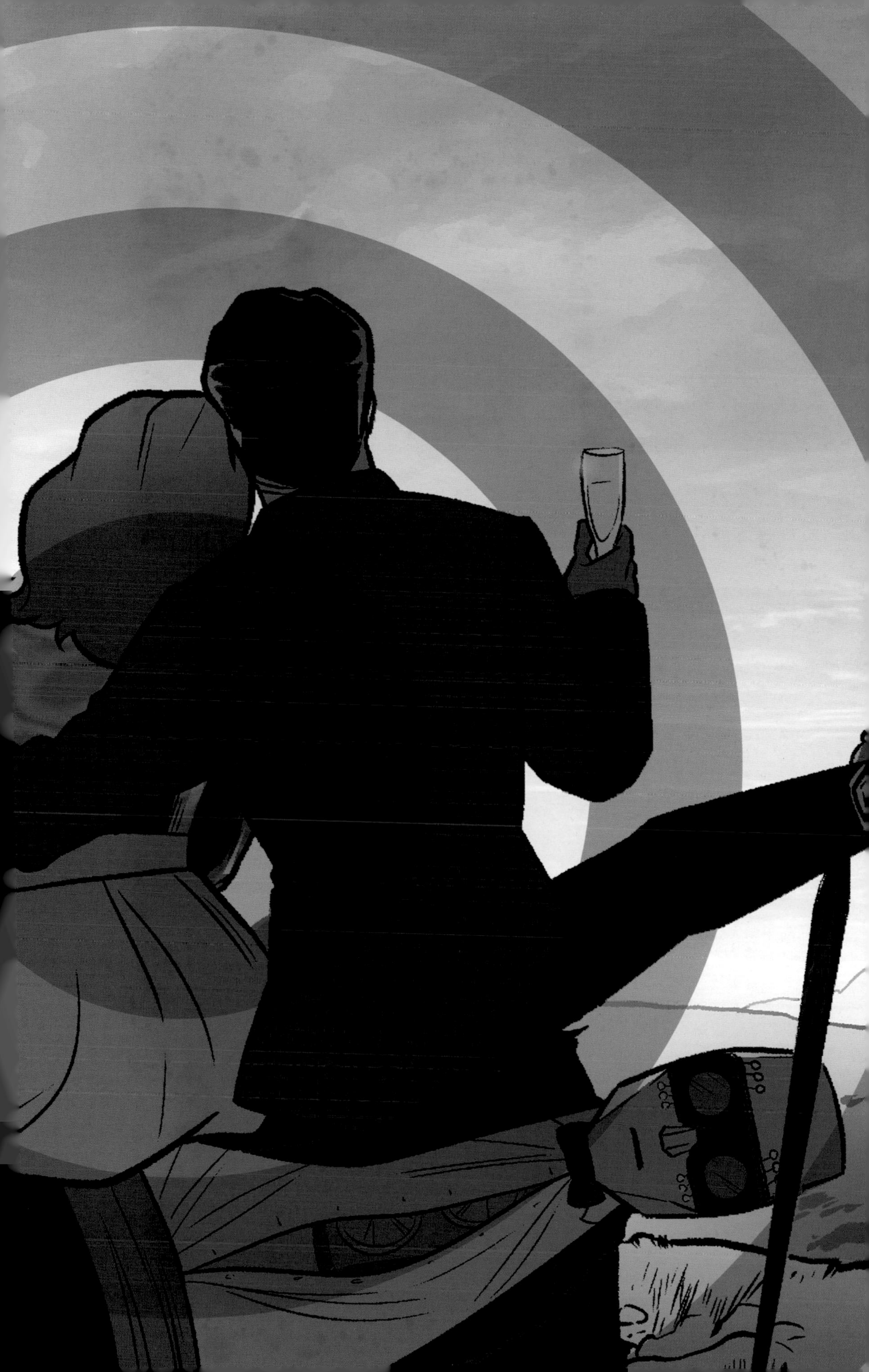

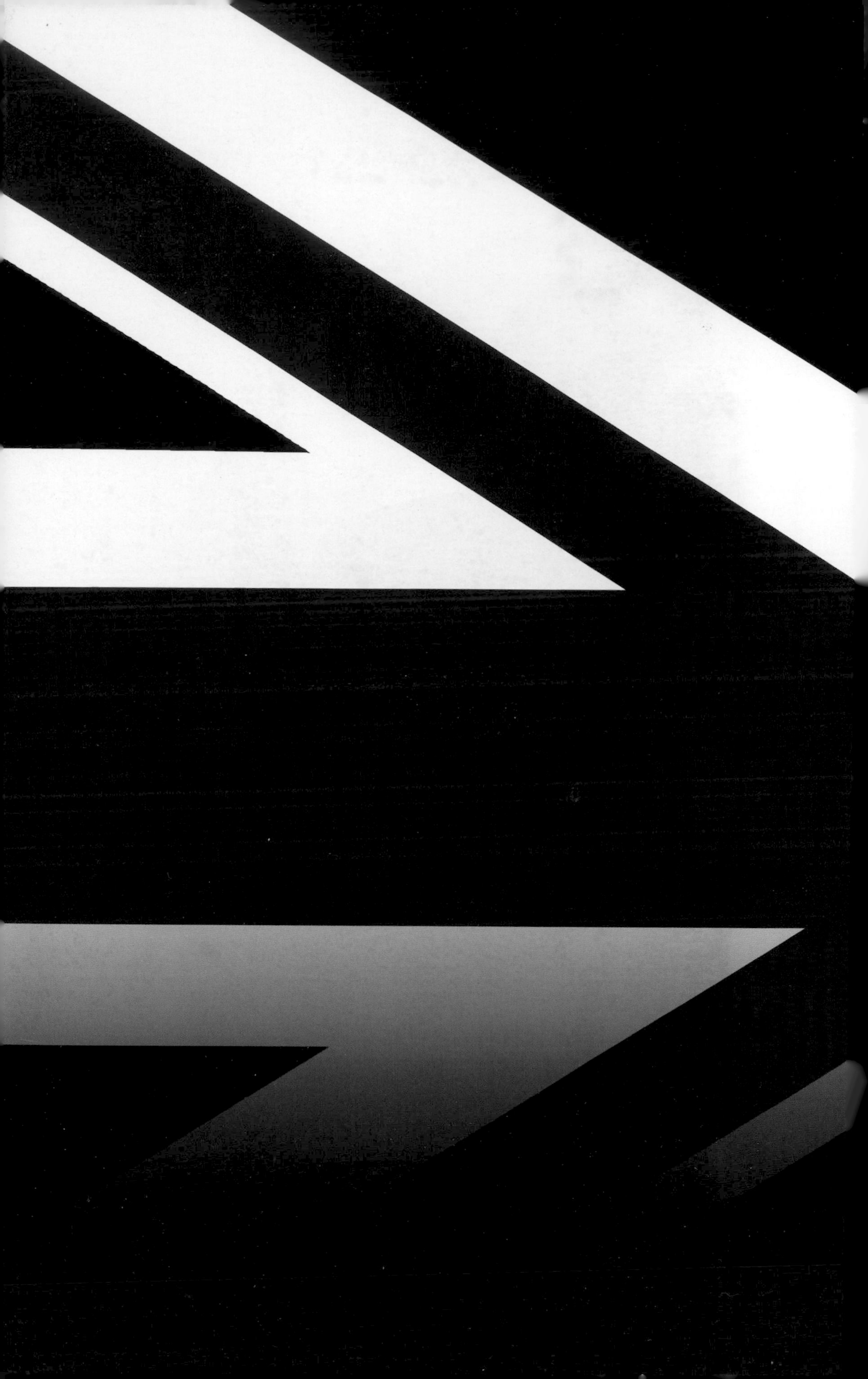